I0211822

SCRIBES OF THE TRIBE

The Great Thinkers on Religion and Ethics

DAVID RICH

Scribes of the Tribe: The Great Thinkers on Religion and Ethics,
copyright © 2019 by David Rich
ISBN 978-1-7322534-6-9
All rights reserved.
Excerpts from *The Great Thoughts* by George Seldes, compilation
copyright 1985 by George Seldes.

Also by David Rich:
Sail the World? – An Absurdly True Story, Prequel to RV the World
RV the World, 2nd Edition
Myths of the Tribe - When Religion and Ethics Diverge
The ISIS Affair - Putting the Fun Back in Fundamentalism
Antelopes - A Modern Gulliver's Travels

Table of Contents

Introduction

> Perhaps an editor might begin a reformation in some such way as this. Divide his paper into four chapters, heading the 1st, Truths. 2d, Probabilities. 3d, Possibilities. 4th, Lies. The first chapter would be very short.
>
> Thomas Jefferson

Religion has an enormous impact on our lives, whether we're religious or not. Daily we decide, with Jeffersonian logic, what probably should be done, what probably shouldn't be done, and what should almost never be done. Sometimes we're right, sometimes we're wrong, and sometimes we know the difference. My Baptist parents had their own answers, and to them these answers were crystal clear, undeniable, and irrefutable.

There are literally thousands of religions in the world—4,300 by one estimation—each one of them considered infallible by its members. As children, we are brought up by our parents, teachers, religious leaders, and schools to believe without question that our particular religion is the best in the world, in fact the only true one on the planet. All other religions are inferior. However, if we as a species can't agree on one ethical value, then humankind is effectively devoid of an ethical core.

Years ago, I became friends with a Catholic lay brother. Besides leading his own parish, Tom was an accomplished economist who oversaw the investment of billions of dollars for a large retirement system. Every month for a year we had dinner, and during that time, Tom kindly provided me with an education in the history of religions and how they relate to current doctrine. The ideas that we discussed eventually led to my book *Myths of the Tribe: When Religion and Ethics Diverge.* (First published by Prometheus Books in 1993, the book was revised in 2019.)

I had just finished writing *Myths of the Tribe* when I discovered a book called *The Great Thoughts,* by George Seldes, the original edition of which was published by Ballantine Books in 1985. I was drawn to the book by its cover, which described it as a

1

compilation of quotations "from Abelard to Zola, from Ancient Greece to contemporary America." The book comprises the ideas that have shaped the history of the world, ideas that continue in central importance today. Impressive. I was particularly attracted by the quotations on religion and ethics, subjects that have fascinated me for decades.

The Great Thoughts is arranged alphabetically by author. Leafing through it, I was convinced the book would be more practical and interesting if humanity's great thoughts were organized in a coherent manner. I bought the book and excerpted the quotes relating to religion (immortality and spiritual beliefs) and ethics (good and evil), arranging them in an intelligible order as a practical guide for the species (excluding thirty-two quotes prevented from use by copyright). They are interspersed here with the discourse on religion and ethics that resulted from my dinners with Tom.

A primary purpose of philosophy is to spur thought and debate from which we can decide whether we have one or more principles in common. Fortunately, one universal ethical value, though often observed in the lurch, has been clearly identified by our great philosophers, and we'll get to that early on. But truth depends on our ability to be objective, and no one can be completely objective. Accordingly, Tom provides a counterargument to my end of the discussion where he deems it necessary.

In a lifetime of travel, during which I've visited and lived in an RV in most of the countries in the world, I've observed many religions close up. My experience has taught me that human beings, for all their differences, are essentially identical, connected by the common wisdom of our great thinkers.

The Origins and Efficacy of Religion

If we go back to the beginning we shall find that ignorance and fear created the gods, that fancy, enthusiasm, or deceit adorned or disfigured them; that weakness worships them; that credulity preserves them and that custom, respect, and tyranny support them in order to make the blindness of man serve its own interests. . . . All religious notions are uniformly founded on authority; all the religions of the world forbid examination, and are not disposed that men should reason upon them.

Paul Henri Thiry Baron D'Holbach

D' Holbach was a radical and wealthy philosopher with great influence on Goethe and Shelley, but was savaged by Voltaire. He was guillotined in 1789.

A great fear, when it is ill-managed, is the parent of superstition, but a discrete and well-guided fear produces religion.

Bishop Jeremy Taylor

Charles I doted on Bishop Taylor,

3

by royal decree making him a doctor of divinity in 1643; by 1650 Taylor was writing popular devotional handbooks that sold well for over a century.

Philosophers agree that the idea of a god or gods sprang from the hopes and fears of our ancestors, no matter the religion and no matter who our ancestors were. Fourteen philosophers are quoted in *The Great Thoughts* on the subject of fear and hope in connection with the origins of religion. They include Spinoza, Sophocles, Butler, and Montesquieu. All sided with D'Holbach, suggesting that fear made us invent our gods. Only Bishop Taylor concluded that fear could be discrete and well-guided to create religion as a positive force.

What can we conclude from the fact that almost all philosophers believe gods neither predated nor created us but were invented to counter our fear of death and the unknown? The dread of death is our strongest emotion, heartier than love, sex, or hate. Our strongest passion requires our strongest response. No response could be stronger than the creation or recognition of a god to which we must eternally genuflect to earn an exemption from oblivion. Tom, my Catholic brother friend, says bowing down is a small part of it; God must have created us, because we surely didn't create ourselves. Darwin is not to the contrary. The characteristics of the poorest god would include the ability to guide evolution, though, until recently, religion didn't think of this explanation. Now many religions embrace evolution as the plan of their particular god, no matter which god out of our thousands of religions.

Gods were created or recognized back when we hadn't the foggiest idea where thunder, wind, sun, rain, and the seasons came from. We reckoned that howling winds, roaring thunder, and whispering breezes were invisible spirits masquerading as demonic or affable gods. Animists still believe this. We concluded a millennium ago that the sun and our mothers were the source of life, accordingly creating sun and mother gods.

The second spark for the awareness or origination of gods came from our dreams of dear departed friends and relatives, proving they lived beyond the grave. In 1995, I visited Etruscan tombs outside Cerveteri, Italy, dating from 600 B.C.E. The Etruscans buried their deceased in large mounds, along with furniture and household furnishings for a comfy afterlife, similar to the practices of ancients the world over. Only gods could guarantee the continued existence of the dearly departed who appeared in our dreams.

Evidence of gods from nature, such as holy stones, rings, water, incense, and crosses, pepper our major religions. Until about 5000 B.C.E. the reigning divinities were sun and mother goddesses. When we finally diagnosed the role of the father in procreation, our gods became male, continuing exclusively male today, though political correctness has removed gender references from some holy books. Our history freezes the origins of our religions in the fears and hopes of our ancestors. This sort of dissection is discouraged by religion because its dogmas are based on the unknown and unknowable. Tom agrees but suggests that spirituality provides a direct line to the unknown and to God with a capital *G*. Tom knows I'm not materialistic, so does that make me spiritual?

Either we created the idea of gods or a God created us. The former seems more likely to me, the latter more likely to Tom. Neither can be established with objective certainty. Following the Jeffersonian admonition, we don't know and have no way of knowing whether a god created the species though many, including Tom, believe it so. We can't conclusively place either religion or atheism in the truth column, though for several good and sufficient reasons many believe it's safer to believe and hedge one's bets. Still, we know the species has created and continues to create gods, excepting whichever true god we believe in and who we believe (no one "knows") is the only true god.

Gods are probably our own creation, making it a hopeful lie that a god created the species, or the portion of the species governed by the particular god. Tom votes hope and probability over lie. The rituals and promises of religion make sense for most of us, including Tom, though we know that dreams are only dreams, providing no evidence of life after death, and that no objective proof exists for the promises of any religion, whether Christian, Hindu, Jewish, Muslim, Roman, Egyptian, Zoroastrian, Buddhist, Mithraic, or the thousands of subdivisions in our major religions. I ask Tom who created his god or did he, she, or it just happen, similar to a big bang?

Religious promises are possibly true in the sense that almost anything is possible. The probability of religious promises being true, however, seems negligible to heathens such as myself. Tom agrees, except for the negligible part.

The Christian religion was partly derived from the primary Roman god Mithra, a sun cult founded in Persia about 1350 B.C.E. The Catholic bishop's hat is a miter, copied from Mithra's headdress. Other sun gods include Jesus Christ (Psalms 84:11, Malachi 4:2, and Revelation 21:23) and the Hindu gods Varuna, Krishna, and Vishnu. All sun gods were born on December 25. Most were worshiped by wise men. All fasted for forty days. Many were violently killed, and all rose from the dead. Worshipers of sun gods traditionally close their eyes when praying. The Christian, Jewish, and Muslim myths were taken from Hindu myths predating them by thousands of years, such as the Garden of Eden (Adami and Heva on the isle of Ceylon) and the great flood (coordinated by Menu, a Hindu holy man saving animals two by two in an ark). Religious myths are myths of the species, inseparable from the gods they represent. Tom says this constitutes near universal evidence that the events must have occurred. We must each draw our own conclusions.

Hope spurs us to progress and achievement. Without hope we'd stagnate, which means hope by itself is no villain. Hope for a superior being who'll solve all our problems, absolving us of personal responsibility and allowing us to live forever, is the fervent hope of almost everyone. Tom says he solves his own problems through conversation with his god.

Hope is the foundation of religion for the majority of us, generally a positive concept superior to many available drugs including work, sex, media, and social standing. Religion unfortunately contains two elements that may overwhelm the value of this hope, elements that tarnish religion, perhaps irremediably. These are explored in depth below. Tom says negatives can be fixed.

Many Eastern religions consider life a torment, believing in neither heaven nor hell. Hindus believe in continuing life and rebirth as punishment for not living a sufficiently good life, the devout achieving, after a thousand rebirths and sufferings, the nothingness that Western religions exist to avoid. A slippery slide to hell may be threatened by parents raising unruly children in the West, such as by my parents on more than one occasion.

No matter occasional protests to the contrary, our fondest desire is to avoid death and live forever at the physical age of thirty or so. To this end we may say goodbye to integrity, hug wishful thinking, and order reality away on the grounds that the fear-filled origins of religion happened too long ago to mean anything in this advanced and enlightened age. Tom says religion is mighty and bona fide and I've closed my eyes to its glory and overwhelming efficacy. I love him dearly and must recognize the possibility. Still, probability is far too strong a word for the efficacy of any religion, because all are based on unverifiable faith, which is defined in one dictionary as "strong belief in God or in the doctrines of a religion, based on spiritual apprehension rather than proof." In other words, belief without any evidence whatsoever.

Identifying the difference between Bishop Taylor's ill-managed fear and a well-guided fear is difficult, similar to finding the difference between superstition and religion. Superstition and religion are grounded on ritual and belief without objective evidence. Many argue that religion is based upon truth while superstition isn't, but how can you tell the difference when there's no objective evidence supporting any religion or superstition? However, the majority of the species believes in some kind of superstition, whether astrology or black cats or talismanic clothing. Tom says religion is goodness and ethics, leaving me struggling for the difference between types of wistful thinking, whether true or false, probably true or probably false, and religion, which often falls short of morality.

We tuck the fear of death out of sight, into our back pockets, living with the quiet desperation that religious promises may only be wishful thinking. Tom says his heart tells him the opposite. No compendium of knowledge—not the Encyclopedia Britannica, nor the Internet, nor the Library of Congress—though filled with religious teachings and tomes, can tell us whether religion prevents death or a soul continues in existence after death. Religious promises of immortality objectively fall into the third or fourth Jeffersonian category; unverifiable as truth, improbable, perhaps possible, but more likely indistinguishable from superstition and lies. Tom disagrees, and I'm glad he does. Agreement would be boring.

Many religious people view unbelievers as ignorant or worse, and vice-versa, making dialogue difficult between the religious and nonreligious. Fortunately, Tom and I don't have that problem. We agree that religion is about the nature of the objectively unknowable, no matter the source of or reason given for religious belief, which does make it similar to superstition. Tom insists that religious experience is reasonable, pointing to examples of faith healing and solace through faith. However, remission of disease occurs as effectively for the positive thinker as for the religious, while solace is entirely a state of mind, unrelated to the efficacy of the belief system providing the comfort. The odds of superstitious or religious acts influencing results can be calculated. Washing my car doesn't make it rain, though experience might make me think otherwise. Belief in a particular religion allows me to honestly pray for rain, health, comfort, assistance, or for the glory of a particular god, the odds of which neither increase nor decrease as a result. Tom says he never prays for selfish reasons.

Prayer often asks an omnipotent god to change its mind and admit the god was wrong. Either the god wasn't paying attention, isn't omniscient, or the only proper prayer is for the glory of the prayed-to god. Tom says prayer is communication with God. Yet, rain dances by Native-American priests and prayers of the faithful don't cause rain any more than superstitious actions increase the odds of winning a bet on a horserace, or wooing a fair damsel or lad. Still, no matter the lack of evidence, few agree that superstitious actions are as effective as religious prayers, though the distinction is illusive to me. Tom has no difficulty with the distinction.

Our Need for Gods

The Being of God is so comfortable, so convenient, so necessary to the felicity of mankind, that (as Tully admirably says) if God were not a necessary being of Himself, He might almost seem to be made on purpose for the use and benefit of man.

John Tillotson, Archbishop of Canterbury

Tillotson was extremely bright, graduating from Cambridge at age nineteen and marrying Oliver Cromwell's niece.

Gods barricade us against the boogeyman and lend force to our curses. Without a god, existence would be meager for many, including most of our friends and relatives, no matter their apparent detachment from or affinity to religion. The concept of a god banishes the riddle of our existence and pretties down the terrors of nonexistence. The notion of a Supreme Being, true or false, bestows hefty psychological goodies.

Tom says life would be ridiculous without religion; for me life without ritual or folderol is sufficient by itself.

Animals learn death first at the moment of death; ... man approaches death with the knowledge it is closer every hour, and this creates a feeling of uncertainty over his life, even for him who forgets in the business of life that annihilation is awaiting him. It is for this reason chiefly that we have philosophy and religion.

9

Arthur Schopenhauer

German   philosopher
Schopenhauer was intrigued by
death as a corrective for life. He
lived his last twenty-eight years as
a recluse, always in competition
with his mother, who was an
established writer and crony of
Goethe's.

Philosophy and religion highlight the gravity of each
individual's impending death. Western religion suggests life would
have no meaning if death were the end, while some philosophers
believe that life is satisfactory by itself. Religion and philosophy
could be seeking the answer to an invalid question based upon a
false assumption that death or life has any significance at all. We
don't know the significance of life, but we can gauge the
probabilities based on what we do know.

Our hope of immortality
does not come from any religion,
but clearly all religions come from
that hope.

Robert Ingersoll

Ingersoll was an American lawyer,
orator, and freethinker. A dashing
colonel in the Civil War, he was a
mouthpiece for Rutherford B.
Hayes and famous on the lecture
circuit for debunking superstition,
which   for   him   was
indistinguishable from religion.

Ingersoll's reference to hoped-for immortality applies only to
Western religions. Non-immortality religions include Buddhism,
Hinduism, Sikhism, and most Eastern religions, encompassing over
half of the world's population. But all religion hopes for something
better, for certainty and peace. However, peace among religions is
almost impossible to achieve, because religions disagree on the
purpose of life and the means of avoiding death, while insisting that

10

their vision of the unknown is the only proper one, allowing no other gods in the presence of their own.

Tom says ecumenicalism has its pluses and minuses.

The Museum of Religion in Glasgow, Scotland, features exhibits on the customs of marriage, birth, death, and dogma of the major world religions. At the exit a bulletin board provides a space for comments by visitors. When I visited in 1995, a note posted by a Christian complained bitterly that other religions were given space, insisting that no other god should be allowed alongside the Christian one. Tom would never write such a note.

> Desire is indeed powerful;
> it engenders belief.
>
> Marcel Proust

> In his flaming youth, Proust surfaced at mid-afternoon and caroused until dawn. After his parents died, he turned to writing and aided the vindication of Dreyfus.

The yearning for immortality fulfills a mental prophesy. Who, besides a potential client for assisted suicide, wants to die? An escape from death is at the top of our wish list, far more urgent than any other hoped-for event. That which is most coveted, such as immortality and the avoidance of death, may fulfill prophesies that create and sustain belief. No one knows for certain whether life exists after death. Because no objective evidence exists to support the possibility, it's probably false.

Tom disagrees but is equally bereft of proof. I don't know and will never know, and Tom won't either.

The Political Uses of Religion

> Religion is the opium of the people. Religion is a kind of spiritual vodka in which the slaves of capitalism drown their human shape and their claim for any decent human life.

11

Lenin

Vladimir llyich Ulyanov Lenin
would never have become a
revolutionary if his oldest brother,
for plotting against the czar, hadn't
been hung by his neck until dead.

Religion unquestionably eases our pain and fear by focusing on a future life, diverting attention from the problems of the only life we know for certain. Tom says the truth of a life beyond this one does tend to diminish current problems. Religion is tough to differentiate from a drug or other pleasurable (or pain-relieving) activity. Tom says any activity—whether religion or any other passion—compulsively pursued, is like a drug. The relief and pleasures of religion are undeniably real, though the efficacy of religious belief is unknown and unknowable, its validity objectively remote—though not a lie, because not intentionally false. Tom says the efficacy of religious belief is well known to him. It may make little ultimate difference how we spend our time or drown ourselves, whether working long hours, taking drugs or pain relievers, philosophizing, watching television or phone screens, working long hours, or immersing ourselves in any of our many religions. No matter the person or the choice, the result is eventual physical death, because life ends. Lenin's accusation that religion creates capitalist slaves would apply equally to addictions stemming from career, sex, mountain climbing, motocross, gambling, or whatever we like to do, no matter under which economic, religious, or governmental system we live. If religion, drugs, making money, or philosophizing please us, we should arguably pursue our own happiness, as long as our actions are ethical, harming no one else.

The wretchedness of
religion is at once an expression
and a protest against real
wretchedness. Religion is the sigh
of the oppressed creature, the
feeling of a heartless world, just as
it is the spirit of unspiritual
conditions. It is the opium of the
people.

Karl Marx

In his "Critique of the Hegelian Philosophy of the Right" (1844), German journalist Karl Marx used the word *opium* in the sense of a pain reliever, for which opium was widely used at the time. The Marx family sprang from rabbis but converted to Lutheran when Marx was age six.

Religions are estimated to spend about one percent of their income on charity. However, since no religion publishes these statistics, they're difficult to accurately estimate. Tom says the one percent estimate is close to accurate, citing the overhead of buildings and ministers. The 99 percent of religion not devoted to charity seeks to obscure the drudgery of human existence while its otherworld core may retard human progress by suggesting we passively accept our problems instead of trying to fix them.

Marx called religion the opium of the people. Whether it wants to or not, the Church consolidates and establishes injustice. It helps men forget their ills instead of curing them. Obsessed with the hereafter, the believer is indifferent to temporal things.

Raymond Aron

Despite this viewpoint, Aron, a French political philosopher and journalist, felt Marxism was anathema because it was totalitarian, a view that destroyed Aron's prestige in leftist France.

No matter whether Christian, Muslim, Hindu, or other, religion tells us to accept earthly conditions as they exist. An ideal philosophy, religious or not, would try to improve temporal conditions instead of passively accepting injustice. Organized religion recognizes the importance of temporal justice but

13

concentrates on temporarily improving the *spiritual* lot of believers or those subject to its recruitment.

Tom says religion is spread thin by providing sustenance to its own members, much less members of other religions and such as me.

> Religion is excellent stuff
> for keeping common people quiet.
>
> Napoleon Bonaparte

> Napoleon was a brilliant general
> but regarded soldiers as mere
> cannon fodder. A coward at heart,
> he abandoned his defeated armies
> on four separate occasions.

The comfort of promised immortality makes true believers relatively indifferent to temporal things. Because there are fewer "true" believers in industrialized nations, religion has less direct impact there but retards progress in the third world, where its influence is strongest. Tom says this isn't entirely accurate but is in any event unintentional. Religion may perpetuate injustice by placing its adherents in camps separate from and theoretically superior to those believing in other religions or no religion at all. This is a major weakness of our many religions, pitting each against all of the others.

> Dogma is less useful than
> cow dung.
>
> Mao Zedong

> Mao idealized Napoleon and
> George Washington.

Religion helps keep us quiet by supporting practically any government action. Tom agrees. For example, dogma was highly useful to politicians such as Mao Zedong because the religious follow the direction of religious leaders who almost always follow the dictates of government, which in turn generally defers to religion as long as religion hews the government's party line. Cozy. Tom bemoans the failure of religion to always follow its own spiritual dictates. Religious dogma is more useful to the politician than fertilizer to a farmer while supremely useful to the true believer's peace of mind.

> Morality is the best of all devices for leading mankind by the nose.
>
> Friedrich Wilhelm Nietzsche

> Nietzsche was uncommonly moral, repudiating his association with Wagner because Wagner was an anti-Semite, also ending ties with his sister when she married an anti-Semite.

By morality, Nietzsche meant religion, which bases its claim for legitimacy on its avowed responsibility for morality. Religion is as closely related to morality as society. The Ten Commandments, for example, consist of four ethical admonitions that are the law in every country in the world irrespective of its dominant religion (don't murder, steal, commit adultery, or give false evidence). The other six Commandments prohibit two mental sins (don't covet the neighbor's house or wife) and contain four prohibitions against tolerating other gods: These four have caused the deaths of millions in the Christian religion, among other religions, and among rival Christian sects, continuing this very instant in time. The ethical portion of the Ten Commandments are the ethics of the species, having no particular connection with any organized religion.

Tom says religion was the original founder of morality, though he knows full well that human ethics predated all religions. Religion, misidentified with morality, seeks to control the lives of most, in partnership with government.

> Our religion, moreover, places the supreme happiness in humility, lowliness, and a contempt for worldly objects. . . . If our religion claims of us fortitude of soul, it is more to enable us to suffer than to achieve

great deeds. . . . These principles
seem to me to have made men
feeble . . . an easy prey to evil-
minded men, who can control
them more securely, seeing that
the great body of men, for the sake
of gaining Paradise, are more
disposed to endure injuries than to
avenge them.

Niccolo Machiavelli

Machiavelli's model for his prince
was Cesare Borgia, son of the
corrupt Pope Alexander III;
perhaps because many of us are
selfish, cowardly, stupid,
treacherous, and gullible, rulers
such as Cesare Borgia must use
hypocrisy, cruelty, and deceit to
instill the fear necessary to rule.

Machiavelli's worldly objects may deserve contempt
because they provide little or no ultimate satisfaction, similar to
humility and lowliness. Great deeds may be only momentous,
unclear as to their greatness a few days or centuries later, and often
purchased with life itself. Religion may have contributed to the
enfeebling of the species but has probably no more softened us as
prey for evil-minded men, except for evil-minded religious men or
evil-minded men who use religious men, than a species without
religion. Because the removal of religion wouldn't remove our other
superstitions, it may have rendered us no feebler than we would
otherwise be. Revenge is an unhappy emotion and usually, in my
experience (and Tom's), unethical.

The Basis for Belief

One must make a distinction between what God Himself has said and what the clergy has said in His name.

Claude Henri de Rouvroy,
Comte de Saint-Simon

The founder of French Socialism, Claude Henri de Rouvroy fought on the American side in the Revolutionary War; he was a captain of the artillery at Yorktown at age sixteen.

The distinction between what a god has said and what the clergy has said in the name of a god renders all gods speechless. God fails to speak to nonfollowers and only speaks on occasions lacking witnesses from outside the particular religion.

Tom says the reality of religion is communication with God.

The godly news of Christianity wasn't written down until dozens of years after it supposedly occurred. On the other hand, the firm belief that a person has been spoken to by a god might convert any individual into clergy, as it did Tom. The only solution to unknowns, such as whether gods exist or talk to clergy, is to calculate the probabilities based on known circumstances. The origins and history of religion render the scenario improbable to me but not to Tom.

Faith may be defined briefly as an illogical belief in the occurrence of the improbable.

H.L. Mencken

Mencken—American editor, critic, and lexicographer— skewered the middle class, prudery, organized religion, and politics in his 1922 satire *Prejudices*.

Faith is defined in dictionaries as belief in the unknowable, unsupported by objective evidence. Tom says religious experience is objective evidence, whereas I call it subjective. Whether belief without hard evidence is foolish boils down to personal choice. No belief that we hold personally is subjectively illogical or we wouldn't believe it. Many of our beliefs, however, may be based on emotion instead of logic. Without empirical evidence of probability any belief is objectively illogical. Religious belief lacks objective evidence and is instead based on desire unrelated to the probability of its validity. Because neither superstition nor religion are supported by evidence, no clear distinction can be made between them, though both may provide comfort without substantial personal harm.

The immortality promised by Western religion seems contrary to common sense and thus improbable. Tom says it might be improbable except for religious experience. There is no evidence that anyone has risen from the dead or possesses an immortal soul.

Tom says Mencken's statement and my myopia ignore religious experience.

> The people in general have not, nor ever had, any reason or motive for adhering to the established religion, except that it was the religion of their political superiors.
>
> John Stuart Mill

English political economist and philosopher John Stuart Mill read Plato and Herodotus in the original Greek at age eight.

J. S. Mill seems correct that our country's dominant religion is usually the same as our political superiors, who include our parents. Our parents grew up with their religious beliefs, obtained from their parents, and passed them along to us. Parents remain our superiors long after our childhoods become history. Our social

18

equals and other political superiors usually believe in the religion of our parents because the dominant religion is an integral part of every society.

> Perhaps it is not without reason that we attribute facility in belief and conviction to simplicity and ignorance; for it seems to me I once learned that belief was a sort of impression made on our mind, and that the softer and less resistant the mind, the easier it was to imprint something on it.

> Michel Eyquem de Montaigne

> The hard-headed French philosopher and essayist Michel Eyquem de Montaigne suffered a non-French-speaking German tutor as a child, learning Latin as his native tongue.

Belief should be based on the probable truth of available evidence instead of the girth of our gullibility. Whether the mind is weak or strong, hope inflames belief. Montaigne may be generally correct that uneducated minds tend more toward faith and belief without evidence than do educated minds. The less we know, the less we're able to assess new information, though we each pick and choose that which supports our preconceived conclusions—Tom and I are both guilty of this tendency. Of course, we should resist bare belief, which is possibility without probable or certain truth, relying only on facts and probabilities. Belief without evidence, except in dire circumstances, has little place in decision-making. Tom says impending death is a dire circumstance and everyone's death is pending.

Hedging Bets

> If there is a God, He is infinitely incomprehensible,

having neither parts nor limits. He has no relation to us. We are therefore incapable of knowing what He is, or whether He is. This being so, who will dare to solve the problem? Not we, who have no relation to Him. . . . You must wager. . . . Which will you choose? . . . Let us weigh the gain and the loss in calling "heads" that God is. Let us weigh the two cases: if you win, you win all; if you lose you lose nothing. Wager then unhesitatingly that He is.

Blaise Pascal

Pascal was a child prodigy and one of the two inventors of the mechanical calculator. He also invented or discovered the barometer, the science of probability, projective geometry, the syringe, hydraulics, the adding machine and the wristwatch, abandoning science for religion at age thirty-one.

In *Pensées*, No. 418, Pascal seems to have gotten it right, identifying one primordial reason we believe in religion: Why not? It can't hurt, though belief without evidence may be contrary to reason and personal integrity. If we're incapable of knowing what a god is or whether it exists (identifying a god with a particular sex militates against the concept) the god idea seems inherently logical. Belief in a muddled concept floats one aimlessly along, leaving us bereft of logic or conscious navigation. But then, the hedging of bets is the most human of actions because it makes sense. Hedging bets succeeds even when the bet hedged is nonsensical. It might be as logical to believe in a unicorn parceling out immortality as to believe in any other unseen and spiritual creature, such as a god, but hedging bets remains a sure thing. Though hedging bets is completely logical, it is difficult to conceive of a god misled by bet-hedging boot-licking sycophants. Uneasy belief haunts many. But then, a merciful god may forgive us anything and everything. Tom says he doesn't hedge bets.

> Men have contempt for
> religion, and fear that it is true.
>
> Blaise Pascal

Many have a general contempt for and fear of religion, though others believe with neither fear nor contempt. The uneducated fear religion, whereas many educated people hold it in contempt, concluding that religious dogma and rules are the stuff of ancient nonsense; other educated people find religion completely logical. Many fear religion because it might be valid. If religion is valid, which religion is the correct one out of this extremely crowded field? Tom bets on Roman Catholicism. Perhaps we're left with the kernel of religion, that a god created us and expects us to be good (whatever that means), requiring us to act ethically. There's no reason not to act ethically, whether religion is valid or invalid. The right thing is right whether religion is balderdash or gospel. Tom says he agrees completely, though many religious would disagree.

> In an absolutely corrupt
> age, such as the one we are living
> in, the safest course is to do as the
> others do.
>
> Marquis de Sade

Donatien Alphonse Francois, Comte de Sade, provided us with the word for sadism (in *La Nouvelle Justine, ou les Malheurs de la vertu*) and died insane.

When safety is first, truth is last, bowing to the corruption that governed then, governs now, and likely shall forever govern our lives evermore. Tom says amen with resonance.

The Nature and Existence of God

> I do not see the difference between avowing that there is no God, and implying that nothing definite can be known about Him.
>
> John Henry Newman

> The English cardinal and writer John Henry Newman was a Church of England cleric before converting to Roman Catholicism in 1845; he had great influence on both religions.

If nothing definite can be said about a god (with or without internal contradiction), perhaps the god can't logically exist. Newman seems to obscure instead of clarifying. This to me makes his statement of little substance. Tom says God is beyond our comprehension, and I feel like resting my case. But we must be sufficiently objective as to have no case.

> IRRELIGION, n. The principal one of the great faiths in the world.
>
> Ambrose Bierce, *The Enlarged Devil's Dictionary*

> Bierce wrote two of the world's most famous short stories: *Occurrence at Owl Creek Bridge* and *The Most Dangerous Game*. Born in 1842, he disappeared in Mexico in 1914.

A 2018 Pew Research poll found that 80 percent of Americans believe in a god (23 percent as a higher power or spirituality; 57 percent the god of the Bible) and 20 percent don't (though 9 percent believe in a higher power). Because religion has had and continues to have enormous influence, particularly in poverty-stricken countries, analysis is hardly wasted. Practical experience suggests that most in the first world are irreligious but won't admit it. We have little faith, which is the mark of a rational creature. Tom says religion is emotional, not irrational.

> The argument that there must be a First Cause is one that cannot have any validity. . . . If anything must have a cause, then God must have a cause. If there can be anything without a cause, it may just as well be the world as God.
>
> Bertrand Russell

> Bertrand Russell's first independent intellectual action was to refuse to accept Euclidean geometry because its axioms required acceptance without proof, without a cause.

Perhaps gods are self-creating or have always existed, birthing from nothing, which is the only possible religious explanation. The probability that a god created itself is difficult to calculate because without evidence gods are on the same footing as a universe just happening or creating itself. Physics theorizes that the universe was created from near nothingness but lacks a theory of where the near nothingness came from. A god creating itself is no more probable than that the universe just happened. Evidence abounds that the universe exists, but there is no evidence that a god exists or created the universe except for the argument that the universe *must* have been created by a god instead of an equally talented unicorn. Tom says I lack spirituality, and I concede his point, scratching my head at his meaning of spirituality, since I have little interest in material things.

The Power of Faith

> There is no creed so false but faith can make it true.

Henry David Thoreau

Thoreau worked as a handyman
for Ralph Waldo Emerson; he was
a quiet worker whose pacifism
inspired Gandhi and Martin
Luther King, Jr.

God exists for those who are able to believe without evidence
and who wish above all that there may be a god. Belief without
evidence may be wishful thinking but provides comfort for
countless millions. Wishing gods into existence is a powerful elixir.
Tom says religious experience proves God for him, and I sincerely
hope for his sake that he's absolutely correct. For me, the concept
is without discernible substance and is meaningless.

The Creation

That the universe was
formed by a fortuitous concourse
of the atoms, I will no more
believe than that the accidental
jumbling of the alphabet should
fall into a most ingenious treatise
on Philosophy.

Jonathan Swift

Jonathan Swift, the Irish satirist,
was ordained an Anglican priest in
1695. For my money, his
Gulliver's Travels is among the
greatest writing in the English
language.

Either the universe and its physical laws are fortuitous or a
particular god, whichever one we choose as our favorite, is
fortuitous. Any god we don't believe in is fortuitous, which includes
the vast majority of the world's gods.

Evolutionary competition creates and destroys species
similar to the human species, creating and outgrowing the gods of
ancient Greece, Rome, Egypt, and Norseland. Religions are

founded on the myths that sustain us today, the meaning of which no religion agrees upon. The Hindu religion is the fountainhead of Western religion, first writing down the stories later adopted by the Jews, Christians, and Muslims in their holy books, about creation and the great flood when glaciers melted, and the origin of the species.

On the ultimate question of universe evolution versus god creation, we simply don't know, but we can calculate the probabilities. We know that before we could write, we created gods, and the gods we believe in today are an amalgam of or substantially similar to the gods we believed in before the Dark Ages.

Gods appear to be a product of our fears and creativity—except for religious experience, says Tom. I ask him whether religious experience is more akin to a dream or a nightmare, and he says I'm a real wisecracker. No one has the slightest idea where the universe ultimately came from. Our guesses and the legends of its origin are as cogent as an accidental jumbling of atoms creating a god.

> No myth of miraculous creation is so marvelous as the fact of man's evolution.
>
> Robert Briffault
>
> Briffault was a British surgeon, a novelist, and an anthropologist who wrote on myths in primitive society (which could easily include our own). His *Rational Evolution* was published in 1930.

A god could as easily ordain evolution as roll up its sleeves and create. Tom wholeheartedly agrees. We can only calculate the probability of a god's existence against the fact of evolution—denied by many religious fundamentalists who could as easily adopt evolution as the handiwork of their god. No evidence has been found for the existence of our millions of gods throughout history, whether Egyptian, Roman, or any of our current candidates; Hindus alone offer 330 million gods. Though evolution may be relatively certain, it neither proves nor disproves a god, though disproving fabulous stories of creation.

Who Created Whom?

> Man has created God, not God man. The priest is the personification of falsehood.
>
> Giuseppe Garibaldi

> Italian patriot Giuseppe Garibaldi fought in South American wars of independence from 1836 to 1848. He was invited by President Lincoln to lead the Union Army in 1861 but declined because Lincoln wouldn't declare it a war against slavery; by 1870 Garibaldi had unified Italy.

Garibaldi's suggested *falsity* of religion never was nor is intentional. Priests, similar to cogs in any bureaucracy, may be required to compromise principle to preserve themselves. Examples include the Curia and the leadership of all organized religions, which are bureaucratic institutions with the weakness endemic to all. Tom wholeheartedly agrees. Falsehood and truth are often in the mind of the beholder. We should strive for certainty, always seeking, upgrading the possible to the probable before believing. We probably created gods, though a god could possibly have created us. The former is certain, and the latter is not uncertain to the point of falsehood.

> We men have made our gods in our own image. I think that horses, lions, oxen too, had they but hands would make their gods like them. Horse-gods for horses, oxen-gods for oxen.
>
> Hesiod

> Hesiod, known as the father of Greek didactic poetry, wrote hundreds of stories, including

Pandora's Box.

The Christian religion says the species was formed in the image of the Christian god, which disregards how nasty we can be and the unknowable nature of any god. It was once considered blasphemous to describe the Christian god with human characteristics, because that would limit the god's character. Gods created by human imagination *always* mirror human attributes. Tom says God's essence is unknowable.

> If we assume that man actually resembles God, then we are forced into the impossible theory that God is a coward, an idiot, and a blunderer.
>
> H.L. Mencken

> Mencken reported the Scopes trial, which he dubbed the "monkey trial," bringing him a notoriety that he loved to feed.

Religion believes that the species can improve to a point nearing perfection, resembling a god. Because few can agree on what constitutes perfection, we might better settle for ethics, the formula for which we may be able to partially agree upon. Tom sadly thinks ethics isn't enough.

> I do not pretend to be able to prove that there is no God. I equally cannot prove that Satan is a fiction. The Christian God may exist; so may the Gods of Olympus, or of ancient Egypt, or of Babylon. But no one of these hypotheses is more probable than any other; they lie outside the region of even probable knowledge, and therefore there is no reason to consider any of them.
>
> Bertrand Russell

The existence of all gods is equally probable because there's neither objective evidence to distinguish them from one another nor proof that they exist, nothing to grab onto. Before the existence of anything can be considered probable some objective proof is required. The foundation of all myth, superstition, and religion is not only impossible to prove but they lack objective evidence and are therefore logically improbable. Tom says what he always says, the same as I do.

The Nature of God

> Religion is the idol of the mob; it adores everything it does not understand.
>
> Frederick II

> To escape the harshness of his father, the future king of Prussia (he would become known as Frederick the Great) tried escaping with his best friend to England and the protection of his uncle George II, but his father uncovered the escape plot, threw Frederick in jail, and made him watch the beheading of his friend.

We adore those things we don't understand, loving the marvelous in direct proportion to its impossibility and, when we have the power, banishing those who disagree with our vision of the unknowable. Religion's perfect knowledge of the unknown and unknowable is foil of knowledge. Tom says that's because religion's importance exceeds that of knowledge.

> The idea of God stands for the possible attempt at an impossible conception. We know nothing about the nature of God.

Edgar Allen Poe

Poe's fiancée married another man
when she mistakenly thought Poe
had abandoned her.

We know nothing about the nature of any god because there's no way for us to find out. Tom says regular church attendance and Bible study may guide us to a religious experience that introduces us to God. I balk on the grounds that the concept of a god is paradoxical because it is contradictory. No being can be good, omnipotent, and allow evil to flourish. A good god surely would avoid the slaughter of beings made in its image and would refuse to discriminate between them based on their wretched understanding of things impossible to grasp. And who created this god, anyway?

And   I   say   to
    mankind, Be not
    curious   about
    God,
For   I,   who   am
    curious   about
    each,   am   not
    curious   about
    God . . .
I   hear   and   behold
    God   in   every
    object,   yet
    understand   God
    not   in   the
    least . . .

Walt Whitman

Whitman's *Leaves of Grass* was
applauded in England but banned
in Boston by the Society for the
Suppression of Vice.

To Whitman and most of us, God is naturally considered the equivalent of nature and its wonders. There is no evidence of a god other than what we perceive in nature, which is evidence of nothing specific. Nothing in nature insists it was created by a god. We reason that nature is marvelous, largely beyond our ability to copy or fully understand, and therefore nature must have been created by a superior being we call God. We assume that nature was created instead of evolving or being evolved, whether under the guidance of a good or bad god or by itself. However, assumptions are neither evidence nor exhibits.

> Whether there are gods or not we cannot say, and life is too short to find out.
>
> Protagoras of Adera

> When Protagoras, a Stoic philosopher, was accused of impiety against the Greek gods, his books were publicly burned and he was exiled from Athens for life.

All the lives ever lived, strung end to end, are too short to resolve whether there are one or more gods. We can only calculate the probabilities based on the available evidence within the little time we have available.

Religion and Superstition

> In dark ages people are best guided by religion, as in a pitch-black night a blind man is the best guide; he knows the roads and paths better than a man who can see. When daylight comes, however, it is foolish to use blind, old men as guides.
>
> Heinrich Heine

> Heine, a German lyric poet and critic, wrote the most popular traditional songs in Europe, inspiring over six thousand

compositions by Schubert,
Mendelssohn, Liszt, and Wagner.

The mostly undisputed good stuff of Western religion are its
few ethical commandments and a theoretical ticket for immortality.
The ethical rules of religion are identical to the ethics of society in
all countries and cultures: Don't pillage, rape, or murder unless told
to do so by government based on real or perceived threats by other
gods, nations, or ethnic groups. The beliefs of all religions are based
on the historical conditions from which they sprang. The Jewish and
Muslim religions forbid their followers to eat pork, a restriction
perhaps based on historical dangers to health that remain partly
valid because of trichinosis in meat inadequately cooked. Individual
health is unrelated to ethics, which defines behavior toward others.
Whether Western religion provides a ticket to immortality is
unknown and improbable. Tom feels his immortality is a slam dunk.

Religions are born and may
die, but superstition is immortal.

Will Durant and Ariel
Durant

Will Durant's bestseller, *The Story
of Philosophy*, allowed the
Durants to quit academia and
devote forty years to writing the
eleven volumes of *The Story of
Civilization*.

Neither superstition nor the species is literally immortal,
though many of us trust superstition in various forms, whether
astrology, repetition, numbers systems, or, some might say,
religion. Tom says religion is ethics and immortality. Religions
seldom die but instead refold and change shape, such as Hinduism
and Zoroastroism into Judaism; Judaism and Mithraism into
Christianity and Islam.

It was either under Persian
influence or by a parallel
development of thought that the
later Judaism came to believe in a
future life, a resurrection, a last

31

judgment, heaven and hell, a cosmic duel between right and darkness, and a divine Savior. A cynic might even say that we owe more to Zarathustra than to Moses. . . . December 25th is the birthday, not of Christ, but of Mithras the Invincible Sun. Isis of many names has acquired a new one as the Madonna.

William R. Inge

As the dean of Saint Paul's Cathedral, the English clergyman and theologian William Ralph Inge was called the gloomy dean because of his pessimism, though he sounds like a realist to me.

The major Western and Middle Eastern religions are related to each other, sharing almost identical myths, changing the names of their celestial actors but boasting nothing new under the sun. A realist might say that religion is the enduring superstition of the species, changing with our myths. Tom says the common roots prove religion's essential truth.

Vain   are   the
     thousand creeds
That   move   men's
     hearts;
     unutterably
     vain . . .

Emily Brontë, Last Lines

Perhaps the greatest and least known of the three famous Brontë sisters, Emily died of tuberculosis at age thirty.

Vanity, conceit, egotism, narcissism, and pride are likely characteristics of the most intelligent species on any planet. We assume, because of and notwithstanding our intelligence, that we can escape death through ritual and old-time religion. We figure the best way to avoid death is by belief and good works, based on the earliest marching orders of our parents and church, no matter the parents and no matter the church, synagogue, mosque, temple, or shrine. Pretending to be gods a-budding is vanity itself, nurturing a hope that we'll never die. We believe we're too precious to die, which is unutterably vain. Tom says we have a right to be vain, having been made in the image of God. I must say, old chap, yon God can be quite the sociopath.

> The rational attitude of a thinking mind toward the supernatural, whether in natural or revealed religion, is that of skepticism as distinguished from belief on one hand, and from atheism on the other. . . . The notion of a providential government by an omnipotent Being for the good of his creatures must be entirely dismissed. . . . The possibility of life after death rests on the same footing—if a boon which this powerful Being who wishes well to man, may have the power to grant. . . . The whole domain of the supernatural is thus removed from the region of Belief into that of simple Hope; and in that, for anything we can see, it is likely to remain.

> John Stuart Mill

> This English economist and philosopher founded one of the first women's suffrage movements in 1867.

There's no middle ground between belief and nonbelief, between theism and atheism. The question of whether a god exists is identical to the question of pregnancy; either there's one or more gods or there aren't. Either the laws of biology and physics govern the universe, or a god governs the universe, perhaps through the laws of physics and biology. God and no god cannot both be true. Mill incorrectly chooses skepticism when his only choice was between belief and atheism, though he may have discerned a lack of evidence for either. Belief in a slight pregnancy is only belief; reality tends to an obligation for child support.

> The devil is at the origin of the first misfortune of mankind. . . . So, we know that this dark and disturbing spirit really exists, and that he still acts with treacherous cunning; he is the secret enemy that sows errors and misfortunes in human history . . . who finds his way into us by way of the senses, the imagination, lust, utopian logic, or disorderly social contacts in the give and take of life.
>
> Pope Paul VI
>
> Paul VI was conciliatory toward other faiths and atheists but not toward birth control, based on his 1968 encyclical.

For this pope, the existence of gods and devils was proved by belief. Our first misfortune came from the picking of a devilish apple of knowledge, proving through myth that a devil exists. More logically, our first fortune was knowledge, represented in Western religion by the forbidden apple. The Garden of Eden myth pegs women as the root of evil, a perception of patriarchal religions frustrated in their dealings with (and celibacy away from) women, blaming women for the first misfortune of *man*kind. Women are the basis for lust, imagination, utopian logic, and disorderly social contacts, the same as men. The real enemy of mankind is ourselves (ask Pogo), which isn't a well-kept secret from males or females. Only we mess up our lives. Until we're entirely responsible for our actions, we tend to dry sticks, leaning on the crutches of religion and superstition.

> Still, instead of trusting
> what their own minds tell them,
> men have as a rule a weakness for
> trusting others who pretend to
> supernatural sources of
> knowledge.

Arthur Schopenhauer

Schopenhauer's idea of the
unconscious influenced Freud.

Trusting others, custom, tradition, and religion is easier and
more socially acceptable than thinking for and depending on
ourselves, though ultimately and practically, we can only trust
ourselves. No other person, organization, or polity can better know
our personal situation or what's best for us. Groups, no matter their
conceptual authority or expertise, are poorly equipped to tell ethical
individuals what to do. Supernatural sources of knowledge remain
forever apocryphal, farfetched, and suspect. Tom disagrees with the
last part.

> My mind is incapable of
> conceiving such a thing as a soul.
> I may be in error, and man may
> have a soul; but I simply do not
> believe it.

Thomas Alva Edison

Edison's first school declared him
addled, so his mother educated
him at home; he named his first
two children Dot and Dash. Edison
is also quoted as saying, "I have
never seen the slightest scientific
proof of the religious theories of
heaven and hell, of future life for
individuals, or of a personal God"
and "Religion is all bunk."

Religion isn't completely bunk if it offers peace of mind and social interaction to those who would otherwise have less or if it tolerates Tom living forever. The idea of a soul lacks foundation, though Tom says religious experience proves its existence. No other evidence supports religious dogma, heaven, the hell denied by nonfundamentalist religions, immortality, or a god. Religion may be, however, worse than bunk if it perpetuates or contributes to intolerance, war, or the poverty to which we'll later see it linked by many philosophers. Tom says the bad parts can be excised. But I can't imagine religion, without frittering away its flock, rejecting prohibitions on birth control; and I can't see any religion (except Buddhism and the Baha'i faith) admitting that other religions are equally valid. Ignoring the question of validity, the almost universal religious prohibition against birth control and every religion's asserted superiority over others are the two glaring flaws of religion.

The Foundations of Religion

My own view of religion is
that of Lucretius. I regard it as
disease born of fear and as a
source of untold misery.

Bertrand Russell

If poverty is related to religious prohibitions against birth
control, then the misery of poverty is bred by religion. Religion
also may actively inspire the misery of war, as it did in Northern
Ireland, the former Soviet Republics such as Chechnya, the former
Yugoslavia, Sudan's Darfur, East Timor, Nepal, Kashmir, every
country in the Middle East, and many in Africa, without mentioning
Israel and the Palestinians. Tom says religion is only an excuse for
war. Too good a one, methinks.

Think of the dull
functioning of dogma, age after
age. How many millions have
been led shunted along dogmatic
runways from the dark into the
dark again . . . endless billions,
and at the gates, dogma,
ignorance, vice, cruelty, seize
them and clamp this or that band
upon their brains.

Theodore Dreiser

Dreiser's novel *Sister Carrie*
(1900) sold well in England but
was condemned in the United
States because its promiscuous
heroine went unpunished.

The dull functioning of dogma may be a relative heaven for
those who would otherwise have difficulty coping without religion.
No matter what bands our brains, we end in the same earthen slot,
though Western religion promises a resurrection no one has ever

seen or experienced. Vice and cruelty that harm others are unethical, which is to say evil. Religion may help keep us ignorant. Science might eventually dispel the dark but can't easily overcome religious us-versus-them divisiveness. Tom says science is a weak sister to religion but both have their place. He's apparently more tolerant than I.

"Our civilization is still in a middle stage," Dreiser wrote in *Sister Carrie*, "scarcely beast, in that it is no longer wholly guided by instinct, scarcely human, in that it is not wholly guided by reason."

We're a primitive species in the first few thousand years of a potential million or billions of years of existence, still governed by superstition. As a result, most of us are unable to mentally separate ourselves from our accidental societies, cultures, races, nations, and religions. Depending solely on ourselves is a fearful business with weighty responsibilities that tempts us to remain as early-stage superstitious beasts, guided by fears of those not culturally, lingually, nationally, racially, and religiously identical to ourselves. Reason, we have little of. Tom tends to agree.

Children Believe Forever

There is no absurdity so palpable but that it may be firmly planted in the human head, if only you begin to inculcate it before the age of five, by constantly repeating it with an air of great solemnity.

Arthur Schopenhauer

Schopenhauer refused to have children, in order to spare them birth into a heartless world.

As kids, we absorb religious and other magical myths like sponges, cherishing them unto death because they're as easy to unlearn as pulling our own teeth. It's tough to scrap myths that justify a fervent hope for immortality, the most unrelenting of our obsessions, though Tom says proper religion isn't selfish.

> Piety is sweet to infant
minds.

> William Wordsworth

> Though Wordsworth married and
> had several children, he lived with
> his sister from age twenty-five.

The make-believe, marvelousness, and mystery of piety are sweet to the human mind, no matter our chronological age. We delight in the unbelievable, in Ripley's *Believe It or Not,* in miracles and ghost stories that send chills arpeggioing up and down the spine. We love to contemplate the known impossible while hoping it's true, beginning with Santa Claus and almost always graduating to the god of our parents. Many outgrow some of these tendencies as adults, but few of us, if any, outgrow them all. Purely rational creatures we are not. Parents and government schools teach the superiority of our nationality and religion, no matter where we grow up. Neither the dogmas of religion nor those of government are founded on empiricism or comparative measurements but instead on nationalism and superstition. We preserve our piety for countries and catechisms to our graves, long after learning there's little dispassionate support for the superstitious parts of religion or the preference for a particular government or bureaucracy in temporary charge of the nation-state where we were accidentally sired. Some kingdoms are better administered than others, but no matter their form, governments, like religions, are buoyed by the myths taught to children that we retain as adults.

> Men will preserve the errors
> of their childhood, of their
> country, and of their age long after
> having recognized all the truths
> needed to destroy them.

> Marquis De Condorcet

> Marie Jean Nicolas Antoine de
> Caritat, Marquis De Condorcet,
> invented the theory that we'll
> gradually approach and attain
> perfection, a doubtful conceit

current today. The French
philosopher wrote *Sketch for a
Historical Picture of the Progress
of the Human Spirit* (1794).

Religions and countries splinter us into contending camps.
We err by believing in the racial, religious, and nationalistic
superiority we learn in childhood and with which we die. This
weakness is almost impossible to fix without extensive foreign
travel. At a minimum we should excise the parts of religion that
contribute to war and poverty, which Tom is all for. Of course, there
might be little left.

The chief cause of human
error is to be found in prejudices
picked up in childhood.

Rene Descartes

Descartes, considered the modern
father of philosophy, had three
visions on November 10, 1619,
that led to his philosophic method.

We ought not to speak
about religion to children, if we
wish them to possess any, and
further . . . they are incapable of
knowing God, even according to
our ideas.

Jean Jacques Rousseau

Neither Rousseau nor his father
forgave Rousseau for his mother's
death, ten days after his birth.

Heaven lies about us
in our infancy!
Shades of the prison-
house begin to

close
Upon the growing
boy.

William Wordsworth

The great secret of Wordsworth's
life was a 1791 affair resulting in a
daughter he didn't meet until she
was age nine.

I count religion but a
childish toy, and hold there is no
sin but ignorance.

Christopher Marlowe

Marlowe almost flunked out of
Cambridge because he was too
busy in the Queen's secret service.

Sin is a religious construct with little connection to morality.
The tension between religion and morality is vivified by the Ten
Commandments, the most serious of which prohibit acknowledging
the gods of any other religion, precepts identical in the three primary
Western religions. These nonethical parts of the Ten
Commandments may immortalize ignorance and war by
evangelizing the obliteration of those tolerating other gods: "Thou
shalt have no other gods before me." Tom can't agree that religion
is a childish toy, though I see the impulses of Western religion as
essentially self-centered, promising we'll live forever as if we are
children in the market for big bridges. Many religious give their
lives to helping others, some only give lip service, and others, for
political gain, pretend to be religious to get ahead.

Religion is comparable to a
childhood neurosis.

The derivation of a need for
religion from the child's feeling of
helplessness and the longing it

41

evokes for a father seems to me incontrovertible, especially since this feeling is not simply carried on from childhood days but is kept alive perpetually by the fear of what the superior power of fate will bring.

Sigmund Freud

Freud smoked twenty cigars a day. He developed cancer of the jaw at age sixty-seven, resulting in thirty-three operations and a prosthesis.

The fruits of religion may be more serious than a mere neurosis if they result in religious wars and relegate many to indigence, assuming most poverty in the third world is caused by religiously induced sexual guilt cheered on by taboos against birth control. Religion and society reflect like mirrors, producing a make-believe infinity no different from a juvenile neurosis. Tom says that kind of religion is only for the spiritually immature. And I ask Tom in his experience as a Catholic brother whether the spiritually immature constitute a majority.

By education most
    have been misled;
So they believe,
    because they
    were so bred.
The priest continues
    what the nurse
    began,
And thus the child
    imposes on the
    man.

John Dryden

The latter half of the seventeenth century was proclaimed the Age of Dryden in England.

We rely on the pabulum fed us in childhood by uneducated parents, bureaucratic religions, and parochial government schools, sanctifying fantasy as wisdom instead of blowing the whistle on our tribal and religious superstitions. Childhood misinformation controls our lives to the crypt. Unlearning the deified debris dispensed by parents, religions, and governments is despairingly difficult if not impossible. Tom says we should keep the ethical parts of religion and get rid of the trash. If only we could agree on which is which.

> Had it not been a law of nature, that any impression, however ridiculous and absurd, and however contrary to fact, may be given in infancy, so as to be tenaciously retained through life, men could not have passed the previous ages of the world without discovering the gross errors in which they have been trained.
>
> Robert Owen
>
> Owen helped reform the early industrial revolution so that six-year-olds were no longer required to work thirteen hours a day.

The gross errors we learn as children can't easily be unlearned, guaranteeing our lifelong belief in the superiority of our government, religion, and ethnic happenstance of birth. No other government, religion, or ethnic group has achieved the heroism of those we memorize myths about in school, church, and at home. To many Frenchmen Napoleon was the greatest man who ever lived, whereas those in other countries may consider him a petty tyrant and bloodthirsty maniac. Similar examples thrive in the history of every religion, ethnic group, and government, other than our own.

> The universe displays no proof of an all-directing mind. . . . Religion is an illusion of childhood, outgrown under proper education.

Auguste Comte

Comte, the French founder of positivist philosophy, was likely the first humanist; his devotion to Clotilde de Vaux made him declare love an essential function of life.

Comte foreshadowed a leading twentieth-century nuclear physicist, Stephen Hawking, who, though warned by Pope John Paul II to avoid searching for the cause of the universe, concluded in *A Brief History of Time* that the universe likely had no creator. The connection of the universe with a god is a concept without logical support but with enormous emotional appeal based on what I call hallucination and Tom calls religious experience. The existence of physical laws is neither inconsistent with nor tied to a law-giver or god. Few outgrow the need for a belief in a god, with or without religious experience, because religious myths foster mental peace. Those believing in a hereafter might logically consider suicide to avoid the harshness of this earthly life, going directly to heaven. However, no one (except a fundamentalist suicide bomber or cult member) believes so completely in religion. An improper education is one with religious, nationalistic, or ethnic biases, which includes all education. The chances of finding an unbiased education or unbiased philosopher are nil. I and all the others are indelible proof.

I am myself a dissenter from all known religions, and I hope that every kind of religious belief will die out. I do not believe that, on the balance, religious belief has been a force for good . . . I regard it as belonging to the infancy of human reason, and to a stage of development which we are outgrowing.

Bertrand Russell

In *Skeptical Essays* (1928), Russell identified his three

passions as "the longing for love, the search for happiness, and unbearable pity for the sufferings of mankind."

Whether religious belief should die out is fairly debatable, but the hypocrisy and immoral portions of organized religion should die yesterday if we could agree on what they are. But it's tough to face the probable reality of death and rot. Delusion is therapeutic for a species not ready for prime-time personal responsibility. Tom says religion has been a dominant force for good, but I see it as causing death through unending conflicts and wars, and widespread poverty, particularly in fundamentalist Africa, by almost universally opposing birth control and sex education. Tom confirms that I'm unrepentant.

And the day will come, when the mystical generation of Jesus, by the Supreme Being as His Father, in the womb of a virgin, will be classed with the fable of the generation of Minerva, in the brain of Jupiter.

Thomas Jefferson

Pro-French Jefferson resigned as secretary of state under Washington because Washington sided with the pro-British secretary of the treasury, Alexander Hamilton.

We've lived a drop in the water bucket of time. When another ten thousand years have passed, Jefferson may be proven correct that our religious myths will fade away. However, we should weigh his prediction as probable, only possible, or a lie. Primary childhood errors may include belief in a superior religion, superior government, and superior race or culture. Countries inhabited by more than one race, ethnic group, tribe, or religion are often rent by violence, war, or chronic dissension, with the exception of first-world countries, whose citizens are often more preoccupied with making money than with racial, ethnic, religious, and national

45

differences. As children, we enlist in the religion of our parents and become lifelong patriots of the fortuitous government of our birth. Few of us research other religions or venture to other countries, knowing as a matter of birthright that our religion and government are the best on earth.

> I believe today that I am acting in the sense of the Almighty Creator. By warding off the Jews I am fighting for the Lord's work.

> Adolf Hitler

> The Austrian-born German chancellor and leader of the Nazi party wanted to be a painter but was denied entry to a Viennese art school. Until his mid-twenties, he lived like a tramp and supported himself by painting postcards.

Hitler's speech before the Reichstag in 1936 illustrates one connection between religion and war. We haven't outgrown Hitler's end-justifies-the-means mien and perhaps never will. For one small example, in 1993, 450 indigenous Tzotzil Indians were expelled from their homes and community in San Juan Chamula, Chiapas, Mexico by their majority Roman Catholic neighbors because the Indians had joined the Protestant church—religious intolerance less destructive than it could have been. The life span of a dominant religion varies in direct proportion to the civilization that believes in it. The Indian subcontinent has sustained Hinduism (spawning Judaism, Christianity, and Islam) for almost six thousand years, while the Egyptian, Greek, and Roman gods were crowded out by Western religions.

We tutor our parents' religion to our children, and they do the same to their children, underwriting our tendencies to war and poverty *ad generatium*. Older folks find it difficult to fathom the ramifications of a god, much less youngsters who at best picture a god as either Santa Claus or a thoroughly good and just parent. Tom says God is better than his parents and he reckons, after hearing some of my stories, better than mine too.

Religious doctrine never submits to verification by scientific or empirical means. No priest or minister designs experiments to compare the power of Jewish prayers with the Christian, Muslim, Hindu, or Zoroastrian kind. Instead of organizing prayer control groups, religions clarify why prayers aren't answered for the unworthy petitioner. Tom says selfish prayers aren't answered, no matter the religion.

No religion touts effective prayers as a selling point or promises that its god answers prayers best, at least avoiding quiz-show religion. Religion could be embarrassed by the idea of prayer that begs (but thy will be done) an all-knowing being to change its "mind" to serve the pressing wants of an unworthy creature out of seven billion others. Tom says prayer is discourse with God. Telling a child to pray, to bank on an invisible and unseeable phantom, may deaden the mind to verifiable reality and responsibility. If good or evil spirits can give us what we want, there's little reason to bother with reality. Tom says wishes are not the proper purpose of prayer. Yet they probably make up 99 percent of prayer.

Faith is a legacy of our parents perpetuated by the fear of death and the desire to live forever. The fear of a superior power requires a talisman to ward off evil spirits, praying for the Redskins to win and the Broncos to lose, invoking protective powers previously wielded by our parents. We pray for the demise of the other team as the other team does unto us, though it might seem beneath a god to choose sides between athletic teams or to sort out the selfishness contained in most prayer. Our father, who art in heaven, give us what we want and protect us from the bad guys.

The Relationship Between Religion and Truth

> The churches are one vast lie; the people do not believe them, and they do not believe themselves; the priests are continually telling what they know well enough is not so, and keeping back what they know is so. The spectacle is a pitiful one.
>
> Walt Whitman

Whitman was hired as a clerk at the Department of the Interior in

January1865, promoted in May,
and fired in June because the
Secretary of the Interior thought
Leaves of Grass was indecent.

The churches are neither intentionally one vast lie nor are priests mostly unbelieving in what they tell their flocks. Still, the spectacle seems a pitiful one to me, if not to Tom. Few profess confidence in churches, though cathedrals in Europe offer a rich reward from an aesthetic viewpoint, ignoring the travail of peasants forcibly conscripted or obliged to tithe to build them. Religion disregards the individual, though, no matter the religion, it establishes a social organization ministering to the psychological needs of many, similar to other bureaucracies of the species. We may disbelieve churches but pay them lip service in order to hedge our bets. The priests don't tell us what they know isn't so but instead hope as fervently as we do that the legends of immortality are true. Priests plainly omit telling us what would disillusion us. No one knows anything about the supernatural, holy ghosts, souls, or other religious mythology.

All the errors of politics and
in morals are founded upon
philosophical mistakes, which,
themselves, are connected with
physical errors. There does not
exist any religious system, or
supernatural extravagance, which
is not founded on an ignorance of
the laws of nature.

Marquis De Condorcet

Condorcet wrote the seminal work
on probability in 1785.

Errors in politics and morals stem at least partially from deliberate actions seeking personal gain, in every government in every country to a greater or lesser degree. All religion was founded on an ignorance of the laws of nature and has always struggled to accommodate science. Billions may believe in eternal life and resurrection of the dead, though the best evidence of their validity is human hope, which may be the primary incitement to religious experience. Tom understands hope.

> It is expedient that there be
> gods, and as it is expedient, let us
> so believe.

> Ovid

> The Roman poet who authored *Ars
> amatoria ("The Art of Love")*—
> which deals, among other topics,
> with how to seduce a married
> woman—was banished by the
> emperor Augustus to Constanta on
> the Black Sea, where he died.

Belief in one or more gods is expedient for religious and political leaders. Without a professed belief in a god, religious leaders would be unemployed and lose their robes, miters, chalices, and relics, and political leaders would lose elections.

> Whoso neglects learning in
> his youth, loses the past and is
> dead for the future.

> Euripides

> Euripides left Athens in 408
> B.C.E. at the invitation of King
> Archelaus of Macedonia and died
> there, perhaps accidentally torn to
> shreds by the king's dogs.

History generally predicts the future because human nature changes glacially, if at all. What we've done before we'll do again, no matter the repercussions. As long as superstition thrives, we don't. Ignorance perverts the history that shapes our future.

Belief Versus Knowledge, Causation, and Evidence

> A wise man, therefore, proportions his belief to the evidence.
>
> David Hume
>
> For some unfathomable reason, corpulent Hume's vacant stare was attractive to women.

Science operates on theories not yet proven true. These propositions are possibly or probably true based on the body of the evidence supporting them. Belief without hard evidence merits further investigation but not unconditional belief. Tom says religious experience is hard evidence supporting individual belief. Without objective evidence to support belief, faith seems irrational to me. Neither the individual nor the species is helped by irrationality. On the other hand, religion causes little harm to the religious individual except to the extent religion causes him or her to have more children than can be financially supported or allows their children to be killed in a war against those of similar or different religions. The negatives of religion may be counterbalanced by the positives of its comfort, whether rationally derived or not.

> The scientific attitude of mind involves a sweeping away of all other desires in the interest of the desire to know—it involves suppression of hopes and fears, loves and hates, and the whole subjective emotional life, until we become subdued to the material, without bias, without any wish except to see it as it is, and without any belief that what it is must be

determined by some relation, positive or negative, to what we should like it to be or to what we can easily imagine it to be.

Bertrand Russell

Russell's father was expelled from his seat in Parliament for advocating birth control; Russell's godfather was J. S. Mill.

No one can completely overcome biases, whether Western versus Eastern culture (European versus Oriental), one religion versus another religion or sect in the same religion, the nonreligious, or nationalistic. We can only make the effort while applying the Russell (or Jeffersonian) formula. Science represents our most objective effort, whereas government and religion represent our most subjective. Tom agrees that religion, government, and ethnic groups are biased in favor of themselves but says we all are and that's a paltry reason to get rid of religion, a preeminent human institution.

To know truly is to know by causes.

Francis Bacon

Bacon entered Cambridge at age twelve and graduated as a lawyer at age sixteen.

All truth results from linking cause and effect. Deviations from this basic theorem are unverifiable and thus merit disbelief. Superstition, astrology, and religion are unverifiable, each based on belief without an objectively identifiable cause. Anything can be believed, such as round bricks and rectangular worlds, but bare belief deserves incredulity, no matter the number of believers. Belief is smoky glass, worthless from the standpoint of determining truth but excellent for excluding light. Only those things with an identifiable cause can reasonably be understood and rationally believed to have occurred. Otherwise, their truth is suspect, requiring pragmatic investigation before belief can be reasonable.

> The scientific attitude implies . . . the postulate of objectivity—that is to say, the fundamental postulate that there is no plan; that there is no intention in the universe.
>
> Jacques Monod
>
> French biologist Jacques Monod believed the origin of life and the processes of evolution to be the purest happenstance. He was awarded the Nobel Prize in 1965.

The cause of the universe is presently unknown. Religion and the big bang theory are two contenders for how the universe came about. Neither are doing well. We still don't understand the most basic force on earth—namely, gravity. Quantum physics hasn't found the cause of gravity, but then, religion has identified the cause of nothing. Tom says, "Be nice."

> Science does not permit exceptions.
>
> Claude Bernard
>
> Bernard was the first French scientist given a state funeral (in 1878).

The plan of the universe has been partially mapped by physics, biology, and other basic sciences. Assuming these laws were handed down by a god violates the rule, if valid, that questions must be answerable. If verification isn't needed for answers, then intellectual chaos results. It shouldn't be an answer to kill each other over whose never-seen god is best or to plunge millions into poverty because religion prohibits birth control.

The Role of Education

> Education, then, beyond all other devices of human origin, is a

52

great equalizer of conditions of men—the balance wheel of the social machinery.... It does better than to disarm the poor of their hostility toward the rich: it prevents being poor.

Horace Mann

Mann became president of Antioch College in 1853, and in his last address to its graduating class said, "Be ashamed to die until you have won some victory for humanity."

In an editorial titled "Education Pays Off," published in the *International Herald Tribune* on January 3, 1996, Mann wrote: "One of the greatest social experiments in American history was the GI Bill after World War II, followed by the massive expansion of inexpensive public universities in the 1960s. In the generation of young Americans that went off to war in 1941, one in sixteen had a college education. By the early 1970s that proportion had more than tripled to one in five. These were also the years of the greatest boom—the greatest increase in public and private wealth—that the country (and the world) has ever seen. That was not pure coincidence."

Equal opportunity for an unbiased education may be the highest objective good, but it is nearly impossible to realize. Everyone doesn't have the same opportunity to attend top universities, much less quality grade schools, where education may matter most. Education means little to those who prefer less intellectual pursuits, such as sports, beer, and pool (all of which I adore). Every country provides education that indoctrinates its youth in the glories of the particular country from the viewpoint of the dominant religion. Religion and government uniformly oppose a truly unbiased education, preferring the uneducated, who are easier to control. Educated parishioners may question the foundations of religion and, because religion has no objective basis, reject it. In order to prevent poverty, most educated people practice birth control, which is contrary to the dogma of all major religions.

He who would prove all

life, leaves it empty. To know the way of everything is to be left with the geometry of things and with the substance of nothing. To reduce the world to an equation is to leave it without head or feet.

Leopoldo Alas y Urena

Leopoldo Alas y Urena, known as "Clarin," was the most influential literary critic and novelist in late nineteenth-century Spain.

To accept the validity of anything without proof avoids reality and promotes fantasy. Life may make more sense to those who have acquired sufficient knowledge to be able to fit new information into a logical structure. The way of things is the substance of life. Without equations and science, the world remains a riddle. Though emotion, intuition, and feelings are rich ingredients of existence, they shouldn't diminish knowledge, reality, and the scientific method. Tom says both realms are necessary for life, though he's not the emotional sort.

Religious Knowledge, a.k.a. Faith

Faith means intense, usually confident, belief that is not based on evidence sufficient to command assent from every reasonable person.

Walter Kaufmann

Kaufmann was born in Germany and raised a Lutheran. He converted to Judaism at age eleven, then lost his belief but remained fascinated with religion his entire life.

Few facts are sufficiently compelling to demand assent from

every reasonable person. Belief in a particular faith is subjectively confident though insufficient to command assent from the overwhelming majority who believe in other faiths. No matter our religion, we're in the minority, because the cumulative members of other religions outnumber our religion by at least five to one, ignoring the effect of belonging to a particular denomination within our many religions. Because no one is completely objective, we often believe in whatever strikes our fancy, rational or not. Belief and faith without verification are irrational. Tom says religious experience justifies belief. Unfortunately, religious experience is completely subjective and can't be objectively verified.

> Intellectually, religious emotions are not creative but conservative. They attach themselves readily to the current view of the world and consecrate it. They steep and dye intellectual fabrics in the seething vat of emotions; they do not form their warp and woof. There is not, I think, an instance of any large idea about the world being independently generated by religion.
>
> John Dewey
>
> A listing of Dewey's publications would fill dozens of pages.

The largest religious idea, at least in the West, is immortality, unfortunately accompanied with tendencies to conflict with or exterminate those believing in other religions, along with general religious prohibitions against birth control that the uneducated and third world take as gospel unto direst poverty. These large ideas affect the lives of everyone and to me appear indistinguishable from evil. Tom says if that were close to the truth, it would be evil, but he doubts the verity.

> There is no expedient to which man will not resort to avoid the real labor of thinking.

Sir Joshua Reynolds

Reynolds' sister kept house for
him his entire life.

Thinking challenges sacred beliefs, which can't be
objectively examined. Tom says we should believe in experience,
whether mystical or subjective. Assessing the validity of bare belief,
one unsupported by verifiable fact, is like scuba diving in molasses
while looking for brown signs written in invisible brown ink.

> . . . there's   a   new
> tribunal now,
> Higher than God's—
> the   educated
> man's.

Robert Browning

In 1846 Browning married the
poet Elizabeth Barrett, a semi-
invalid six years older, and they
moved to Italy for her health.

Education is the key to a satisfying and productive life for
many if not most, the same as many see religion. Bare belief is the
flip-side of education, perhaps explaining why the beliefs of one
religion are the abomination of other religions.

> Philosophy makes no secret
> of the fact. Her creed is the creed
> of Prometheus—'In a word, I
> detest all the gods.' This is the
> device against all deities of heaven
> or earth who do not recognize as
> the highest divinity the human
> self-consciousness itself.

Karl Marx

Marx was a kind and patient father
and devoted husband who often
protested that he wasn't a Marxist.

The gods were likely concocted whole-cloth from fear of the unknown and death. No other evidence explains their origins. Philosophy insists on logic or evidence before accepting a hypothesis as probable. The various gods of our many religions would be more laudable if they refused to pit the species against itself or encourage poverty by taking an icepick to condoms. But then, gods flow from human consciousness, and human consciousness is all we really have.

> True ideas are those that we can assimilate, validate, corroborate, and verify. False ideas are those that we cannot. That is the practical difference it makes to us to have true ideas; that therefore is the meaning of truth, for it is all that truth is known as.
>
> Wi
> lliam
> James

> James destroyed his health on an expedition to the Amazon with Louis Agassiz but recovered it upon marriage.

Religion and superstition can't be validated, corroborated, or verified, though they are easily assimilated by the vast majority. The distinction between religion and superstition is unclear. Because no religion can be verified, no religion is entitled to claim superiority over any other, making Jews and gentiles, Muslims and Buddhists, indeed all our 4,300 world religions, equal. Tom goes along with the spiritual essence of this.

Who Could Believe a Lie?

> The size of the lie is a definite factor in causing it to be believed, for the vast masses of the nation are in the depths of their hearts more easily deceived than

they are consciously and intentionally bad. The primitive simplicity of their minds renders them a more easy prey to a big lie than a small one, for they themselves often tell little lies but would be ashamed to tell a big one. . . . All propaganda must be so popular and on such an intellectual level, that even the most stupid of those towards whom it is directed will understand it. Therefore, the intellectual level of the propaganda must be lower the larger the number of people who are to be influenced by it. . . . Through clever and constant application of propaganda, people can be made to see paradise as hell, and also the other way round, to consider the most wretched sort of life as paradise.

Adolf Hitler

Hitler didn't smoke, drink, or chase women, making him the ideal politician for the prudish masses. Rudolf Hess, Hitler's cell mate, to whom *Mein Kampf* was dictated, is generally credited with being its chief author. Robert Payne wrote that Ilse Hess claimed she and Rudolf spent countless hours on the manuscript galleys, but Payne believed *Mein Kampf* to be largely Hitler's.

Hitler was a premier psychologist. Most of us refuse to lie in big things but hesitate less to lie in small matters of little or no importance. We give liars and truth-tellers the benefit of the doubt because we can't easily tell the difference, usually assuming that others tell the truth until that assumption is disproven. When proof is unavailable and belief is based on the assurances of elders, imams, rabbis, and priests, religion, superstition, and lies thrive. Telling a probable lie about every individual's greatest desire, to avoid death, results in belief for most of us. Religion tells us that the only world we know for certain is misery and torment, which it assuredly can be, while an improbable afterlife is paradise, mythical or not. Religion and superstition operate on the level of the masses, impressing those who can't see beyond material trappings and ritual. The most impressive structures on earth are cathedrals and mosques (excluding secular temples dedicated to capitalism), built on the bones and sweat of peasants to impress us, the forbears of our sacrificed ancestors. Religion is probably a grand lie that we all yearn to believe. No one knows for sure. Its clever and constant repetition, beginning in childhood, keeps us convinced. However, because it has no factual foundation, it should be considered as probably false. Tom says religion isn't false, but he can offer no proof of its truth beyond personal religious experience.

Our age is the age of criticism, to which everything must be subjected. The sacredness of religion, and the authority of legislation, are by many regarded as grounds for exemption from the examination by this tribunal. But, if they are exempted, they become the subjects of just suspicion, and cannot lay claim to sincere respect, which reason accords only to that which has stood the test of a free and public examination.

Immanuel Kant

Kant lived and worked his entire life in Konigsberg, Prussia, now Kaliningrad, the single Russian enclave entirely within Western Europe.

Religion and ethics are my favorite subjects for criticism and analysis. Religion is often exempted from criticism because it offers nothing objective to criticize. Religious analysis, no matter how subdued, is often seen as directed against society's code of morality and thus considered the equivalent of sedition or heresy. Many can't rationally discuss their faith because faith is the flip side of logic, leaving nothing for discussion. Beyond, "I believe," nothing rational can be said, no matter the belief. Belief and faith are justly suspect and difficult to sincerely respect. Tom understands the problem for those of little faith.

Infallible Religion

There faithfully adhering to the tradition received from the beginning of the Christian faith, for the glory of God our Savior, the exaltation of the Catholic religion, and the salvation of the Christian people, the Sacred Council approving, we teach and define that it is a dogma divinely revealed; that the Roman Pontiff, when he speaks *ex cathedra*, that is, when in discharge of the office of the pastor and doctor of all Christians, by virtue of his supreme Apostolic authority, he defines a doctrine regarding faith or morals to be held by the universal Church, by the divine assistance promised to him in blessed Peter, is possessed of that infallibility with which the divine Redeemer willed that his Church should be endowed for defining doctrine regarding faith and morals; and that therefore such definitions of the Roman Pontiff are irreformable of themselves, and not from the consent of the Church. But if any one—which may God advert—presumes to

contradict this our definition; let
him be anathema.

Pope Pius IX, *The Dogma
of Papal Infallibility* (1870)

Papal infallibility when speaking *ex cathedra* was early
applied when Pope Pius IX declared the immaculate conception in
1854. The pope and leaders of fundamentalist religions, and perhaps
all religions (ask any which part of their dogma isn't the truth),
consider themselves infallible when speaking within the scope of
their churchly offices. The dogma of papal infallibility governs the
largest Christian sect, condemning other religions as fallible, though
modern Catholic doctrine rejects condemnation of other religions.

Nothing rational can be said about belief without evidence.
In *The Riddle of the Universe,* the German biologist Ernst Heinrich
Haeckel wrote: "The famous encyclical and syllabus which the
militant Pope Pius IX sent out into the entire world—were a
declaration of war on the whole of modern science; they demanded
a blind submission of reason to the dogmas of the infallible Pope."

As for morality, religion is difficult to distinguish from evil
if it promotes conflict and wars between those believing in different
religions or relegates a single person to poverty by nixing birth
control. The morality of religion—that we shouldn't kill each other
(though seemingly urged to do so by religious commandments
forbidding other gods), steal, lie, or cheat—is universal in all
societies, no matter the local religion.

Anathema lost its sting when religion lost the power to burn
at the stake. Tom says papal infallibility is in error, which is why
I've used a pseudonym, so Tom isn't drummed out of the Roman
Catholic Church.

But Christ could certainly
not have established the Church.
That is, the institution we now call
by that name, for nothing
resembling our present conception
of the Church—with its
sacraments, its hierarchy, and
especially its claim to
infallibility—is to be found in
Christ's words or in the
conception of the men of his time.

61

Leo Nikolayevich Tolstoy

In 1873, twenty years before Tolstoy said this, the puritan aunt who raised him died, his wife became gravely ill, two of his children died, and he wrote *Anna Karenina*.

Gods through popes and ayatollahs declare themselves infallible, which gods are by definition, whereas popes and ayatollahs simply aren't. Infallibles are know-it-all objects of derision. Neither Christ, Mohammed, Abraham, Confucius, nor Buddha declared themselves infallible, though infallibility follows naturally from the basic premise of all religions. Because of their intimate connection with a god, religious leaders may deem themselves equally infallible. Neither infallibility nor the bureaucracies of religion are established by the Bible, the Koran, or any other holy book. The spirituality integral to religion is antithetical to religious bureaucracy, but without its bureaucracy religion might molder away, though Buddhism (the least bureaucratic religion) hasn't, nor has Islam, the world's fastest growing religion, allowing up to four wives and prohibiting birth control, projected to leave Christianity in its taillights by 2050. Tom isn't an organization man, even for religion, though he says he knows full well what spirituality is, even if I don't. I'm guessing that it's similar to ethics, with religious overtones, instead of simply nonmaterialistic.

To require uniformity in the appreciation of sentiments or the interpretation of language, or uniformity of thought, feeling, or action, is a fundamental error in human legislation—a madness which would be only equaled by requiring all to possess the same countenance, the same voice, or the same nature.

Josiah Warren

Warren became an Owenite in

1825, selling his lucrative lamp
factory and moving to New
Harmony, Indiana.

The possibility is remote that we might achieve consensus in
thought, action, and feeling but could perhaps settle for one core
principle governing ethics. Because religion is based on faith,
agreement on the principles, goals, and methods of 4,300 disparate
branches is doubtlessly impossible. Debate and experimentation can
achieve uniformity and resolve disagreement only in disciplines
based on evidence.

> *Homo sapiens*, the only
> creature endowed with reason, is
> also the only creature to pin its
> existence on things unreasonable.
>
> Henri Bergson

> To avoid receiving preferential
> treatment, Bergson, a French
> philosopher and 1927 Nobel Prize
> recipient, resigned his university
> and academy positions when the
> Vichy government came to power;
> he caught a chill while registering
> as a Jew and died.

We all base our existence on things unreasonable; for
example, living our lives as if they continued forever. We're the
only species theoretically capable of recognizing what's reasonable,
but we seldom agree on the difference between reason and
unreason. My position is reasonable, and yours is unreasonable;
that's as far as we're able to go. We should establish the whys and
wherefores of what we believe in order to determine our basic
principles, if any we have. By the beginning of the twenty-first
century we should have an inkling of what's objectively
unreasonable in religion and ethics. Tom says, hear, hear.

> The man of belief is
> necessarily a dependent man. . . .
> He does not belong to himself, but
> to the author of the idea he

believes.

Friedrich Nietzsche

Nietzsche spent his last ten years in a mental institution under the care of his anti-Semitic sister, who bequeathed his walking cane to Hitler.

We should believe nothing unless based on probability. Beliefs based on superstition, absurdities, and possibilities should be shelved until the probability of their truth is established. More mistakes are made by relying on beliefs that are possibly true than on those that are probably true. Those relying on probabilities are independent, belonging to themselves and not to those selling beliefs based on mere possibility, myth, or flat-out lies. Tom says religious experience establishes the validity and probability of religion, zooming beyond the limits of my reason.

Rely Only on Established Fact

Shake off all the fears of servile prejudices, under which weak minds are servilely crouched. Fix reason firmly in her seat, and call on her tribunal for every fact, every opinion. Question with boldness even the existence of a God, because, if there be one, he must more approve of the homage of reason than that of blind faith.

Thomas Jefferson

Jefferson was elected vice president under John Adams because he came in second in the election for president, with three less electoral votes than Adams.

Servile prejudices are exhausting to eradicate, often serving as operating systems, without which we would founder. Life demands that others be deemed inferior; that our culture, nation, and religion be deemed better than all others. Those who disagree, consisting of the vast majority outside our nation and religion, are obviously inferior because they're not us; they're them. Until such myopia is smashed, we remain hopelessly prejudiced, unable to meet Jefferson's suggestion that prejudices be obliterated. Tom emphatically agrees.

We should require facts to support every proposition, impossible for most of us, because it would exclude the possibility of a god's existence. Hedging bets isn't homage unless our god is stupider than we are; fat chance. Gods preferring faith to reason are arguably dumber than other gods. Tom agrees with this one. Faith is blind because not based on fact. Tom says religious experience is fact. Blindness doesn't exclude the possibility of truth, but it removes the probability, and Tom isn't blind.

> Herein is the strength of the Catholic Church; herein she differs from all Protestant mockeries of her. She proposes to be built upon facts, not opinions; on objective truths, not on variable sentiments; on immemorial testimony, not on private judgment; on convictions or perceptions, not on conclusions. None else but she can make this profession.
>
> John Henry Newman
>
> Fifteen years before being made a cardinal in the Roman Catholic Church, Newman was attacked for having previously been an Anglican; he responded with "An Apology for My Life" (1864), which silenced his critics.

No religion is based on fact but instead on the teachings of a founder whose beliefs have evolved beyond recognition. The immortality promised by Western religion and the nirvana of Hinduism are based on immemorial testimony and perceptions stemming from private subjective judgment, not on fact or objective truth. Tom says I stubbornly ignore religious experience. And then we discussed hallucinations and the like.

> The only good is knowledge, and the only evil is ignorance.

> Diogenes Laertius

> Laertius wrote the most important source of the history of Greek philosophy and philosophers.

Of course there are evils other than ignorance, unless harming others proceeds solely from ignorance. Questions arise, such as is all knowledge good, such as how to make pipe bombs? Tom says that's nitpicking because you know what he means, that ignorance is bad, which he would have expanded if you'd have given him the chance.

> Make reason thy guide.

> Solon

> This Athenian statesman lived prior to written history and biography, which began with his poems and laws.

Of course, Tom and I agree that reason should always be one's guide, though Tom, as usual, cites the reasonableness of religious experience. And I respond, it's all in your head. Tom smiles and suggests a beer break. Prost.

> The truth wears longer than all the gods; for it is only in the truth's service, and for love of it, that people have overthrown the gods and at last God himself. 'The Truth' outlasts the downfall of the

world of gods, for it is the immortal soul of this transitory world of gods; it is Deity itself.

Max Stirner

Stirner was a true anarchist, the forerunner of twentieth-century anarchism, who felt the only value was the individual, with no value residing in abstractions such as social class or the state.

Truth may be the greatest god, though belief in gods likely can't be overthrown. Most would say that religious belief shouldn't be overthrown, but most haven't a clue how many there are. If the species excised superstition, what portion of religion would remain? Tom says lots, while I say near nothing. Western religion bases original sin on the eating of an apple from the tree of knowledge, transparently symbolic. Knowledge is the forbidden fruit of Western religion. Tom says the tree represents materialism instead of knowledge. Reason requires reliance on probabilities; not on possibility or myth. Tom says religious experience is real, beyond probability. Religious experience is absolutely real to the person experiencing it, similar to any highly emotional moment, but not necessarily related to either reality or reason.

We work by exorcizing incessant superstition that there are mysterious tribal gods against you. Nature has neither rewards nor punishments, only consequences. You can use science to make it work for you. There's only nothingness and chaos out there until the human mind recognizes it.

Edwin H. Land

Land invented, among other things, the Polaroid camera, polarized sunglasses, and 3D movies.

Logic establishes no factual link among religion, nirvana, immortality, the veneration of cows, holy water, or the signing of crosses. The superstitious trappings of organized religion argue against a religious monopoly on truth or keys to eternal life. The universe appears to consist primarily of nothingness and chaos. Tom says the Christian god and, perhaps, other gods make sense from nothingness and chaos. I say prove it, while Tom and I have dinner at a nice little Italian restaurant.

> Wisdom is not acquired
> save as the result of investigation.
>
> Shankara Acharya
>
> Acharya was responsible for the
> main current of "modern" Indian
> thought, distinguishing between
> Hinduism as believing "Atman
> (Soul, Self) exists," and Buddhism
> that there is "no Soul, no Self."

Little if any wisdom flows from divine revelation. Most wisdom flows from knowledge gained through investigation and experience. Tom says religious experience establishes knowledge through personal investigation. But religious experience can't be articulated, much less quantified. The knowledge required for membership in any organized religion is unqualified as wisdom, excepting a few wise rules evolved from historical experience—that we shouldn't kill, steal, covet, or lie is ignored by society, religion, and the individual when it suits our interests. Our interests are often served better by wars between governments, always supported by religion, by the declaration of birth control as a venal sin, by capital punishment, wars, and other glaring exceptions to basic religious commandments. The sacraments, prayers, and rituals of religion appear largely unrelated to wisdom, particularly in those religions that promise immortality, support wars against other religions, and prohibit birth control. Tom says immortality is real, but he agrees that religion encourages conflict and that having children one can't afford to raise and educate may induce poverty. There's little we can't agree upon. Just the core.

The miseries derived to mankind from superstition under the name of religion, and of ecclesiastical tyranny under the name of church government, have been clearly and usefully exposed. We begin to think and to act from reason and from nature alone. This is true of several, but still is by far the majority in the same old state of blindness and slavery; and much is to be feared that we shall perpetually relapse, while the real productive cause of all this superstitious folly, enthusiastical nonsense, and holy tyranny hold a revered place in the estimation even of those who are otherwise enlightened.

Edmund Burke

As a member of Parliament, Burke supported U.S. independence and the repeal of the Stamp Act, which brewed the U.S. revolution.

Enlightenment is subjective. One person's enlightenment is another's superstition and vice versa. The feud between religion and science demands closure. Many principles are capable of agreement. Science helps produce knowledge, certainty, and material advancement; religion contributes peace of mind, though hazarding potential poverty, while science provides the means for avoiding too many children; both science and religion may contribute to conflict and war. Uttering science and religion in the same breath shouldn't compromise reason. Tom agrees.

I don't know about God . . . The only things I know are what I see, hear, feel, and smell.

Günter Grass

Grass is the literary spokesman for Germans who grew up in the Nazi era and survived; he wrote on the unease of Poland after German unification.

The only things we know for certain are those things we experience personally, and we still may be easily fooled. Many have religious experiences, the meaning of which may be rationally debatable. We've seen mirages and fantasies as real as eating breakfast. We feel something profound when overcome with the emotion of religious experience. Integrating the rational portion of the mind with religious experience may be impossible.

That there is a Devil is a thing doubted by none but such as are under the influence of the Devil. For any to deny the being of a Devil must be from ignorance or profaneness worse than diabolical.

Cotton Mather

Mather graduated from Harvard (his father was president of Harvard) with an M.A. at age eighteen. A Congregational minister, he believed in witches and smallpox vaccinations, the latter incensing the city of Boston.

Belief in spirits, benign or malevolent, buggers reality. The justification for bare belief is afforded by belief itself. Believing in a devil is as reasonable as believing in a god. Both are contrary to logic but appeal to our delight in the magical and marvelous. Their truth is unknowable except through science or, some might say, religious experience. I'm skeptical about truth residing in the latter, but Tom isn't.

For the crowd, the incredible has sometimes more power and is more credible than Truth.

70

Menander

Menander's work as a comic
dramatist greatly influenced,
albeit quite indirectly, European
comedy beginning with the
Renaissance.

For all of us, the incredible often has more power than truth.
Truth is relatively boring when compared to gods, devils, and the
occult. Seriously debating their existence (or nonexistence) might
remove much romance from our lives. I'm not a romantic though
always overly optimistic. Tom is a romantic and perhaps overly
pessimistic.

If we must play the
theological game, let us never
forget it is a game. Religion, it
seems to me, can survive only as a
consciously accepted system of
make-believe.

Aldous Huxley

Huxley became partially blind
while a student at Eton and could
barely read during his tenure at
Balliol College, Oxford. He later
taught George Orwell.

Make-believe is satisfying though not particularly conducive
to mental health, whereas reality needn't detract from our well-
being. Tom says religious experience isn't mere make-believe, and
we make our usual progress toward synthesis.

If Jesus Christ were to come
today, people would not even
crucify him. They would ask him
to dinner, and hear what he had to
say, and make fun of it.

Thomas Carlyle

This Scottish historian and
sociological writer suffered from
gastric ulcers; he called economics
the dismal science.

Many of Christ's reported teachings were ethical and
idealistic. The Christian churches have perverted his message
through ritual and myth, removing its force and efficacy. Tom says
right on, brother. (Mort Sahl said if Christ were born in the twentieth
century, instead of little golden crosses we'd wear tiny electric
chairs.)

The myth of the conception
and birth of Jesus Christ is mere
fiction, and is at the same stage of
superstition as a hundred other
myths of other religions.

Ernst Heinrich Haeckel

Haeckel originally wanted to be an
artist but upon reading Charles
Darwin in 1859, abruptly changed
his mind.

Religion is inseparable from myth. The idea of Christ seems
too good to be true. Otherwise, we would not believe. The myths of
Christianity are indistinguishable from the myths of Judaism, Islam,
Hinduism, Egyptian gods, and the rest. Tom says yes, religions are
the building blocks of human experience and spirituality.

Religious feeling is as much
a verity as any other part of human
consciousness; and against it, on
the subjective side, the waves of
science beat in vain.

John Tyndall

This British physicist was the first
to demonstrate why the sky is
blue.

Religious feeling can't be denied. Neither can hot flashes, drug-induced hallucinations, or wishful fantasies. Religion to me looks like the antithesis of reason, though Tom says otherwise.

> I sometimes think that God, in creating men, somewhat overestimated his ability.
>
> Oscar Wilde

> Gilbert and Sullivan satirized Wilde and his Aesthetic Movement in *Patience*, making Wilde a celebrity before he had published a single word.

Believing the species has outstripped its gods is as egocentric as believing a god exists in the image of the species, precisely Wilde's point. If a god created the species, either it made a tactical error or it is a sadistic jerk. If a god didn't create the species, then all is well with the world and we can rest without fear of divine retribution, hell, eternal punishment, and eternal life. Tom says we should skip the bad parts, but he still fancies the eternal-life part.

> A deaf, dumb, and blind idiot could have made a better world than this.
>
> Tennessee Williams

> Williams began writing while working at a St. Louis shoe factory.

The earthly world is a marvel. Only the fearful, the untraveled, and perhaps Tennessee Williams think otherwise. The religions and governments of the world that contribute to human suffering are an abomination, which is likely what Williams meant. We don't get along with each other because of nationalism, religion, greed, and ethnic prejudice, though I find individuals essentially the same in every country everywhere; most of us are decent folk seeking a better life for ourselves and our families, sprinkled with a few stinkers.

> All the philosophers of the world who had a religion have said in all ages: 'There is a God; and one must be just.' That, then is the universal religion established in all ages and throughout mankind. The point in which they all agree is therefore true, and the systems through which they differ, therefore false.
>
> Voltaire

> After complimenting the English, Voltaire was forced to flee 1734 Paris.

Religions universally agree that God (or gods) exists and is (or are) just, except toward other gods. No one, religious or philosophical, has satisfactorily defined justice. Though no evidence of any god has ever been found, a universal concept of justice lurks beneath the surface of philosophy and religion. Justice may be incompatible with the retribution demanded by religions and governments and derails when it tries to protect the individual from himself. Tom rather agrees.

Revel in the Impossible

> It is certain because it is impossible.
>
> Tertullian

> Because Tertullian, after initially converting to Christianity, rejected it as too lax, he wasn't considered as a father of the church until the nineteenth century.

Religious belief couldn't be more succinctly described. Tom adds: or more inaccurately. We marvel at whatever contradicts common sense. Tom says magic sometime works; I can't disagree with the power of the human mind, or its ability for wishful thinking.

> Earth to earth, ashes to ashes, dust to dust; in sure and certain hope of the Resurrection unto eternal life.
>
> Book of Common Prayer

Resurrection is certain because it's likely impossible, having no known occurrence outside of religious myth. The fact of the human body's decomposition after death is religious proof of immortality. A more imaginative myth is difficult to conceive. Most believe they'll live forever. Tom says yea, and I say nay. Neither of us knows or likely ever shall.

> Men willingly believe what they wish.
>
> Caius Julius Caesar

After years of battle, Caesar finally conquered Gaul (northern Italy, France, Belgium, and a bit of the Netherlands), camping on the Rubicon; the Senate ordered him to relinquish his command, but he instead crossed the Rubicon, signaling the dawn of civil war.

We refuse to believe that which contradicts our hopes, opting for the religious myth of immortality without supporting evidence. We believe what we need to believe because it's easier than confronting reality. Tom says immortality is reality, though he doesn't really know either.

> Every great scientific truth goes through three states: First, people say it conflicts with the Bible; next, they say it has been discovered before; lastly, they say

they always believed it.

Louis Agassiz

This Swiss-born naturalist rejected
Darwin's *Origin of the Species*
because he believed all creation
was by a god.

Hypocrisy is the philosophy of the species, in society and
religion. All religions dismissed Darwinian evolution as in conflict
with the Bible, but after evolution became generally accepted,
religion generally decided evolution to be the handiwork of their
god. Now nonfundamentalist religions say they've always believed
in evolution. Fundamentalist sects, no matter the religion, believe
evolutionary theory devilish, similar to Agassiz.

Religion and Education

The rivers of America will
run with blood filled to their banks
before we will submit to them
taking the Bible out of our schools.

Billy Sunday

William A. ("Billy") Sunday was
a professional baseball player until
he became an evangelist; he led
over three hundred revivals with
an estimated attendance in excess
of 100 million people.

The Bible and other holy books should be taught in school as
the myths they are, analyzing their interrelationships and continuing
impact on the species. Permitting prayer in public schools is a major
policy goal of many politicians. Only common courtesy prevents
bloodletting. Tom says prayer shouldn't be required in public
schools, because that which is forced is scorned and devalued.

The exclusion of Christ
from the history of man is an act
against man.

Pope John Paul II

This long-lived pope was fluent in Latin, Polish, Italian, English, French, German, Spanish, and Portuguese.

All history is incomprehensible without Christ.

Ernest Renan

During his first lecture at the College de France, Renan, a philologist and historian, called Jesus "an incomparable man," and the cleric faculty suspended him as an atheist.

History is incomprehensible without Christ, other religious leaders, and religious events. However, religious history couldn't be objectively taught in any public school in any country, because no one could agree on the curriculum. I would vote for including the entire history of all religions along with their origins, evolution, charitable acts, and atrocities resulting in unending wars and poverty, while most would likely vote to exclude this portion of religious history. Government schools, in deference to religion, never accurately teach religious history. The only means of understanding the history of religion is through individual research and self-teaching. Tom agrees but says religion has overcome its dark past while I continue to overemphasize it. The religious present seems little better to me.

Let them innovate in nothing, but keep the tradition.

Pope Stephen I

The details of Stephen I's papacy are known only through three reports by his archenemy, Bishop St. Cyprian of Carthage.

Religion universally advocates the status quo, avoiding change. We may need the status quo for stability, but we equally need change for progress. Religious tradition includes archaic ideas badly needing riddance, such as prohibitions against birth control, religious infallibility, and commandments that other gods, sects, and religions be exterminated. Without its missionary zeal, religion might wither away; Tom toasts missionaries.

> As a rule people are afraid
> of truth. Each truth we discover in
> nature or social life destroys the
> crutches on which we need to lean.

> Ernst Toller

> Toller was a German playwright,
> poet, and pacifist whose
> autobiography was titled *I Was a
> German.*

Truth is merciless. Recognition of truth requires personal responsibility, as opposed to blaming events on the supernatural, superstition, gods, devils, holy or unholy ghosts, and similar. The truth is that spirits probably don't exist, whether called souls, gods, devils, or angels; no evidence of their being has ever been found, not a scintilla, though Tom insists that personal experience establishes the existence of religious precepts.

> Faith branches off from the
> highroad before reason begins.

> William James

> James said that impersonal reason
> is an illusion because emotion and
> thoughts are inseparable.

Reason is learned through experience and documentation, not by bare belief, no matter its sincerity. Belief not based on probability is the low road. Tom says that for him, personal experience creates probability.

> Men fear thought as they

fear nothing else on earth—more than death. Thought is subversive, and revolutionary, destructive and terrible; thought is merciless to privilege, established institutions, and comfortable habits; thought is anarchic and lawless, indifferent to authority, careless to the well-tried wisdom of the ages. Thought looks into the pit of hell and is not afraid. . . . Thought is great and swift and free, the light of the world, and the chief glory of man.

Bertrand Russell

Russell's primary thoughts as a child centered on sex, religion, and mathematics, a rather heady mix.

For most of us, thought isn't as easy as Russell makes it sound.

Nobody thinks clearly, no matter what they pretend. Thinking's a dizzy business, a matter of catching as many of those foggy glimpses as you can and fitting them together the best you can. That's why people hang on so tight to their beliefs and opinions; because, compared to the haphazard way in which they're arrived at, even the goofiest opinion seems wonderfully clear, sane, and self-evident. And if you let it get away from you, then you've got to dive back into that foggy muddle to wangle yourself out another to take its place.

Dashiell Hammett, *The*

79

Clear thought fails to respect persons or institutions that order our respect without scrutiny. We're mostly religious because we're mostly unthinking. However, many religious are intellectuals and scholars who have concluded that faith has merit though it can't be tested by scientific method. They are possibly, though not probably, correct. This gap can never be closed unless we agree that probabilities negate the viability of bare possibilities. Tom says religious experience establishes probability, and I say not. We have complete freedom of choice.

> A fact never went into partnership with a miracle. Truth scorns the assistance of wonders. A fact will fit every other fact in the universe, and that is how you can tell whether it is or is not a fact. A lie will not fit anything except another lie.
>
> Robert Ingersoll

> Ingersoll single-handedly popularized intellectual criticism of the Bible, humanistic philosophy, and scientific rationalism.

Religious dogma fits no known fact. *Whopper* is too strong a word to describe myths, religious or otherwise, which were spun from our anxieties and infatuation for the sensational, thus not constituting deliberate falsehood. Religion is speculation unconnected to verifiable truth. Tom says no way.

> As a rule we disbelieve all facts and theories for which we have no use.
>
> William James

> James founded scientific (laboratory) psychology but

considered it "a nasty little
subject" compared to philosophy
and religion.

If we wish to avoid death, we have little use for the fact of
putrefaction after death, and who doesn't want to avoid death? We
cling to the ancestral myths that promise life forever if we follow
rituals and keep the faith. Tom says myths contain truth or they
wouldn't endure. I ask how he knows, and the answer is the same.

Religion is nothing but the
shadow cast by the universe on
human intelligence.

Victor Hugo

Hugo's father was a general in
Napoleon's army, whereas Hugo
championed the downtrodden,
universal suffrage, compulsory
education, and minority rights.

Religion purports infallibility and a monopoly over human
intelligence, though it's difficult to conceive of thousands of
different religions all being right or having a major connection to
human intelligence. More than a mere shadow on human
intelligence, religion is a hurricane against it.

A thinker (and what is an
artist if not a triple thinker?)
should have neither religion nor
fatherland nor even any social
convictions.

Gustave Flaubert

The French government tried
Flaubert for immorality when he
published *Madame Bovary*, and he
barely escaped conviction.

Allegiance to a religion or country requires belief in its
superiority. We can't be Roman Catholic without believing that

Baptists, Muslims, and Jews belong to an inferior religion. Most can't be Americans or Germans without believing that citizens of other countries are backward, less intelligent, or at least culturally inferior. Our allegiance better belongs to the species instead of to our artificial division into hundreds of countries, thousands of religions, and other pigeonholes unrelated to character. Tom agrees, almost entirely (because Roman Catholic is obviously the one), and he still gives communion on Sundays.

> In religion, man denies his
> reason. . . . Miracle owes its origin
> to the negation of thought.

> Ludwig Feuerbach

> This German philosopher denied
> he was an atheist, though he said
> God was an illusion.

Hope blossoms through religion, though neither are related to reason and thought. Religious thought is about the unknowable, like debating the number of angels that would fit on the head of a pin. Belief negates thought when not based on probability. Tom says religious philosophy is as intellectually advanced and as honest as nonreligious philosophy.

> The light of faith makes us
> see what we believe.

> Thomas Aquinas

> Aquinas synthesized classical
> philosophy with Christianity,
> which is to say that he
> Christianized Aristotle.

We believe what we need to believe—that we'll live forever if we do thus and so, no matter the sense of it all. If we have faith, we can believe anything, no matter its connection with reality. Because beliefs are unsupported by objective reality and therefore can't be tested, no belief can be ranked against other unsubstantiated beliefs. This means that the validity of all religions is identical. Islam is as valid as Hinduism, Zoroastrianism,

Christianity, Scientology, Mormonism, or a thousand others. Without a verifiable basis in reality, we can't rationally distinguish between beliefs. Tom disagrees, based on his experience.

> Let the convinced Christian believe, for that is the duty he has taken upon himself. The non-Christian has forfeited the grace of faith. (Perhaps he was cursed from birth in not being able to believe but only to know.)
>
> Carl Gustav Jung
>
> Jung believed that each of us has a strong need for religious belief, which is required in order to tap into Jung's theory of the collective unconscious.

Belief limited to knowledge may be a blessed curse while belief without evidence may be irrational, the equivalent of building a house on shifting sand or, more aptly, air. Non-Christians are a vast majority of the species, comprising Hindus, Muslims, Buddhists, Hindus, and the nonreligious, all, in Jung's view, having forfeited the grace of faith. Tom says the Jung statement is intolerant, but he does believe that certain knowledge can flow from religious experience.

> Nothing in the world is more dangerous than a sincere ignorance and conscientious stupidity.
>
> Martin Luther King, Jr.
>
> King was arrested at a lunch-counter sit-in on the pretext that he had violated probation from a months-earlier traffic violation; John F. Kennedy got him released from jail eight days before the 1960 presidential election,

swinging the black vote and
perhaps Kennedy's election as
president.

Views on race, religion, sex, nationality, and other
stereotypical views of the individual are often based on sincere
ignorance and conscientious stupidity, unrelated to character or
honesty. The fallacy of so judging an individual's worth is
illustrated where the tectonic plates of the world's major religions
grind together, in the Middle East and Africa, now filtering
worldwide. Neither Martin Luther King nor Tom would agree that
religion is sincere ignorance and conscientious stupidity. I wouldn't
use the word *stupidity*—more like contented sightlessness.

Superstition . . . religion
which has grown incongruous
with intelligence.

John Tyndall

Tyndall was an Irish surveyor who
became one of the world's leading
physicists, making formative
discoveries in magnetism and
infrared radiation.

The part of religion congruous with intelligence may be
limited to the religious ideas mirroring the moral principles of the
species, no matter the local religion. And these predate all religions,
though practiced in the breach ever since. Tom says he understands
the difficulty of one who has had no connection with religious
experience—and buys the next round.

Can there exist a people free
from all superstitious prejudices?
That is to ask: can there exist a
nation of philosophers?

Prejudices are what fools
use for reason.

Voltaire

Though vehemently opposed to organized religion, Voltaire was a deist, believing the universe was created by a god.

Prejudices let us cope with diversity, others, and the unknown. We internalize myths about the characteristics of other religious, ethnic, and national groups, judging their members accordingly, though our stereotypes are absurd when applied to the individual. Philosophers may possibly be less prejudiced than nonphilosophers, or perhaps they try harder to avoid stereotypes and prejudices, but we don't know that.

For some reason or other man looks for the miracle, and to accomplish it he will wade through blood. He will debauch himself with ideas, he will reduce himself to a shadow if for only one second of his life he can close his eyes to the hideousness of reality. Everything is endured—disgrace, humiliation, poverty, war, crime, *ennui*—in the belief that overnight something will occur, a miracle, which will render life tolerable.

Henry Miller, *Tropic of Cancer*

Tropic of Cancer was based on Miller's experience in depression-era Paris, living hand to mouth.

The human understanding is no dry light, but receives infusion from the will and affections; whence proceed sciences which may be called 'sciences as one would.' For what a man had rather were true he more readily believes. Therefore,

85

he rejects difficult things from impatience of research; sober things, because they narrow hope; the deeper things of nature, from superstition; the light of experience, from arrogance and pride; things not commonly believed, out of deference to the opinion of the vulgar. Numberless in short are the ways, and sometimes imperceptible, in which the affections color and infect the understanding.

Francis Bacon

Bacon discovered that freezing a chicken stopped it from decaying, whereupon he caught a chill and died.

Wherefore Miracles?

No miracle has ever taken place under conditions which science can accept. Experience shows, without exception, that miracles occur only in times and in countries in which miracles are believed in, and in the presence of persons who are disposed to believe in them.

Ernest Renan

Renan attended seminary but lost his faith, leaving the Catholic church in 1845; he thought God might exist but was extremely well-hidden.

We love miracles, building on our feeling as wee tots that we'll live forever, reveling in the marvelous and chasing miracles because we delight in the magical. But life might be better without a dependency on miracles. Denying miracles would remove the downside of genuflecting to those who demand belief through enchantment. Reality isn't so hideous that we need miracles and religion. The negatives of religion—the creation of poverty throughout Africa and Asia by prohibiting birth control for the uneducated and third world; then the intolerant competitive nature of religion leading to inquisitions, interminable conflicts, and war— overshadow miracles created by religious belief. How relevant can it possibly be that someone sees the image of Jesus on a tortilla, and a crowd agrees? Tom says religion helps him cope, and I ask at what price. A miracle restrains his hand.

> . . . science . . . is so greatly
> opposed to history and tradition
> that it cannot be absorbed by our
> civilization.

> Max Born

> After fleeing the Nazis in 1933,
> this German-born physicist taught
> philosophy at the University of
> Edinburgh from 1936 until his
> retirement in 1953, when he
> returned to Germany. He was
> awarded the Nobel Prize in 1954.

Most people are more attached to religion, based on its history and tradition, than to science and the scientific method, which accepts only the provable and probable.

> The doctrine of first cause
> and the very idea of miracles
> vanish with the notion of causality.

> Charles Sanders Peirce

> Pierce was the father of
> pragmatism. *Webster's*
> *Biographical Dictionary* called

him "the most original thinker and greatest logician of his time." He refused to permit his writings to be published until after his death and spent his last twenty-six years as a poverty-stricken recluse.

The doctrine of first cause presumes a god created the universe because only a god could create a universe, avoiding the questions of who or what created the god and whether a god must have a cause. The notion of causality applied to the origin of the universe consternates religion, science, and philosophy. The simple fact is that no one knows how (or why, assuming a why is necessary) the universe came into being. Science tries objectively to find the answer. Religion identified numerous answers centuries before the Dark Ages, and its conclusions continue infallible though we lacked the foggiest notion of cosmology back then. Miracles caused by spirits, gods, and ghosts are similarly suspect. No miracles have been verified except by the religious entity gaining prestige through the miracle's occurrence. Ever.

The many instances of forged miracles, and prophecies, and supernatural events, which, in all ages, have either been detected by contrary evidence, or which detect themselves by their absurdity, prove sufficiently the strong propensity of mankind to the extraordinary and marvelous, and ought reasonably to beget a suspicion against all relations of this kind.

David Hume

The author of *An Inquiry Concerning Human Understanding* (1748), Hume became rich, spending the last seven years of his life entertaining friends such as Adam Smith and writing an autobiography of five startling pages.

No religious spirit has ever appeared to a person outside that religion. The archangel Gabriel has never appeared to a Christian, and the Virgin Mary has never appeared to a Muslim. All miracles appear to originate in the mind, indistinguishable from hallucinations, drug euphoria, or sleep or food deprivation. From a scientific point of view, there's no difference between a man who fasts and sees heaven and a man who drinks alcohol and sees snakes. According *The Book of Lists 3* the Virgin Mary made 232 appearances in thirty-two countries between 1928 and 1975, all to Roman Catholics. She failed to appear to Jews, Protestants, Muslims, Buddhists, Hindus, or atheists. Tom says he knows that, and I know he does.

> Miracles arise from our ignorance of nature, not from nature itself.
>
> Michel Eyquem de Montaigne

> Montaigne invented the essay, writing in his famous ivory tower, though he found time to serve as the mayor of Bordeaux from 1581 to 1585.

Miracles arise from our credulity, hopes, and fears. We wish to believe that a god exists to rescue us from the oblivion of death. Miracles are a sign that a god exists, supporting our hope for immortality. Nature abhors a miracle, making fun of bare belief when a miracle is revealed as balderdash. Nothing has ever occurred contrary to the laws of nature, though Tom says God has. Religion is compatible with human nature but opposed to physical laws and the scientific method. The Christian gospels were written down years after the events they describe. We know from our childhood game of gossip (where a word or phrase is whispered through ten or more people) that oral storytelling is a grossly unreliable witness to events occurring seconds earlier, much less years.

> To prove the Gospels by a miracle is to prove an absurdity by

something contrary to nature.

Denis Diderot

Diderot wrote, edited, and
published the first encyclopedia
with a little help from his friends,
such as Rousseau, writing to
support a mistress.

A miracle drips magic and holiness though credible only
when supported by objective evidence. The incredible explained by
bare belief strains credibility. Religious myths are similar to
flickering shadows in Plato's cave, explained by silhouettes and
whispers of wind. The voice of a god shimmering in light would
convert most anyone, similar to a hallucinogenic episode or a
religious experience based on faith. Drugs are drugs.

The more the fruits of
knowledge become accessible to
men, the more widespread is the
decline of religious belief.

Sigmund Freud

Freud turned psychology (then a
branch of philosophy) on its ear by
insisting that unselfishness can be
self-punishment, kindness
superiority, altruism self-
centeredness, and male celibacy a
flight from women.

No matter the accessibility of knowledge, the majority will
never become well-educated. Education is a product of the state,
always biased toward the particular state and its dominant religion.
State schools educate few well and those few accidentally, because
of their own ability and ambition, while leaving the rest uneducated.
Thus, religious belief will likely never waste away. The hope for
immortality and fear of death outweigh education. Even an
extensive and relatively unbiased education doesn't necessarily
extinguish religious belief. Many religious, such as Tom, are
incredibly well-educated, intelligent, and nobody's fool. They

believe in religion no matter its conflict with reason. Their belief is based on religious experience, spirituality, morality, and tradition, though organized religion may truly reflect only the first and last.

> Whatever a man prays for, he prays for a miracle. . . . 'Great God, let not two times two make four.'

> Ivan Turgenev, Fathers and Sons

> Turgenev challenged Tolstoy to a duel after Tolstoy fell asleep reading *Fathers and Sons,* but the duel was never fought because Tolstoy didn't receive the challenge until after he arrived in Paris.

We pray for the nullification of physical laws during football games, shipwrecks, wars, and personal jealousies, among other circumstances. The Christian, Jewish, and Muslim gods have led their converts against each other in innumerable bloody battles, the gods taking turns winning, leading one to suspect that the victor actually depends on which armies are more skillful, lucky, or numerous.

We experience the desperately hoped for, clawing for immortality and a reprieve from death. It's easier to believe in eternity than investigate the probability. Our backgrounds indelibly color our experience, perceptions, and hopes. The environment of a black South African protestant diverges beyond understanding from that of a Japanese Shinto, Indian Hindu, or Italian Catholic. These differences may be nearly unbridgeable due to nationalism, ethnicity, and religion, though our hopes and needs are essentially identical. We crave acceptance by our local society, no matter the cost, acquiring belief in the superiority of local myth, religion, superstition, and nationalism. These divisions are high profile, indelibly coloring our attitude toward others.

A miracle cured dozens of diseased and crippled peasants in 1987 Guatemala after they viewed an image of Christ that appeared on the side of a church. The faithful continued to believe the miracle after a rainstorm revealed a Willie Nelson poster that had been covered by recent whitewash. Cured is cured. Mental processes and imagination are sometimes stronger and more productive than medical care. Mind over matter often works, such as when a ninety-pound mother lifts a car off her child. Yet a religiously recognized miracle seems slim evidence for a particular god.

The Logic of Prayer

> PRAY, v. To ask that the laws of the universe be annulled in behalf of a single petitioner confessedly unworthy.
>
> Ambrose Bierce, *The Enlarged Devil's Dictionary*
>
> Bierce lived in England from 1872 to 1875, writing for the London magazines *Fun* and *Figaro*.

Prayer, whether Christian, Jewish, Muslim, Buddhist, Hindu, or other, asks an all-knowing god to change its mind, to entertain begging, and reassess facts previously overlooked by the one true God who knows everything and is omnipotent. Only petty gods enjoy boot-licking sycophants. Tom says prayer is communication.

> If God listened to the prayers of men, all men would quickly have perished: for they are forever praying for evil against one another.
>
> Epicurus
>
> Epicurus wrote over three hundred books, but only fragments survive, perhaps related to his view that the world is made up of atoms continually being created and destroyed.

Gods must have their hands full weighing the merits between contending prayers. A proper god would either ignore both sides or

92

position a lightning strike against the more selfish or vindictive. Tom says such prayers don't qualify as prayers.

> To deny the possibility, nay, actual existence of witchcraft and sorcery is at once flatly to contradict the revealed word of God in various passages of both the Old and New Testament.
>
> Sir William Blackstone

> Blackstone's four volumes of *Commentaries on the Laws of England*, published between 1765 and 1769, remain the foundation of legal education in England, Canada, and the United States, including the law school I did little more than attend.

Denying the existence of unicorns, devils, and other spirits contradicts the revealed word of various gods. Belief in the Christian god requires belief in billions of spirits called souls, angels, devil(s), and three gods, which include a father, a son, and a holy ghost, who are actually one god, thus raising questions whether a holy ghost is similar to a regular ghost and how to tell the difference. Though these questions may be irreverent, they bear asking. Many Biblical scholars interpret these texts as allegorical. Where allegory stops and reality begins is a difficult distinction to draw. Tom suggests prayer.

The Greatest Good: Knowledge, Religion, or What?

> I give instruction concerning mighty things and proceed to free the mind from the closely confining shackles of religion.
>
> Lucretius

In the first century B.C.E.,
Lucretius wrote the six-volume
poem *On the Nature of Things,*
describing Epicurean philosophy,
which included atoms, mortality
of the soul, and gods unconcerned
with human affairs.

Mighty things are defined subjectively and, for Lucretius, divorced from religion. Religion has precipitated massacres, bloodshed, wars, and poverty, things that qualify as other than mighty. The mightiest thing creditable to religion is perhaps its proclaimed concern for the poor, contradicted by religious prohibitions against birth control. Tom says religion soothes poverty but can't deny its possible role in poverty creation.

Education is danger. . . . At
best an education which produces
useful coolies for us is admissible.
Every educated person is a future
enemy.

Martin Bormann

Bormann succeeded Rudolph
Hess as Hitler's chief of staff after
Hess's quixotic 1941 flight to
Scotland. The quote is from a
letter to his wife, Gerda.

The educated dislike dictators, whether in government, religion, or other bureaucracies. Government schools educate the masses as useful coolies through high school, teaching obedience to and respect for a government that may deserve neither. Education beyond government-mandated curriculums may produce people unbound by customary thought. The educated are dangerous because they accord respect only to those institutions earning respect, no matter their historical demands for genuflection. Stuart Wavell, writing in *The Sunday Times* (London), on September 3, 1995, observed that global access to new ideas, such as online, "may open up closed societies to heretical ideas and threaten their governing cliques. . . . The Internet is the most dangerous new technology challenging autocratic regimes, because they have little control over what goes in or out." As a result, many governments, such China, control the Internet absolutely. Mr. Wavell adds that one extremely popular topic is religion because, according to one observer, "If people made some of these religious comments face-to-face, they would have hit each other." Or shoot each other. Tom says he tries to avoid the temptation, and I do appreciate it.

> Vice is ignorance. Virtue is knowledge.
>
> Plato

> Plato witnessed Socrates' trial in 399 B.C.E. Athens and fled to Italy, Sicily, and Egypt when Socrates drank hemlock. He returned to Athens fourteen years later and founded the Academy.

Ignorance may as competently avoid vice as knowledge is no guarantor of virtue. The relationships between vice and ignorance, knowledge and virtue, are insufficient to usefully predict behavior. Only the individual (not classes of individuals, whether based on educational level, race, religion, nationality, or ethnicity) may accurately be judged according to vice or virtue. Tom says amen, and I feel anointed.

> Education makes people easy to lead, but difficult to drive; easy to govern, but impossible to enslave.
>
> Henry Brougham

> This wit, orator, lawyer, politician (lord chancellor of England), scientific theorist, translator of Demosthenes, and novelist designed the first four-wheeled carriage for a single horse, called a Brougham.

An unbiased education makes people difficult to lead and

impossible to drive; difficult to govern, because they have their own ideas, and impossible to enslave for a significant period of time. Government (and religious) schools make people easy to lead, relatively easy to drive (such as the hype leading any country into war), simple to govern like sheep, and to enslave such as any country under a nationalist fever. Government education is no guarantor of freedom but insures more freedom than no education at all; but there is little practical alternative to government-sponsored education.

> There is nothing which can better deserve our patronage than the promotion of science and literature. Knowledge is in every country the surest basis of public happiness.
>
> George Washington

> The English tomb of Washington's family featured a coat of arms in the shape of a shield covered with stars and stripes.

Knowledge may be a great source of happiness for those inclined in that direction; others may prefer beer and billiards. Happiness is a uniquely individual matter. Public happiness is a misnomer, because only individuals can be happy. Whether government should support science and literature is a difficult question, because government support often means government control and research or writing that benefits the government.

> Beware you are not swallowed up in books! An ounce of love is worth a pound of knowledge.

> Passion and prejudice govern the world; only under the name of reason.

> In 1735 Wesley—the English divine and founder of Methodism—became the pastor of a new settlement, Savannah, Georgia. In 1774 Wesley was among the first in England to speak out against slavery.

Those suggesting we beware of books are likely either religious or a particular type of government leader, such as Wesley and Bormann. Tom says this is sadly true but doesn't happen often. Love of others may be key to individual happiness but is far beyond the modest scope of an analysis of the relationship between religion and ethics.

We enjoy a particular talent for rationalization, often able to justify anything that furthers our interest. Though reason may conceal passion and prejudice, only reason is likely to deliver us from both. Prejudice is the opposite of reason, because it judges people and situations not personally known, based on group affiliation.

> Human history becomes more and more a race between education and catastrophe.
>
> H.G. Wells

> Wells's father was a professional cricketer and his mother a domestic maid.

A universally unbiased education might help avert any number of catastrophes, from war to poverty. Because an unbiased education is impossible for the majority (or even a tiny minority), Wells's statement may be a harbinger of doom, but we're individually doomed anyway; Tom votes not.

The Sources of Knowledge

> Possibly if a true estimate

97

were made of the morality and religions of the world, we would find that the far greater part of mankind received even those opinions and ceremonies they would die for, rather from the fashions of their countries and the constant practice of those about them, than from any conviction of their reason.

John Locke

Locke's parents were Puritans, but he pioneered separation of church and state and was quoted on the greatest good in the Declaration of Independence: life, liberty, and the pursuit of happiness.

Locke is jarringly accurate. Custom governs more surely than government and laws, and is closely akin to religion. Religion and government manage us through tradition, historical precedent, and a near universal acquiescence in their command, rather than by reason. We reason little, instead choosing the easier course of avoiding confrontation with the behemoths of religion and government, which is usually an excellent idea. Tom says religion is reasonable but government often isn't. It seems to me that neither are notable for reasonableness, especially the fundamentalist and intolerant ones.

He who knows only one religion knows none.

Max Muller

Muller was the foremost expert of his time on Eastern religions, editing the fifty-one volumes of *The Sacred Books of the East* (1879–1904).

We can't know Christianity without understanding its

98

intimate Jewish, Hindu, Mithraic, Islamic, and other interconnections. We can't know religion in general unless we understand the history of the major religions and their thousands of offshoots. Tom agrees, which means I can't help but love the guy, and adds, but no one has the time.

> Burn the libraries, for their value is in this one book [the Koran].
>
> Omar I

> The second caliph and captor of Jerusalem, Omar I married Mohammed's daughter Hafsa in 625, conquered much of the Middle East, and was assassinated by a Persian slave.

Fundamentalists, no matter their religion, defend their particular holy book similarly to Omar I. When religion claims infallibility and a monopoly on truth, other books are relative trash, and many are heretical.

> Anyone who stops learning is old, whether at twenty or eighty. Anyone who keeps learning stays young. The greatest thing in life is to keep your mind young.
>
> Henry Ford

> This American automaker's greatest educational gap was his notorious anti-Semitism; by the early 1920s he'd published ninety articles against the Jews, including the infamous "The Protocols of the Elders of Zion."

The continual acquisition of knowledge is a fountain of youth. Seniors with active minds (a coterie of nuns in Pennsylvania translating Greek into English, for example) stand half the chance of developing Alzheimer's disease as the general public—though we should perhaps distinguish knowledge of popular entertainment from that which pieces together the puzzle of the world. On the other hand, an aging mind cushions the free fall into oblivion. Tom asks, curiously, what oblivion?

Religion and Superstition Versus Reason and Knowledge

> The priesthood have, in all ancient nations, nearly monopolized learning. . . . And ever since the Reformation, when or where has existed a Protestant or dissenting sect who would tolerate A FREE INQUIRY? The blackest billingsgate, the most ungentlemanly insolence, the most yahooist brutality, is patently endured, countenanced, propagated, and applauded. But touch a solemn truth in collision with a dogma of a sect, though capable of the clearest proof, and you will soon have disturbed a nest, and the hornets will swarm about your eyes and hand, and fly into your face and eyes.
>
> John Adams

The second U.S. president was a fourth-generation American, born in Quincy, Massachusetts; he died the same day as Thomas Jefferson, on the fiftieth anniversary of signing the Declaration of Independence, a year after his son became president.

Our ancient priests began the collection of human knowledge, mixed with the myths of the species, until science began to branch off from religion in ancient Greece. Religion has poorly withstood competition from science, persecuting science during the various Inquisitions, banning and burning scientific books. It did, however, kindly commute Galileo's sentence of death at the stake when he stated, "I, Galileo, being in my seventieth year, being a prisoner and on my knees, and before your Eminences, having before my eyes the Holy Gospel, which I touch with my hands, adjure, curse and detest the error and the heresy of the movement of the earth"—that it revolved around the sun instead of being the center of the universe as taught by the Christian Church.

Religion discourages free inquiry because free inquiry always questions religious dogma. Religious intolerance encourages brutality toward other religions and the nonreligious. Those not believing in the god of a particular religion are considered less human by its members, often unworthy of basic human courtesy or subject to random mutilation. This has been the history of religion since its inception and will likely continue until its demise, which is unlikely in a species that delights in the marvelous.

Hornets of financial ruin fly into the eyes and face of the heretic or nonbeliever, who now may only suffer social leprosy instead of banishment or death. A few hundred years ago, religious dissenters were subject to some of the most horrible deaths ever concocted by human ingenuity. The slaughter continues where major religions meet, in much of Africa, India and Pakistan, Israel and Palestine, and the Middle East. Religion excommunicates dissenters when it has no power to execute. The believers in any dogma, whether religious, scientific or other, can be similarly intolerant when central tenets are challenged. The sole difference between religion and science: scientific conclusions require proof and evidence, whereas no proof or evidence are necessary for religious conclusions. Tom blandly says religious experience is proof of religious efficacy.

> They [the clergy] believe that any portion of power confided to me, will be exerted in opposition to their schemes. And they believe rightly: for I have sworn upon the altar of god eternal hostility against every form of tyranny over the mind of man.
>
> Thomas Jefferson

Jefferson believed the biggest problem in the United States

would be keeping church and state
separate. Ignoring slavery, he was
right.

Jefferson spins a web by opposing unidentified clerical schemes with vehemence sworn on the altar of god, lower case. I don't know what Jefferson meant, but Tom says the clergy must accede to the altar of god, just like Jefferson.

One single well-established
fact, clearly irreconcilable with a
doctrine, is sufficient to prove that
it is false.

John Stuart Mill
Proof is antithetical and impertinent to superstition, astrology, and organized religion, which are based on hope without provable foundation, contrary to science and established fact.

Nor do I seek to understand
that I may believe, but I believe
that I may understand. For this too
I believe, that unless I first believe,
I shall not understand.

Saint Anselm, Archbishop
of Canterbury

Saint Anselm wrote the first
argument for the existence of God
based on reason: that everyone
recognizes greater beings and the
greatest is God, thus proving the
existence of God.

Religion requires belief before understanding, because without belief religion is unintelligible, which includes every religion other than our own. No religion would attract a purely rational person, but then none of us are purely rational. Western religion attracts belief by banking on the universal desire to avoid death. Few accept the inevitability of death against the possibility of eternal life promised by Western religion. Hope reigns, avoiding reality to extend life indefinitely. Few, if any, accept or understand religion without first believing without evidence.

> It is the heart which
> experiences God, and not reason.
> This, then, is faith: God felt by the
> heart, not reason.
>
> Blaise Pascal
>
> Pascal's father, a civil servant and
> an amateur scientist, recognized
> the genius of Pascal and his two
> sisters early, quitting his job to
> devote himself full time to their
> education.

The heart yearns for life eternal. Gods, through religious dogma, promise immortality, targeting the heart to convert incredulous minds that should know better. A god can't easily be comprehended by reason, particularly the kind that not only tolerates war and poverty but is a prime contributor.

> To understand via the heart
> is not to understand.
>
> Michel Eyquem de
> Montaigne
>
> Though a humanist, Montaigne
> died accepting the full rites of the
> Roman Catholic Church.

> But inasmuch as He is the
> one true God, wholly
> incomprehensible and
> inaccessible to man's
> understanding, it is reasonable,
> indeed inevitable, that His justice
> also should be incomprehensible.
>
> Martin Luther

In 1534 Luther, father of the
Reformation, created the written
German language by translating
the Bible into German when
"Germany" was three hundred
autonomous states.

It's unreasonable to label a god or religion as "reasonable."
Because reason is the antithesis of religion it's impossible, for
example, to rationally determine which god is "the one true God"
out of the literally millions of gods revered by our thousands of
religions. Luther's statement is jumbled because a true god
"incomprehensible and inaccessible to man's understanding" can't
be understood. Incomprehensible justice isn't justice. Tom as a
loyal Catholic brother rather agrees, but then, Luther started the
Protestant/anti-Catholic thing.

The most frightful idea that
ever corroded human nature—the
idea of eternal punishment.

John Morley

Morley quarreled with his father
over religion while at Oxford and
was forced to leave the university
early without an honors degree;
his father had wanted him to
become a clergyman. He instead
became secretary of state for
Ireland and later, India.

Eternal punishment is unrelated to justice. Retribution is
appropriate, if ever, only by government against intentional,
reckless, or negligent harm of another. Eternal punishment is the
ultimate retribution and is levied only by religion, which often
threatens damnation for acts that harm no one other than the actor.
A sin that harms no one else is a silly sin. Tom says perhaps, not
entirely, but maybe mostly.

God will not have that we
should attain a higher knowledge
of things.

Martin Luther

> Luther vowed that if he survived a
> horrendous 1505 thunderstorm, he
> would become a monk; in 1525 he
> married a former nun and fathered
> a son.

A higher knowledge of things is contrary to religions that consider knowledge the forbidden fruit causing the downfall of the species. Knowledge is the opposite of superstition, which is difficult, if not impossible to distinguish from religion. Neither the Koran nor the Bible portrays education positively, or even mentions education. Religion appeals to the uneducated and poverty-stricken. Those who've moved away from religion are usually better educated and wealthier. Thus, gods of all religions must dislike the well-educated.

> When the consensus of
> scholarship says one thing and the
> Word of God says another, the
> consensus of scholarship can go
> plumb to hell for all I care.

Billy Sunday

> Sunday was a decisive force in
> establishing Prohibition in the
> United States.

Authenticating the word of a particular god is tougher than plumbing hell. If we had indisputable evidence that a particular command came from a god, we'd be fools not to follow it. We don't know any possible words of a god, much less probable ones. When the possible word of a god conflicts with the consensus of scholarship, the word is contrary to reason.

> If the work of God would be
> comprehended by reason, it would
> be no longer wonderful, and faith
> would have no merit if reason
> provided proof.

Pope Gregory I

This former president of Rome
sprang from a wealthy family (his
father was a senator and his great
great-grandfather was Pope Felix
III); he donated the family fortune
to the church.

Incomprehensible things are those things theoretically
existing though no evidence supports their existence. Evidence
supporting belief replaces belief with fact. If fact isn't always
superior to belief then philosophy and science are giddy. A rational
mind can't reasonably believe the merely possible when opposed
by a probable or established fact. The incomprehensible is contrary
to good sense, no matter its fascination and mystery, which should
be distinguished from reality. Proof establishes knowledge,
requiring no faith. Only the unknowable requires faith. Tom says
religious experience establishes knowledge guided by faith. Tom
and I seem to have clearly identified our differences, and they
apparently consist of religious experience.

The most serious parody I
have ever heard was this: In the
beginning was nonsense, and the
nonsense was with God, and the
nonsense was God.

Friedrich Nietzsche

Nietzsche called Christianity "the one great curse . . . the one
immortal blemish of mankind."
Tom says that at times, Nietzsche was worse than giddy.

Our nada who art in nada,
nada be thy name. Thy kingdom
nada, thy will be nada as it is in
nada. Give us this nada our daily
nada and nada us our nada as we
nada our nadas and nada us into
nada but deliver us from nada;
pues nada. Hail nothing full of
nothing, nothing is with thee.

Ernest Hemingway, *A Clean Well-Lighted Place*

Hemingway published this parody thirty-three years after Nietzsche's death, illustrating how little new has recently been said. Of course, what is said counts for less than how it is said.

A sarcastic comment may simulate a flash of erudition while adding little to debate. Making fun of a philosophical or religious proposition sheds little light on its validity. Still, Hemingway makes a point. If a god is indistinguishable from nothingness the synonym adds force. Christian and other gods are indistinguishable from nothingness in the sense that they are nowhere evident, except in the mind, which in a real sense is true of everything we perceive. The personification of gods through their ministers, parishioners, and society prove they're far from nothingness. When the majority believes in something, whether the belief is probable, possible, or gullible, the fallout affects us all.

We should always be disposed to believe that that which appears to us to be white is really black, if the hierarchy of the Church so decides.

Saint Ignatius of Loyola

Saint Ignatius spearheaded the Counter-Reformation, founding the Society of Jesus, the Jesuits, dedicated to education, good works, and helping the underprivileged. His quote accurately describes the history of organized religion.

Only the institution matters; the individual is less important because real individuals buck the unthinking obedience demanded by religion, government, and other bureaucratic groups that scorn verifiable truth in favor of authority. Identification with these institutions obscures reality by elevating belief without evidence over reality. The only valid belief is based on probability. That which appears white should be considered white until we find firm evidence that it's black. Only proof establishes the validity of belief. Tom says religious experience is proof of revealed religion but not proof that black is white, no matter what organized religion decrees.

> Reason is, of all things in the world, the most hurtful to a reasoning human being. God only allows it to remain with those he intends to damn, and in his goodness takes it away from those he intends to save or render useful to the Church. . . . lf reason had any part in religion, what then would become of faith?
>
> Voltaire

> Voltaire was educated at a Jesuit school until age sixteen.

If faith is the opposite of reason, then faith is foolish on its face. Reason is seldom hurtful, though it may remove the fervent hope of immortality. Reason is otherwise a basic necessity of life, because without reason we're helpless. Reason protects us by providing shelter and sustenance, making life feasible. Without reason, life would be a gray gob of gibberish. A god has nothing to do with our ability to reason, unless we believe god made our brains, which a majority believe without evidence. Gods are traditionally above micro-management, though some religions believe gods predestine our actions. No evidence of predestination or of a god-made brain exists. Such an explanation for human behavior is improbable.

> The nature of the universe has by no means been made through divine power, seeing how great are the faults that mar it.
>
> Lucretius

Lucretius saw religion as a
monster, partly because it
threatened eternal punishment.

Only a game-playing god would create a world with much of
its made-in-the-image creatures miserable; what kind of jerk is that?
A masochistic god that no one can understand is unworthy of
genuflection. On the other hand, the universe appears flawed only
from the viewpoint of animals who know they soon die. The
universe otherwise ticks along with perfect consistency, based on
the laws of physics, biology, and the rest of the sciences. The only
flaw in the universe is that we must compete among ourselves and
with other species for room to live and thrive, and then we die.

In the long run nothing can
withstand reason and experience,
and the contradiction religion
offers to both is only too palpable.

Sigmund Freud

Freud believed that all neuroses
were the result of repressed sexual
development and was intolerant of
other opinions, the latter a failing
of us all.

Religion has successfully contradicted experience and reason
with little adverse effect to itself but with misery for the species in
the short run of human existence, a few thousand years out of the
five thousand million years the earth has existed, or the fifteen or so
billion years the universe has existed. The death of religion at the
hands of reason and experience is unimaginable. Tom says rightly
so, because religious experience properly shapes reason.

Ignorance and superstition
ever bear a close and mathematical
relation to each other.

James Fenimore Cooper

Cooper's first successful novel,
The Spy (1821), was a sea yarn

fictionalizing the exploits of John
Paul Jones, a genre I enjoy.

Cooper didn't consider religion synonymous with superstition, and neither does Tom, who distinguishes religion from superstition based on religious experience. Some may have a mystical experience when superstition works, such as for a compulsive gambler. The distinction between superstitious belief in a Holy Ghost betting system (wins come in threes) and the religious belief in a Holy Ghost, is unclear. No evidence exists that washing my car makes it rain or that crossing myself and performing rituals on prescribed occasions buys immortality. There may be an arguable difference between religion and superstition, but their relative validity at best boils down to personal religious experience. Tom agrees but wouldn't put it quite like that.

An individual can't be called ignorant solely on the basis of a belief in religion—witness Tom and other highly educated religious leaders. However, because faith and any other belief without evidence are the opposite of reason, the link between religion, superstition, and ignorance seems less than fanciful.

> By reason only can we attain to a correct knowledge of the world and a solution of its great problems. Reason is man's highest gift, the only prerogative that essentially distinguishes him from the lower animals.
>
> Ernst Heinrich Haeckel

Haeckel briefly practiced medicine until his father let him travel to Italy, where he painted and considered becoming an artist.

None of our major problems—such as disease, famine, war, racism, or poverty—have been solved by religion, prayer, or fervent belief. Instead, they have often been triggered by religion. The divisiveness of religion and its general prohibition against birth control promote the incidence of war and poverty. The world's problems are solvable only by reason and science. If reason is the sole distinction between the higher and lower animals, then bare belief lowers us to the level of dumb animals.

> Evolution excludes creation
> and all other kinds of supernatural
> intervention.
>
> T. H. Huxley
>
> After submitting papers to the
> Royal Society describing a four-
> year voyage to Australia, the
> British biologist received
> honorary doctorates from the
> universities of Breslau,
> Edinburgh, Dublin, Cambridge,
> Wurzburg, Oxford, Bologna, and
> Erlangen.

A god could have created evolution, the laws of physics, and the big bang, though no evidence of this exists. Religion must embrace these possibilities or it might, however unlikely, fade away. The alternative is to deny evolution, as fundamentalists do. Tom is no fundamentalist.

> The Bible must be put away
> in libraries where it belongs. Filed
> to gather dust beneath appropriate
> labels: Mythology, Ancient
> History, Superstition, Folk-lore,
> Pre-scientific Philosophy, and so
> on.
>
> Philip Wylie
>
> Wylie wrote the popular Crunch
> and Des fishing stories; his most
> successful book was *A Generation
> of Vipers* (1942), based on the
> psychology of Carl Jung.

The Bible shouldn't be filed to gather dust, because it contains the myths of Western civilization and much wise counsel. Still, the Bible and other religious writings are properly categorized as myth, ancient history, superstition, folklore, and prescientific philosophy, which many religious recognize, including Tom.

Philosophy removes from
religion all reason for existing.

Benedetto Croce

Croce, the foremost Italian philosopher in the first half of the twentieth century, published the journal *La Critica* for forty-one years, featuring his own writing.

Philosophy might eventually remove the reason for religion's existence, but it hasn't yet succeeded and won't, I believe, in the foreseeable future. Tom says it never will, and I suggest that never is a mighty long time. Though reason has little relationship to religion, religion is far from the verge of disappearance. The primary legitimacy of religion is based on such as the ethical portion of the Ten Commandments, which was firmly established in human society long before the religion of anyone living today. The species would do better without the war and poverty that flow from religious competition.

Reason is the greatest
enemy that faith has; it never
comes to the aid of spiritual things,
but—more frequently than not—
struggles against the divine Word,
treating with contempt all that
emanates from God.

Martin Luther

Luther's faith led him to advocate
persecution of the Jews when they
refused to convert to Christianity.

It's tough to tell what comes from a god, because just saying that something did, doesn't make it so. The only evidence of godly sayings comes from those dependent on the tithes of the particular god's followers. The difference between faith and superstition is near impossible for anyone to agree upon or even discern, unless superstition is bad faith and religion is good faith; the distinction seems elusive. Tom says religion is proved by religious experience, whereas superstition lacks such experience, and this is the proof. One problem with religious experience is that it can't be communicated. Things that can't be concretely described make their existence difficult to credit. For example, the primary definitions of *spiritual* include pious (or religious), supernatural, incorporeal, priestly, and not materialistic. Reason supports ethics and charity but little else related to organized religion. But then, reason should treat nothing with contempt but instead listen, analyze, and critically respond in a soft voice. Only violence and dishonesty are proper grounds for contempt.

> The deeper our insight into the methods of nature ... the more incredible the popular Christianity seems to me.

> John Burroughs

> This American naturalist was buddies with Walt Whitman, John Muir, and Teddy Roosevelt.

Religion constantly adjusts to science. An early Christian episode tried to gag Galileo, a practice that continued with Darwin and Hawking. Religion denies science, then says it always believed last decade's discovery because its god caused it to happen. Religion evolves through science. Tom says many scientists are religious. No one is perfect, though 93 percent of the members of the National Academy of Scientists are atheists or nonreligious.

> Whoever wants to be a Christian should tear the eyes out of his reason.

> Martin Luther

> Luther coined the phrase "hocus pocus" as a parody on the Latin *hoc est corpus*, the culmination of the Roman Catholic mass.

Religion can't compete with reason, or vice versa. Reason

destroys religion, and religion destroys reason. The only choice is between religion and reason. Tom chooses both.

> Experience witnesseth that ecclesiastical establishments, instead of maintaining the purity and efficacy of Religion, have had a contrary operation. During almost fifteen centuries has the legal establishment of Christianity been on trial. What have been its fruits? More or less in all places, pride and indolence in the Clergy, ignorance and servility in the laity, in both, superstition, bigotry and persecution.

> James Madison

> The fourth U.S. president drafted the guarantee of religious freedom for the Virginia (and U.S.) Constitution but failed in re-election to the Virginia Convention because he didn't provide free whiskey for the electors.

Leaders of any bureaucracy may reap pride and indolence, whether leading legislative, executive, military, judicial, or religious orders, and their followers may often be ignorant and servile. Superstition and religion are difficult to tell apart. Pitting our religion versus their religion naturally breeds bigotry, intentional or not. Religion persecutes by ostracizing other religions, sects of the same religion, and the nonreligious, primarily in countries with an economic standard below that of the first world. Where capitalism produces prosperity, religion is mostly winked at, observed to get ahead, but not to the point of ostracizing other sects and the nonreligious, who are the majority of its customers. Religion has involuntarily mellowed because it has lost the power to burn at the stake, outside of the Middle East and parts of Africa.

The less men reason, the

more wicked they are. Savages, princes, nobles, and the dregs of the people, are commonly the worst of men, because they reason least.

Paul-Henri Thiry, Baron D'Holbach

D'Holbach contributed 376 articles to Diderot's *Encyclopedia,* mostly translations from German on chemistry and science.

Reason has little relationship to practical ethics or how most of us behave, feeding wickedness as well as goodness. Only a failure to act ethically is wicked. Good old Tom agrees.

Knowledge alone effects emancipation. As fire is indispensable to cooking, so knowledge is essential to deliverance.

Shankara

Over three hundred works are attributed to this ninth-century Hindu philosopher, and at least eleven biographies were penned on his life, all featuring improbable anecdotes and legendary stories, written centuries after his death.

Knowledge is an essential ingredient for the happiness and fulfillment of a reasoning species. Knowledge may emancipate us, but, in some sense, so do alcohol and drugs such as television, phones, religion, and philosophy. Everyone needs their own drug for deliverance. Knowledge is a drug for many, perhaps the most benign drug, except from the viewpoint of organized religion and many governments.

> So long as the priest, that professional negator, slanderer and poisoner of life, is regarded as a superior type of human being, there cannot be any answer to the question, 'What is truth?'

> Friedrich Nietzsche

> Nietzsche was born in a Lutheran parsonage in Rocken, Prussia, and was named after the king of Prussia.

Ministers, rabbis, ayatollahs, imams, and priests are considered superior because they claim a stairway to heaven and a pipeline to a god, moral superiority, and spiritual truth. Gods are unknowable and likely can't be pipelined, while religion has no necessary relationship to morality or truth. Some religious leaders lead exemplary lives and others don't, the same as regular people. It's not exemplary to prohibit birth control if that results in millions starving or to support any and all wars suggested by the government in power. Religious leaders often act as professional negators, damning as sinful whatever their religious tradition defines as wrong, no matter its connection with immorality. Birth control is a sin in the three largest world religions: Christianity (based on its largest sect, Roman Catholicism), Islam, and Hinduism. Birth control is defined as sinful by religion because it would otherwise keep new Christians, Muslims, and Hindus from being born in the war of numbers among our uber-competitive world religions. Tom nods unhappily.

Religious leaders may be professional slanderers by condemning the majority who fail to follow the particular religion's tenets. This attitude, though likely necessary to the survival of religion, skews the lives of those following rules lacking logic, rules which can financially or mentally cripple. The religious are caught in an artificial corral that narrows the possibilities of their single life on earth for an unconfirmable afterlife. Still, a belief in immortality relieves the religious from the fear of death and makes them on average more content than the nonreligious, though few if any believe with sufficient fervor to accelerate the process. If happiness is the primary goal of life, then the religious may have found the key. A release from a fear of death, however, is counterbalanced by a life that can easily be poisoned when mothers are prohibited from using birth control or when sons are given a one-way ticket to war by religion in cahoots with government. Religious tradition is largely responsible for these poisons; the priest is only a cog in the religious machinery. Tom says he sometimes feels like a cog, but he mostly likes his job.

The Source of Our Opinions and Beliefs

> The majority of men . . . are not capable of thinking, but only of believing, and . . . are not accessible to reason, but only to authority.
>
> Arthur Schopenhauer

When Peter the Great visited Schopenhauer's hometown of Danzig in the winter, the czar picked a bedroom that was so cold that the day was saved only by Schopenhauer pouring barrels of fine brandy on the tile floor, setting it alight, and presto, warm bedroom for the czar.

We bow to authority more easily than to reason because authority relieves us of the necessity of thinking for ourselves, of self-reliance, which may be difficult at best. Nothing is more insular than relying on individual reason, which any reasoning person recognizes as perilously fallible. Even when capable of thinking, we're often reluctant to act contrary to the currents of social and religious opinion. This reticence is understandable though cowardly.

> We are all tattooed in our cradles with the beliefs of our tribe; the record may seem superficial, but it is indelible. You cannot educate a man wholly out of the superstitious fears which were implanted in his imagination, no matter how utterly his reason may reject them.
>
> Oliver Wendell Holmes

Holmes's poem *Old Ironsides*

119

(1830) saved the 1812 U.S.S. *Constitution* from destruction; Holmes was among our most beloved Supreme Court justices, a brilliant jurist.

We're tattooed in our cradles with the belief that our parents' religion, ethnicity, and nationality are superior to all others, while other religious, ethnic, and national tribes believe precisely the same. Disabuse of such belief is nigh impossible. The only antidote is an unbiased education and wide-ranging travel, both accessible to few. We all retain prejudice against individuals of other races, religions, and nationalities; it's inherent in the individual and the species. We universally feel others to be inferior in honesty, dependability, and intelligence, suspecting they bathe less. Though these notions are facially silly when judging the individual, because they're often found facially reliable (based on self-fulfilling prophesies), we retain them in perpetuity. The primary reason for our stick-to-us-ness is that race, religion, and nationality seem divinely inspired. Most religions, races, and governments denigrate others, a natural reaction among competitors, though hardly sporting. Nationalities, rival cities playing football, and ethnic groups look down on their opponents, though after the Holocaust and various civil rights movements, it's less socially acceptable to admit disliking another racial or religious group. Christian fundamentalists find it difficult to believe that Hindus are just like them, the same as fundamentalist Muslims distinguish Jews and every possible vice versa. Fears based on superstition are sheer prejudice unsupported by evidence. The belief that others are inferior is superstitious braggadocio, a pigeonholing of group characteristics, when groups consist entirely of people like you and me who are incredibly diverse in character. Our irrationality is indelible, and Tom quite agrees, though he suggests I let him do the preaching from now on.

So that, in effect, religion, which should most distinguish us from the beasts, and ought most particularly to elevate us, as rational creatures, above brutes, is that wherein men often appear most irrational, and more senseless than beasts themselves.

Credo, guia impossible est (I believe, because it is impossible) might, in a good man, pass as a sally of zeal; but would prove a very ill rule for men to choose their opinions and religions by.

John Locke

Locke was an anti-philosopher, suggesting that our capacity is so limited that full understanding is beyond our powers; he despised atheists.

Hope for immortality makes us easily accept the religion of our parents and their parents before them, *ad ancestrium*. Instead of religion, intelligence is what distinguishes us from beasts. Religion maintains our connection with beasts, tying us to bare belief when we should instead be guided by reason and intelligence. To say we believe because belief is impossible smacks of astrology and raw superstition. Tom says belief is rational and that religious experience alone distinguishes us from the beasts.

A political or religious system may burn or imprison those who investigate its principles; but it is an invariable proof of their falsehood and hollowness.

Percy Bysshe Shelley

Shelley was expelled from Oxford after five months' attendance for refusing to answer questions about a pamphlet he wrote entitled "The Necessity of Atheism."

Shelley's statement provides small consolation for the dissident. Force is nasty stuff, justified only in self-defense, but remains the political and religious justification for burning and imprisoning dissidents. Force by one nation, religion, or race against another litters our history, and no nation, religion, or race is immune. The individual may ethically exert force commensurate with and sufficient to repel force but only in self-defense; the justification of group force is more complex and almost always unethical. Tom agrees, except perhaps when his country or religion suggests otherwise.

> To believe is very dull. To
> doubt is intensely engrossing. To
> be on the alert is to live, to be
> lulled into security is to die.

> Oscar Wilde

> Wilde's parents were remarkable.
> His father was Ireland's leading
> ear and eye surgeon and wrote on
> archeology, folklore, and Jonathan
> Swift. His mother was a poet and a
> Celtic scholar.

We traditionally believe little of what we hear, half of what we see, and carefully selected portions of what we read. Doubt is the spice of life. Bare belief is boring because unrelated to reality. Only the real is truly interesting, whereas bare belief is ephemeral and insubstantial, though seldom fleeting. Only probabilities deserve belief. Tom says religious experience establishes probability. Lord, find us another chorus!

> The most costly of all
> follies is to believe passionately in
> the palpably not true. It is the chief
> occupation of mankind.

> H. L. Mencken

> Mencken ruined his early sterling
> reputation by satirizing the Great
> Depression and the New Deal.

Bare belief is usually the flip side of truth. Belief consists of anything being possible, a twin to gullibility. Truth can only be winnowed from the probable—those theorems with no known exception, instead of those things lacking any evidence whatsoever. Truth can be difficult to identify, which makes belief far easier to latch onto. Much effort, thought, discussion, deliberation, and debate with those as infallible as ourselves is imperative before we can commit to truth, avoiding too easy roads that promise everything but deliver nothing beyond comfort. One chief occupation of mankind is belief without verification based entirely on hope. Hope isn't necessarily devoid of truth but is usually on the lighter side. Unless supported by religious experience, says Tom.

> From the death of the
>   old   the   new
>   proceeds,
> And the life of truth
>   from the death of
>   creeds . . .

> John Greenleaf Whittier

> Whittier was successively a poet
> and a journalist; an abolitionist; a
> writer and a humanitarian; and a
> Quaker poet.

Truth may occasionally replace discarded beliefs and creeds but is itself often displaced by other bare beliefs and creeds. Tom says truth is verifiable from experience, mystical or actual.

> I believe that religion,
> generally speaking, has been a
> curse to mankind—that its modest
> and greatly overestimated services
> on the ethical side have been more
> than overcome by the damage it
> has done to clear and honest
> thinking.

> H. L. Mencken

> Mencken's fondness for things
> German blinded him to the
> emerging Nazi threat in the 1930s.

Ignoring the befuddled-thinking part, religion delivers nothing ethical beyond the ethics of the species. No country legalizes murder, theft, adultery, or false evidence, no matter its dominant religion, form of government, or economic system, leaving the ethical parts of the Ten Commandments a pale shadow of the ethics of the species. Instead of anchoring ethics, religion fosters unending conflicts, promoting war by pitting *us* against *them*, and banishing the uneducated and the third world to misery by blackballing birth control. Mencken may be too kind to religion, which should be portrayed as evil if it in fact perpetuates penury and death, and after traveling the world for decades, I find that it does. On the other hand, religion does no necessary damage to clear and honest thinking. Only the individual damages the clarity and honesty of his or her thinking. Religion has no effect beyond that allowed by the individual. Societal reverence for religion, however, seems to force many to obey the arbitrary dictates of our thousands of religions and their peculiarly different conception of sin, which has little connection with reason. Tom mostly agrees.

> The various modes of worship which prevailed in the Roman world were all considered by the people as equally true; by the philosophers as equally false; and by the magistrate as equally useful.
>
> Edward Gibbon

> Gibbon's famous *Decline and Fall of the Roman Empire* features a continuous chronicle from the second century to the fall of Constantinople in 1453, the title referring to the loss of intellectual freedom caused by the "triumph of barbarism and religion."

We consider our own religion infallible, though most philosophers consider religion silly while government uses it to keep us in line. Because religion is eternally in cahoots with government, it risks its reputation for its theoretical relationship with morality.

The Internal Inconsistency of the Concept of Gods

> Then God, if he is good, is not the author of all things, as the many assert, but he is the cause of a few things only, and not of most things that occur to men. For few are the goods of human life, and many are the evils, and the good is to be attributed to God alone; of the evils the causes are to be sought elsewhere, and not in him.
>
> Plato

Plato was born when his mentor, Socrates, was forty-two.

A god without universal effect isn't a god, and a god that allows evil is a terrorist. The species has wrestled forever with this paradox, which has caused many philosophers to conclude that a good god can't logically exist. Plato overstates the proposition, however, because most things that happen to us are our own doing, directly or indirectly. If many of the things that happen are evil, they may be our own fault. Tom agrees that we must take personal responsibility for our actions.

> The gods can either take away evil from the world and will not, or, being willing to do so cannot; or they neither can nor will, or lastly, they are able and willing. If they have the will to remove evil and cannot, then they are not omnipotent. If they can but will not, then they are not benevolent. If they are neither able nor willing, they are neither omnipotent nor benevolent. Lastly, if they are both able and willing to annihilate evil, why

does it exist?

Epicurus

> Epicurus thought the gods had no
> interest in humans, neither
> punishing wrongdoers nor
> rewarding the just, and thus there
> was no reason to dread death.

A god by definition has the power to take evil from the world, but every god believed in by our thousands of religions refuses to excise evil, which either smacks of a game or they don't exist. No god worthy of respect tolerates evil or plays games. We worship gods based on the fears of our primitive ancestors, who discovered the key to eternal life through ritual and religious belief promising eternal bliss. Tom says he completely trusts the last part.

> The problem of
> evil . . . Why does God permit it?
> Or, if God is omnipotent, in which
> case permission and creation are
> the same, why did God create it?

Sir William Temple,
Archbishop of Canterbury

> Temple's private secretary was
> Jonathon Swift.

Religion tells us that gods allow evil to test the individual. Gods must be crazy to allow evil to test their handiwork. Or perhaps we're entertainment for our gods. We're better off relying on ourselves.

> If the works of God were
> intelligible to man, if good and
> evil are what we think they are, a
> god who is both omnipotent and
> benevolent is a contradiction.
> Humanly speaking, good and evil
> are antithetical.

126

Charles P. Curtis

Either the idea of a god is illogical, founded on the fears of our ancestors (and our current selves), or we can't understand good and evil. Many benevolent and principled people make do without belief in a god, perhaps for two reasons: The idea of a god is illogical and unrelated to morality. Tom says religious experience outweighs logic, and without God there would be no morality.

There is no possible source
of evil except good.

Saint Augustine

Saint Augustine's embrace of Platonic philosophy as the cornerstone of Christianity dominated Europe for almost a thousand years.

If a god created everything that exists, then a god created evil. Because a god is presumed to be good, then the source of evil must be good. Religion explains the paradox by declaring we can't tell good from evil; the evil we experience is actually good camouflaged by a god working in mysterious ways. The distinction between good and evil is crystal clear to me, though the god concept seems impossible.

If there is a God, whence proceed so many evils? If there is no God, whence cometh any good?

Boethius

Anicius Manlius Severinus Boethius, commonly known as Boethius, was born four years after the fall of the Roman Empire, and his writings single-handedly transmitted Greek thought—including philosophy, music, and math—to the Middle Ages, influencing Thomas Aquinas and

127

Chaucer.

Good and evil likely proceed more from ourselves than from a god and constitute a simple definitional problem. Gods are defined as good and devils as evil, though no one has ever seen either of these invisible friends or enemies. Tom might reluctantly concede the disconnection of religion from morality but not from immortality. Tom's getting older.

> Faith in immortality, like belief in God, leaves unanswered the ancient question: Is God unable to prevent suffering, and thus not omnipotent? Or is he able and not willing it and thus not merciful? And is he just?

> Walter Kaufmann

> Kaufmann was raised as a Lutheran but converted to Judaism at age eleven, later discovering that his grandparents were Jewish. His 1950 book rehabilitated Nietzsche after Nietzsche's gross misinterpretation by the Nazis; Kaufmann brought existentialism to the U.S.

> How are we to explain it [evil], the existence of God being taken for granted, except by saying that another will, besides His, has had a part in the disposition of his works, that there is a quarrel without remedy, a chronic alienation, between God and man.

> John Henry Newman

> In 1879 this former Anglican bishop was ordained a Roman

Catholic cardinal.

Man is a powerful creature if he can work evil in the face of an omnipotent god that is supposedly good. Alienation and quarrelsomeness are unrelated to the power of a god except for one thriving on retribution and pettiness, which would be startling from a just god. Tom says there's no will besides His, so it's okay if I say this stuff.

> It is absurd to call him a God of justice and goodness, who inflicts evil indiscriminately on the good and the wicked, upon the innocent and the guilty. It is idle to demand that the unfortunate should console themselves for their misfortunes in the very arms of the one who alone is the author of them.
>
> Jean Meslier
>
> Meslier was a French abbé who, after his death, was discovered to have authored an essay extolling atheism. He prayed, "Protect me, O god, from thine divineness."

Seeking mercy from the merciless is bad strategy. Religion says we're unequipped to distinguish good from evil because a god may do bad stuff for good reasons, which is incomprehensible to a logical mind. Embracing an irrational god is insanity. Tom says God isn't that bad.

> When we claim that 'God does not exist,' we mean to deny by this declaration the personal God of theology, the God worshiped in various ways and diverse modes by believers the world over, that God who from nothing created the universe, from chaos matter, that God of absurd

attributes who is an affront to
human reason.

Benito Mussolini

Mussolini was an aggressively
unruly child, twice expelled from
school for knifing fellow students.

We believe a god exists because no one, except indirectly
through evolution, has suggested an alternative explanation for our
existence. Religious theories of creation are as good as any other.
Stephen Hawking suggested a big bang theory—now generally
accepted but by no means established—and the pope told him to lay
off. However, the landscape in particle physics and quantum
mechanics changes rapidly, and who knows what's coming next?
The religious creation theory was recorded in Hindu literature three
thousand years before Christianity, featuring a Hindu Adami and
Eva in the Garden of Eden on Ceylon, now Sri Lanka. The attributes
of a god make the concept impossibly confusing and an affront to
human reason, the same human reasoning that plucks religious rules
and dogma from thin air. Tom's not personally offended.

The place wherein Thou
(God) art found unveiled is girt
around with coincidence of
contradictories, and this is the wall
of Paradise wherein Thou dost
abide. The door thereof is guarded
by the most proud spirit of Reason,
and unless he is vanquished, the
way will not lie open.

Nicholas De Cusa

This French cardinal and
theologian (1401–1464) was the
model of a renaissance man. He
also said that a learned man is one
aware of his own ignorance.

Reason is anti-religion. The two share an uneasy co-
existence. Paradise resides in fantasy, myth, and thousands of

religions based on contradictions and coincidence. Yet the banishment of reason buys paradise and peace of mind for many, ranking high among life's greatest comforts for most. Reason provides comfort to the religious and the nonreligious. The illogic of religion disqualifies it from dispensing morality and renders religion unethical because it promotes conflicts unto war and the poverty flowing from bans on birth control. Tom says religion may have two minor flaws, but that's all.

> The efficacy of religion lies precisely in what is not rational, philosophic, nor eternal; its efficacy lies in the unforeseen, the miraculous, the extraordinary. Thus, religion attracts more devotion according as it demands more faith—that is to say, as it becomes more incredible to the profane mind.

> Henri Frederic Amiel

> Amiel was a professor of aesthetics and philosophy at the University of Geneva. He considered his life a failure, and he only become famous when his journals were published posthumously.

The irrational naturally attracts an infant species. The extraordinary, miraculous, and unforeseen are favorites on the six o'clock news and the programs that follow. The bigger the lie, the more believable or entertaining. Religion may be mass participation in the magical, Hollywood at its most garish, *The Greatest Story Ever Told*. Religion and entertainment prosper by appealing to the lowest common denominator of the profane mind, as well as to the educated. Tom says religious experience is miraculous and quite unprofane. I find sympathy with his position, though I find no objective evidence for fantastical belief.

> Study is the bane of boyhood, the oil of youth, the

indulgence of manhood, and
restorative of old age.

Walter Savage Landor

This quarrelsome writer was best
known for his multi-volume
fiction of conversations between
famous personages.

The ultimately valuable gains momentum with age. Most of
us may have disliked grammar and other subjects in school, but
many thrive on higher education, continuing the indulgence through
adulthood and finding it restorative in old age. Only a small
percentage continue education throughout their lives. Education is
the golden ideal of the educated but holds little appeal for many,
including the religious, the nonreligious, and those preferring
television, cellphones, and other entertainment. Tom is big-time on
education, a minority among the religious.

In the realm of science all
attempts to find any evidence of
supernatural beings, of
metaphysical conceptions, as God,
immortality, infinity, etc., thus far
have failed, and if we are honest,
we must confess that in science
there exists no God, no
immortality, no soul or mind as
distinct from the body.

Charles Proteus Steinmetz

Steinmetz discovered and created
the formula for alternating current
at age twenty-eight, though neither
he nor it were understood for
years.

Science can't document immortality, any god of our many
religions, or miracles and visions. Gods undetectable by objective
means seem imaginary. Either science is a failure or religion is in
the process of being debunked. Tom says God must be experienced

in order to believe and that science can't experience God. No question about that.

> The Roman Church has never erred, and, according to the scripture, never shall err.
>
> Pope Gregory VII
>
> This pope began the ban against married priests, because the church was losing property through inheritance.

Error in myth is impossible to detect. Tom says religious experience is undeniable. I agree, but it may exist only in the mind.

> Even God cannot make two times two not make four.
>
> Hugo Grotius (Huig van Groot)
>
> This father of modern international law graduated from the University of Leiden at age fourteen, edited an encyclopedia at age fifteen, and entered a diplomatic mission to King Henry IV of France, who called him "the miracle of Holland."

Any god by definition could change the rules and make two plus two not equal four. No god has bothered to do so in this particular universe.

> O my brothers, God exists. There is a soul at the center of the nature and over the will of every man, so that none of us can wrong the universe.
>
> Ralph Waldo Emerson

Emerson's 1838 address at
Harvard University claimed Jesus
wasn't divine and that organized
religion was corrupt, alienating
many of his friends.

Reality refutes Emerson. We follow the rules of the universe
because we have no choice. Whether our actions are right or wrong
should be determined by ethics without genuflection to religion or
the idea of a soul. The existence of a god appears improbable.
Wronging a non-animate object such as a universe is difficult to
comprehend. Tom says my literalism wears, and suggests a
cabernet.

Philosophy has no end in
view save truth; faith looks for
nothing but obedience and piety.

Baruch Spinoza

This greatest of Jewish
philosophers insisted on making
his living by grinding glass lenses,
and the dust killed him at age
forty-five.

Few human endeavors have truth as their singular end,
human nature being inherently me-centered. Faith is estranged from
truth by belief without evidence. Belief is unimportant, unless sifted
from probabilities based on experience and impartial perception.
Tom relies on religious experience, which is scarcely objective.
Tom nods wisely.

Does Religion Answer the Meaning of Life?

> To be thoroughly religious, one must, I believe, be sorely disappointed. One's faith in God increases as one's faith in the world decreases. The happier the man, the farther he is from God.
>
> George Jean Nathan
>
> Theater critic Nathan championed the plays of Strindberg, Ibsen, Shaw, O'Neill, O'Casey, and Saroyan.

Sociological and psychiatric studies find the religious happier and healthier than the nonreligious, perhaps because life's traumas shrink when contrasted with the prospect of a sunny afterlife, whether it exists or not. Carl Sagan concluded in *Channeling and Faith Healing—Scam or Miracle* that "some illnesses are psychogenic. Many can be at least ameliorated by a positive cast of mind. . . . Conceivably, endorphins—small brain proteins with morphine-like effects—can be elicited by belief . . . hope can be transformed into biochemistry." Sagan noted that 100 million people visited Lourdes, France, in the 136 years before 1994, hoping to be cured of disease; the Roman Catholic Church has authenticated sixty-four miraculous cures, less than the odds of winning the lottery or spontaneous remission of cancer; more might have been cured by staying home.

Hope, no matter its source or validity, reduces stress, perhaps lengthening life. The religious who are unsure of their afterlife destination suffer higher stress than the nonreligious. Most religious are happy and secure in their belief, trying to do right according to the teachings of their faith. We're a superstitious lot, and religion is our primary superstition. Happiness, in the final analysis, is an individual matter. Tom tops up the cabernet.

> If you wish to strive for peace of soul and pleasure, then believe; if you wish to be a devotee of truth, then enquire.
>
> Heinrich Heine

> Heine's prediction that whoever burns books will burn people came true during the Nazi era; the Nazis also banned his songs, the most popular in Europe, or designated them as "Author unknown."

Peace of mind or soul and pleasure in the belief of eternal life provides happiness for many, if not most. Truth is unrelated to belief in myth, because truth depends entirely on verification, which excludes spiritual experience confined to the mind, impossible to objectively verify, and unrelated to objective reality. Tom says I just don't know, not having had the experience. Actually, I was baptized at age twelve and recall the religious experience leading up to that event as euphoria in joining a holy club, and the serious wet T-shirt worn by my girlfriend, Ruth, that resulted from the same ceremony. I've backslid since and back then was already on my way.

> The humble, meek, merciful, just, pious and devout souls everywhere are of one religion, and when death has taken off the mask, they will know one another, though the diverse liveries they wore here make them strangers.
>
> William Penn

> The founder of Pennsylvania called the New World Indians the lost tribes of Israel, attracting religiously oriented settlers to Pennsylvania, which Penn only visited twice, briefly.

As far as we know, death removes no mask. Penn's adjectives are a semantic dance: Humbleness and meekness may be false or justly deserved modesty. Mercifulness and justness are positive attributes of morality, but their definitions can't be universally agreed upon. Piety and devoutness relate solely to religion and its antique constructs of morality. The assumption of an afterlife is a gigantic leap of faith unrelated to reason or verification. Tom says religious experience verifies and I'm the poorer without it. Prost.

> Necessity teaches us that . . . if God is the author of good, he is also the author of evil . . . God made man such as he is and then damned him for being so.
>
> Percy Bysshe Shelley

> Shelley's poem *Queen Mab* attacked the evils of commerce, war, eating meat, the church, monarchy, and marriage, ending with great hope for mankind once these evils were expunged.

An irrational god who plays games with its creation deserves no respect. Gods damn us for acting without reason while at the same time demanding piety without reason. Still, man's nature is no excuse for unethical acts. The individual is responsible for his or her actions, which should never harm another; amoral acts can't be blamed on a god or other entity, imaginary or not.

Is Religion Class-Driven?

> As a general rule the classes that are low in economic efficiency, or in intelligence, or both, are peculiarly devout.
>
> Thorstein Veblen

> This brilliant writer on economics

led a grossly unsettled personal
life as a serial philanderer; an
eminent fellow economist called
him a "visitor from another
world."

Many poor are devout because religion is their main comfort.
It may be as difficult for a rich man to be devout as to pass through
the eye of a needle because the monied have little need for religion.
Many poor are economically inefficient because they are burdened
with children they might otherwise have avoided by ignoring
religious bans on birth control, as we do in the first world—an
observation based on my decades of living in Africa, Asia, and the
Americas. Religion is the prime comfort and cause of the poor.
Intelligence is largely irrelevant to the equation.

> Formal religion was
> organized for slaves; it offered
> them consolation which earth did
> not provide.
>
> Elbert Hubbard

> Hubbard wrote fourteen volumes
> of *Little Journeys,* pleasant
> biographies of famous persons,
> strewn with comments and satire;
> he died in the sinking of the
> *Lusitania.*

Religion offers consolation for almost everyone, while the
rich live in luxury. Happiness may consist of doing that which
provides the most satisfaction and could be the loftiest goal,
assuming we harm no one else along the way. Religion is unrelated
to morality, because it demands obedience, with only lip service
paid to never harming others. (Case in point: bans on birth control
that result in children being born to parents who can't financially
support them.) Religion provides consolation for slaves while
creating them in abundance. Tom says he's not a slave, but he may
be in a minority.

> Our religion, moreover,
> places the supreme happiness in

humility, lowliness, and a contempt for worldly objects. . . . If our religion claims of us fortitude of soul, it is more to enable us to suffer than to achieve great deeds. . . . These principles seem to me to have made men feeble . . . an easy prey to evil-minded men, who can control them more securely, seeing that the great body of men, for the sake of gaining Paradise, are more disposed to endure injuries than to avenge them.

Niccolo Machiavelli

Machiavelli was one of the least Machiavellian of his time, a nice guy whose vividly pornographic correspondence has yet to be published.

Most religions preach humility and a contempt for worldly objects. Humility, in moderation, may be a valuable attribute, and worldly objects may deserve avoidance, if not contempt. Religion accordingly girds its followers for suffering, which is a useful trait in a dog-eat-dog world but often tardy in ferreting out the intentions of evil men.

Mandates and Promises of Religion

To maintain that Slavery is *in itself sinful*, in the face of all that is said and written in the Bible upon the subject, with so many sanctions of the relation by the Deity himself, does not seem to me to be little short of blasphemous! It is a direct imputation upon the wisdom and justice, as well as the declared

139

ordinances, of God, as they are
written in the inspired oracles, to
say nothing of their manifestations
in the universe around us.

Alexander H. Stephens

Because of his boyish
countenance and only weighing a
hundred pounds, Stephens was
often mistaken for a boy. The vice-
president of the Confederate States
of America, he served in the U.S.
House of Representatives from
1843 to 1859 and from 1873 to
1882, after which he became
governor of Georgia.

Religion supports the government because it has no choice if
it wishes to survive. Accordingly, similar to government, religion
has no particular relationship to morality or ethics. The ordinances
of the various gods, declared by the clergy, may resemble slavery.
Tom says not by him as clergy.

O Grave! where is
thy Victory?
O Death! where is
thy Sting?

Alexander Pope

This English poet was a great
satirist who, because he was
Catholic, was denied a formal
education; at age twelve he was
stricken with a disease that stunted
his growth at four feet six inches.

To the sincerely religious, death should have no sting. But
then death has no sting, with or without eternal life; death erases
every sting. If there is no eternal life, the deceased never knows the
difference. If there is, they keep really quiet about it while the
nonreligious, Buddhist, and other Eastern religious lose big-time.

Logic suggests we hedge our bets for a possible shot at eternity. Logic, however, ignores integrity if the sole reason for belief is to earn immortality. Western religions preach immortality for all, though a warmer sort is promised by religious fundamentalists for nonbelievers and other pagans like me.

> You will eat, bye and
> bye
> In the glorious land
> above the sky,
> Work and pray, live
> on hay,
> You'll get pie in the
> sky when you die.
>
> Joe Hill, "The Preacher and
> the Slave"

> Born Joseph Hillstrom in 1879, American labor organizer Joe Hill was a Swedish immigrant who allegedly robbed and murdered a grocery clerk in Salt Lake City; he was executed by firing squad in Utah, in 1915, despite mass public demonstrations and a plea by President Woodrow Wilson.

The distinction between pie in the sky and religiously promised immortality is difficult to pinpoint. Neither have been experienced and likely never shall. The iffiness of religious promises make them as remote as a fountain of youth.

> Life and death are but phases of the same thing, the reverse and obverse of the same coin. . . . I want you to treasure death and suffering more than life and to appreciate their cleansing and purifying character. Death which is an Eternal verity is revolution, as birth and after is slow and steady evolution. Death

is as necessary for man's growth
as life itself.

Mohandas Gandhi

For twenty-five years Gandhi
acted as the Rosa Parks of South
Africa, and when he left, General
Smuts said, "The Saint has left our
shores, I hope forever."

Some suggest that only the British would have put up with
Gandhi in India, while North Korea, China, or Syria would have let
Gandhi live about ten seconds. Almost a trillion people have been
born while the same number, less those fortuitously still alive, have
experienced a probable final death. Ancients myths are likely less
truthful than logic, experience, and common sense. Burying friends
and relatives after watching them lose their mental and physical
abilities points more toward the finality of death than immortality
and a never-seen resurrection. Without death the earth could sustain
only a few generations. Though grossly unappreciated, death is the
ultimate cleanser. Tom is banking on resurrection.

Immortality is the glorious
discovery of Christianity.

William Ellery Channing

Channing founded Unitarianism
and spent his life trying to
eliminate slavery, drunkenness,
poverty, and war, avoiding
doctrine.

Immortality was discovered by Christianity's forebears,
Mithraism, Zoroastroism, and a dozen others. These predate
Christianity by thousands of years, teaching immortality, the
granddaddy of all floods, and creation long before their adoption by
Christianity. Nothing in religion is new under the sun. Tom says
that confirms its validity.

Would Immortality Be a Good Thing?

> If life were eternal all interest and anticipation would vanish. It is uncertainty which lends it satisfaction.
>
> Kenko Hoshi
>
> Kenko's fame is based on *Tsurezuregusa*, a collection of 243 short essays, published posthumously; these essays treat the beauty of nature, the transience of life, traditions, and friendship, and are a part of current Japanese high school curriculum.

If life were truly eternal, we would be fat slugs and worse procrastinators than ever. The looming end of life, no matter how much we try to ignore the certainty that it could occur at any second, lends urgency and color. The uncertainty of life doesn't as much lend satisfaction as it creates value, the push to get on with things, to create, to progress, occasionally mend relationships, to learn and build for future generations, who replace us with regimental regularity. Meanwhile, we consist only of the quick and the dead as doornails.

> A man who is good for anything ought not to calculate the chance of living or dying; he ought only to consider whether in doing anything he is doing right or wrong—acting the part of a good man or a bad. . . . For the fear of death is indeed the pretense of wisdom, and not real wisdom, but a pretense of the unknown; and no one knows whether death, which men in their fear apprehend to be the greatest evil, may not be the greatest good.

143

Socrates

Socrates was a foot soldier in the
Peloponnesian   War,
distinguishing   himself   for
courage.

Calculating the chances of living or dying has definite value, such as when deciding whether to enlist in an army or walk a tightrope over the Grand Canyon. Otherwise, fearing death is like trembling at taxes. Reality is. The fear of death changes nothing and is thus unhelpful. We fear death because the only evidence we have is that death is the end. Socrates glosses over this unexceptional experience and ultimately faced it like a true hero. In a hundred years, few now alive will still be around, and they will likely feel poorly, if at all. We know the body rots at death, inviting worms, and the brain is damaged beyond functioning, within a single minute. There have been no verified exceptions, ever. But death cleanses the species, winnowing the old from vibrant youth, spurring evolution and Lebensraum, protecting the environment better than the EPA. Death is a necessary good, completely painless a split second after it occurs. Death is less painful than our fear of death. Tom says I've convinced him that death is a completely positive experience.

I died as mineral and
    became a plant,
I died as plant and
    rose to animal,
I died as animal and I
    was human,
Why should I fear?
    When was I less
    by dying?

Jalaoddin Rumi

Rumi composed over 25,000
couplets of poetry and recited
them continuously, in his bath, at
breakfast, out shopping; a real
loud mouth.

We evolved to fish from less, dying in order to evolve over a billion years. We would stagnate if we stopped dying, sinking under our own detritus. Myths similarly evolve, dying, embellishing, and expanding. Tom says the Christian myth is the be-all end-all of myth.

> If we had the offer of immortality here below, who would accept this sorrowful gift?
>
> Jean Jacques Rousseau

At age seven Rousseau was placed with a village pastor whose sister beat Rousseau, occasioning him dandy sexual pleasure.

Immortality here below might be pleasant if we stayed as physically fit as a twenty-year-old, as productive as a thirty-year-old, and as wise as we become later on, if ever. Otherwise, immortality on earth would be a sorrowful gift for the individual and disastrous for the species. Tom says immortality is a done deal after death and hopes it doesn't get too hot for me. I suggest a cold beer.

> I believe that the evidence for immortality is no better than the evidence of witches, and deserves no more respect.
>
> H. L. Mencken

Mencken was the foremost authority on the idioms, expressions, and language variations in the U.S.

The Bible and other religious books feature witches, virgin mothers, holy ghosts, angels, souls, and other supernatural beings. Evidence of immortality may reside in wishful thinking, a probable myth for a believe-anything-is-possible species, fitting us like a body bag. Tom says immortality is probable because he's already there.

145

The Evidence for Immortality and God

Hope springs eternal
    in the human
    breast:
Man never is, but
    always to be
    blest.
The soul, uneasy and
    confin'd from
    home,
Rests and expatiates
    in a life to come.
All Nature is but Art
    unknown to thee;
All chance direction,
    which thou canst
    not see;
All discord, harmony
    not understood;
All partial evil,
    universal good:
And spite of pride, in
    erring Reason's
    spite,
One truth is clear,
    Whatever is, is
    right.

Alexander Pope

Pope translated *The Iliad* (six volumes) and *The Odyssey* (five volumes) into heroic couplets, writing as if Homer were from eighteenth-century England.

Whatever is, is too late to avoid, which doesn't make it right. Religion says evil is camouflaged as good while reason says evil is evil and good is good. The first problem is agreeing on definitions. Religion predicts we'll enjoy blessings in a life no one has experienced while billions of our kind have rotted to dust. But then, if we can clone dinosaurs, a god could clone a speck of dust and award eternal life to all. Just because a god hasn't yet bothered doesn't mean it won't happen, though the possibility seems impossibly remote. Tom says it's only remote for those of little faith.

> The imaginary flowers of religion adorn man's chains. Man must throw away the flowers and also the chains.

> Karl Marx

> Marx was exiled from France and then Belgium at the instance of the Prussian government, forced to spend his life from 1849 in England, the bastion of capitalism.

Religion is a scented flower of consumer fraud. Reason suggests we toss fantasy and face reality, but fantasy is far sweeter, so we likely never will. The hope of angels and anthems is more pleasant than the reality of death. Of course, Marx was a hopeless utopian, fond of visualizing impossible solutions to practical problems. We can no more throw away the fantasies of religion than operate under an economic system without incentives. Tom says religion is reality and communism is fantasy while I suggest both are hopelessly clueless.

> Religion is the root of human existence.

> Wilhelm Schlegel

> Schlegel was the finest translator of Shakespeare (seventeen plays) into German and also fashioned excellent translations of Dante, Boccaccio, Petrarch, Cervantes, and Tasso.

Religion is the root of human existence. We thrive on beliefs that promise to deliver us from death and the traumas of life. Unless we detox from religion, we will never avoid religious conflicts, wars, and poverty-inducing bans against birth control. Tom says our roots may need pruning but they don't need to be chopped off.

> Human salvation demands the divine disclosure of truths surpassing reason.
>
> Thomas Aquinas

> Aquinas defended Aristotelian thought against the Platonic thought of Franciscan Bonaventura.

No truth surpasses reason, because reason is the search engine of truth. We cling to the idea of immortality because it's all we have. Divine disclosure is undocumented, though Tom says it's utterly valid.

> The impossibility for me to prove that there is no God proves to me His existence. . . . I feel that there is a God, and I do not feel that there is none; that satisfies me, all the reasoning in the world is useless; I conclude there is a God.
>
> Jean de la Bruyere

> Jean de la Bruyere was a French essayist and moralist whose eight editions of *The Characters, Manners of the Age* is a classic of satiric French literature.

Those suggesting the existence of the unproven bear the burden of proof. Otherwise, truth would be forever illusive, because anyone saying anything would be presumed correct until the contrary was proved, which is illogical. Bruyere's statement is nonsense. When reasoning is useless, only voodoo remains. Probably there's no god, though it can't be proven either way. The existence of a god is less likely than the nonexistence of a god.

Feelings prove nothing, though Tom insists on religious experience as proof.

> Thus, there is no human nature, because there is no God to have a conception of it. Man simply is. . . . Man is nothing else but that which he makes of himself. That is the first principle of existentialism. . . . Dostoyevsky said, 'If God did not exist, everything would be possible.' That is the very starting point of existentialism. Indeed, everything is permissible if God does not exist, and as a result man is forlorn, because neither within him or without does he find anything to cling to.
>
> Jean-Paul Sartre

> The French army drafted Sartre in 1939. He was captured by the Germans in 1940, released in 1941, and joined the Resistance.

We are what we make of ourselves, as illustrated by Dale Carnegie and similar positivists. The probability of no god neither negates human nature nor requires us to be forlorn. We simply are, independent of our desperate hankerings for security and happiness. However, the poverty suffered by most of us prevents positivism from being a potent force outside of the "haves." If a god likely doesn't exist, everything is possible and everything not unethical should be permissible. With or without a god, ethics exists, and we'll soon look at what ethics is and isn't. The species shouldn't be forlorn; life and oneself are sufficient. There's no hard evidence of existence other than this life, though Tom strongly disagrees.

> As the moral precept is at the same time my maxim, reason commanding that it should be so, I

shall inevitably believe in the existence of God, and in a future life, and I feel certain that nothing can shake this belief, because all moral principles would be overthrown at the same time, and I cannot surrender them without becoming hateful in my own eyes.

Immanuel Kant

The German philosopher explored all known proofs for the existence of a god and concluded they were all invalid due to the nature of reason, yet he still believed.

Kant's reasoning begs critique. Because the existence of a god is improbable, reason alone should withhold belief. Gods were created from a lack of knowledge. We should give up gods for two reasons. The idea of a god is without supporting evidence and unrelated to morality, except a negative relationship caused by religious intolerance and interdictions against birth control. Striking gods from our consciousness would be a positive act, instantly abolishing religious wars and potentially allowing individual control of reproduction. Dashing false hopes would salute reality. Tom says religious hope is the only real hope.

A good man never dies.

Callimachus

Callimachus was the librarian for the Alexandria Library, the most extensive in the Hellenic world; he wrote 120 volumes describing its contents, discovered a mere two hundred years ago.

Everyone dies when their heart stops beating. Tolstoy illustrated the reality of death in *The Death of Ivan Ilyich*. We're mostly forgotten before our funerals are over, and memories fade as rapidly. A year after our death few will remember us and the memory of the few becomes dull and infrequent. A hundred famous folks end up in history books, but most dim to obscurity in a few hundred years. Would we rather have been Einstein than who we are, remembering that Einstein is dead? Tom says immortality changes all that. It certainly would.

I cannot imagine a God who rewards and punishes the objects of his creation, whose purposes are moulded after our own—a God, in short, who is but a reflection of human frailty. Neither do I believe that the individual survives the death of his body, although feeble souls harbor such thoughts through fear of ridiculous egotisms.

Albert Einstein

At age twenty-six, Einstein was a bored, unhappily married, poorly paid clerk in the Berne, Switzerland, patent office; then he published three papers that laid the foundation for lasers, television, and his 1921 Nobel Prize.

Instead of us being made in the image of a god, gods are made in our image. The idea that an unknown and unknowable entity would preserve the flesh of a remote planet in a remote solar system on the edge of a remote galaxy on the edge of an immense universe is insufferably egotistical. It seems masochistic to believe that a supernatural entity would punish us for impulses that harm no one else. We should perhaps dismiss the concept of a god that grants immortality to boot-licking sycophants. Tom says that's not him.

And a summary explanation of this whole inexplicable problem is found in a single little word: *There is a life after this life: and all that is not punished and repaid here will be punished and repaid there.*

Martin Luther

A 1510 visit to the Vatican
shocked Luther because of its
worldliness and lack of
spirituality, but Luther found
revolt extremely difficult.

Punishment after death is difficult to dread, like a dead horse
afear'd of a beating. Under Luther's theory, many souls exist to be
punished. A god who gets his rocks off on eternal damnation is a
poor excuse for a god. Other than fundamentalists, most religions
have rejected the idea of hellfire. Removing the concept of hell
removes anxiety from the nonreligious but leaves less incentive for
the religious. Tom says hell was a myth but immortality isn't. The
logical difference is elusive.

It is ridiculous to suppose
that the great head of things,
whatever it be, pays any regard to
human affairs.

Pliny the Elder

Pliny the Elder left his command
of the Western Roman Navy to
observe the eruption of Vesuvius
and died from the fumes, survived
by thirty-seven volumes of natural
history.

The religious presume themselves fashioned in the image of
their god, who pays constant attention to a borderline intelligent
species on a remote planet circling a dim and minor star on the edge
of an enormous galaxy dwarfed by trillions of larger galaxies. But
then, by definition, gods count grains of sand, and thus keeping
track of minor species on small planets is a piece of cake. Perhaps
a god must pay attention to something, though gods knowing
everything have to be terminally bored. Tom says fantasy footwork
contributes nothing to philosophy.

God foreordained, for His
own glory and the display of His
attributes of mercy and justice, a
part of the human race, without
any merit of their own, to eternal
salvation, and another part, in just
punishment for their sin, to eternal
damnation.

John Calvin

This French Protestant reformer
established a theocracy in Geneva,
requiring everyone to attend
church and morning prayers,
outlawing Christmas as the devil's
mass.

Calvin's god was a real asshole. This religious vision is
fortunately archaic, except among a few million fundamentalists,
primarily Islam and Hindu. Before contemplating the horrific
substance of Calvin's vision, sin should be defined. Fortunately, sin
is easier to define than ethics, because sin is based entirely on
religious doctrine, varying among our thousands of religions
without end. Muslims define the consumption of alcohol as sin
while many Christians use alcohol in communion with their god.
Because sin is unrelated to ethics, the Calvin quote is substanceless
nonsense. A god glorying in sentencing its creation to eternal
damnation without consideration of merit is repulsive, but compare
Einstein's sentiments above. Tom agreed until I raised the Einstein
quote.

The end of life would be
much less frightening if it were not
called death any more. The fear of
death is the source of all religion.

Maurice Maeterlinck

This Belgian dramatist's prose
blended pessimism with an
interest in nature and was
unappreciated until the 1930s,

though he received the Nobel
Prize for Literature in 1911 and
was internationally known by the
1890s.

Religion erases the fear of death by calling it eternal life; still,
a rose by any other name . . . We cling to the impossible because
that's all there is. Hope shrieks to avoid death but without objective
support. The fear of death is the source of most Western religions;
Eastern religions instead fear life. Religion substitutes hope for
reality but exacts the temporal lives of its converts. Tom says it's
worth it.

And indeed it is old age,
rather than death, that is to be
contrasted with life. Old age is
life's parody, whereas death
transforms life into a destiny. In a
way, death preserves life by giving
it the absolute dimension—'As
unto himself eternity changes him
at last.' Death does away with
time.

Simone de Beauvoir

Beauvoir was a friend and
associate of Sartre, and wrote
heaps on aging.

Death is often a welcome release from old age. Without death
we would be stuck with bedpans, wheelchairs, and perpetual
slobbering. Death completes life, opening the way for younger
generations, which similarly ignore their fate. Religion embraces
death by saying yea to the resurrection of an unverified soul. Tom
is counting on it.

To desire immortality is to
desire the perpetuation of a great
mistake.

Arthur Schopenhauer

In his late teens Schopenhauer
toured Europe with his father, an
aristocratic Pole, and his mother, a
writer, and was deeply affected by
the wretchedness of the poor.

An eternally healthy life wouldn't necessarily be a mistake,
except ecologically. Creatures who know they die do everything
they can to avoid death, many joining health clubs, jogging, and
eating right. Because no other species anticipates death, less
cognizant animals are delivered from the guilt, regimentation, and
solace of religion. Tom says he's quite comfortable, unguilted, and
unregimented by religion and its promise of eternal life.

Go and try to disprove
death. Death will disprove you.

Ivan Turgenev

Turgenev spent most of his life
pursuing Pauline Viardot, an opera
singer, placing his illegitimate
daughter in Pauline's care.

Death disproves everyone. No objectively verified
exceptions exist. Hope and religion disdain proof by promising
resurrection without objective verification. Tom smiles smugly and
hopes retirement in Phoenix acclimatized me.

Needless to say; since
Christ's expiation not one single
Christian has been known to sin,
or die.

Voltaire

For statements such as these the
Catholic church refused to allow
the burial of Voltaire in Paris until
thirteen years after his death. He
probably didn't notice.

Voltaire had fun with semantics, coloring me envious. No

religion promises that its converts will neither sin nor die. Religion says we can find the strength to avoid its artificial sins through dogma, promising that the faithful will live forever. Eastern religions promise Nirvana after a millennia. Voltaire's point is cleanly made; the religious constitute a cross-section of the community as gullible as the rest of us. Religion doesn't change us from bad to good but enlists us into a socially acceptable club to which Tom is happy to belong.

> It is the final proof of God's
> omnipotence that he need not exist
> in order to save us.

> Peter De Vries

> This American novelist was noted
> for good-humored satirical stories.

No religion admits its god doesn't exist, though some religions suggest that nonbelievers may be saved by good works, or at least by not committing bad works, however defined by the particular religion. Belief is no longer necessary to salvation, which makes Tom feel better about me.

> A man's first and greatest
> victory must be won against the
> gods.

> André Gide

> This French novelist and essayist,
> born in 1869, satirized his
> puritanical Protestant upbringing.
> Gide was gay—difficult back
> then. He married his cousin
> Madeleine, the only love of his
> life.

Our emancipation may demand dead gods or at least the exorcism of superstition. Vanquishment of the gods, whether a victory or not, can be achieved by few. Not by Tom, and he feels better for it.

156

People today live without faith. On the one hand the minority of wealthy, educated people, having freed themselves from the hypnotism of the Church, believe in nothing. They look upon all faiths as absurdities or as useful means of keeping the masses in bondage—no more. On the other hand, the vast majority, poor, uneducated, but for the most part truly sincere, remain under the hypnotism of the faith. But this is not really faith, for instead of throwing light on man's position in the world it only darkens it.

Leo Tolstoy

Tolstoy spent his entire life looking for its meaning and finally decided that a new religion of Jesus Christ was needed to give happiness on earth instead of postponing it to heaven, to which Tolstoy gave up everything, left on a train, and died a week later.

Faith is belief in the improbable without objective proof. Most wealthy have little attraction to faith, which is evidence of little or nothing. The majority poor are mostly over-childrened and undereducated, which explains their poverty. Perhaps education, instead of faith, would do more to improve their earthly lot. Faith seems without exception to darken the path to knowledge. Tom says, bah, humbug, and his erudition is undeniable.

Not one man in a thousand has the strength of mind or the goodness of heart to be an atheist.

Either we have an immortal soul, or we have not. If we have

157

not, we are beasts; the first and
wisest of beasts it may be; but still
beasts.

Samuel Taylor Coleridge

Because of financial difficulties,
Coleridge dropped out of
Cambridge in his third year and
enlisted in the Dragoons under the
name Silas Tomkyn
Comberbache; he was discovered
by friends, his enlistment bought
out, and he was reinstalled at
Cambridge. Coleridge wrote the
mysterious poetry of *Kublai Khan*
under the influence of laudanum, a
tincture of opium popular in the
day.

Strength and goodness may be required to resist evil and
superstition, no matter their guise. The majority give lip service to
strength of mind and goodness of heart, assuming without
examination that these reside in the dogmas of religion. It's difficult
to buck the majority, no matter the rationality of its beliefs. Tom
says he feels rational, and I so testify.

Whether we have an immortal soul—shorthand for saying
we're immortal—is unrelated to whether we're beasts, which in this
context seems to mean "bad animals." Semantics is everything. If
beasts mean animals without a soul, the concept of a soul being
substantiated only in the imagination, then it probably makes little
difference whether we're soulless or soulful. No one knows before
death whether there's a soul, and after death it's too late. The
hedging of bets is an attractive proposition for the wisest of beasts.
Tom says he's not hedging his bets; his belief is based on personal
experience.

Animals have these
advantages over man; they never
hear the clock strike, they die
without any idea of death, they
have no theologians to instruct
them, their last moments are not

158

disturbed by unwelcome and unpleasant ceremonies, their funerals cost them nothing, and no one starts lawsuits over their wills.

Voltaire

The works and ideas of Voltaire, Locke, Hobbes, and Rousseau were the leading lights of the American and French revolutions.

And then after the death of many animals, they're eaten. I followed a truckload of pigs on their way to market in Coimbra, Portugal. They oinked and scrambled, pink ears flapping and snouts snuffling over the tailgate, enjoying their last ride. If they heard a clock strike, they wouldn't know it or care; their ride was a minor episode in a tiny consciousness; no theologians would meet them at the slaughterhouse to say last rites; the slice of the knife would evince momentary surprise with pain and that for a split second; they would forgo funerals, instead displaying their body parts at the local market, and not even a lawyer would represent them. These are not advantages, except perhaps for the absence of theologians and lawyers. The clock bequeaths an awareness of death without which we would accomplish less than we do now. Our last moments need not be disturbed by intrusive ceremonies and moaning, our funerals personally cost us nothing, and lawyers need us. We are animals, smarter than pigs but suffering the burden of our intelligence and its accompanying superstitions. Tom says theologians are okay.

Without philosophy we should be little above animals.

Voltaire

Through successful investments and inheritance, Voltaire was rich enough to live far above the standards of any animal.

Only intelligence distinguishes us from other animals. Religion and philosophy are emblems of that intelligence, the same as science and other imaginative or thinking disciplines. Religion is a stepchild of philosophy, the sort that demands belief without logic. Tom says his belief isn't without logic.

> I think I could turn
> and live with
> animals,
> they are so placid and
> self-
> contained . . .
> They do not lie
> awake in the dark
> and weep for their
> sins,
> They do not make me
> sick discussing
> their duty to God,
> Not one is
> dissatisfied, not
> one is demented
> with the mania of
> owning things,
> Not one kneels to
> another, nor to his
> kind that lived
> thousands of
> years ago,
> Not one is
> respectable or
> unhappy over the
> whole earth.
>
> Walt Whitman, Leaves of
> Grass
>
> A bard of democracy, Whitman
> wrote about the equality of race
> and class and, progressively for his
> time, of sex and the body.

Many animals are neither placid nor self-contained but instead obsessed with their next meal, similar to poor humans. Still, animal needs are simpler than worries occasioned by sin, the

160

obsession for material things, and bowing to kings and popes. Perhaps happiness and self-respect depend on the avoidance of these obsessions. Tom agrees, though he says the pope's okay. Come on, Tom; just okay?

The Perception of Atheists in Society

> Depend upon this truth, that every man is the worse looked upon, and the less trusted, for being thought to have no religion; in spite of all the pompous and specious epithets he may assume, of *Esprit fort*, Free-thinker, or Moral Philosopher; and a wise Atheist (if such a thing there is) would, for his own interest, and character in this world, pretend to some religion.

> Philip Dormer Stanhope

> Stanhope, the fourth Earl of Chesterfield, was best known for his guide to manners such as *Letters to His Son*, which explained the art of pleasing and the key to worldly success.

An atheist is unwise to broadcast his or her pitiful disbelief in a god. Society ostracizes atheists and the nonreligious, barring them from public office as inferior, simply because they refuse to believe without evidence or probability of truth. Tom says religious experience establishes truth and he wouldn't vote for me either.

> It is true, that a little philosophy inclineth man's mind to atheism; but depth in philosophy bringeth men's mind about to religion. . . . The causes of atheism are: divisions in religion, if they be

161

many . . . scandal of
priests . . . custom of profane
scoffing in holy matters . . . and
lastly, learned times, specially
with peace and prosperity; for
troubles and adversities do more
[to] bow men's minds to religion.
They that deny a God destroy
men's nobility; for certainly man
is of kin to the beasts by his body;
and, if he be not of kin to God by
his spirit, he is a base and ignoble
creature.

Atheism leaves a man to
sense, to philosophy, to natural
piety, to laws, to reputation, all
which may be guides to outward
moral virtue, though religion were
not; but superstition dismounts all
these, and erecteth an absolute
monarchy in the minds of man.

Francis Bacon

Though Bacon founded the
scientific method, his essays on
atheism and superstition weren't
particularly consistent, concluding
that only verified discovery
counts; he also floated the original
idea of evolution, foreshadowing
Darwin by hundreds of years.

A little philosophy, spiritual feeling, and education may
incline the mind to religion, while immersion in philosophy and
history may lead some to atheism. The history of religion reveals
two primary defects: intolerance, inviting perpetual conflict unto
war; and its stance against birth control and sex education,
relegating many to poverty. Religious fallibility is illustrated by
eternal divisions in religion. The scandal of priests reflects the state
of the species; we're all weak, subject to social scandal, with little

natural connection to morality, doing what we can get away with. Though its natural for males to impregnate a female, it's scandalous for a priest, and particularly scandalous to molest children of any sexual persuasion. The custom of profane scoffing in holy matters comes from our inability to understand our thousands of religions. Hard times may bow our minds to religion as an escape from reality, the same as drugs of any kind, whether work, sex, money, or single malt. The denial of a god is unrelated to the nobility of the species. An individual is neither base nor ignoble by rejecting a particular religion, or all religions. Tom agrees but suggests that religion provides answers for many, a suggestion I can't deny.

The distinction between superstition and religion is slippery. Both erect absolute monarchies in the mind proportional to the strength of personal belief. If atheism leaves the species to sense, to natural piety, or ethics, then atheism may be superior to superstition and religion. Atheism is arguably an inwardly moral virtue lacking the superstitious core of religion while retaining a natural ethics uncomprehended but actively pretended to by religion. Ethical commandments are ignored by religion in cahoots with government. "Thou shalt not kill," embraced in theory by all religions, is practically replaced by the indiscriminate slaughter of religious others. Religious wars have been fought continuously since religion began, and they continue where the tectonic plates of our major religions abut. Though it claims to have cornered the morality market, religion is often the antithesis of ethics. An us-versus-them mind-set creates confrontations between governments and ethnic groups, justified and overheated by religion. Tom says religion has a few weaknesses but they're overwhelmed by spirituality and the promise of immortality. Geez, Tom, good thing you don't live in the Eastern world.

> We know . . . that man is by
> his constitution a religious animal;
> that atheism is against not only our
> reason, but our instincts; that it
> cannot prevail long.

> Edmund Burke

> Burke supported British intervention in the French Revolution on the grounds that democracy is dangerous because

163

ruled by numbers, an argument
warmly responded to by Thomas
Paine in *The Rights of Man*.

We're superstitious and religious animals, which doesn't make us right. Atheism may go against our instinct but not against our reason. Religion and superstition are against reason because no verifiable basis for either exists, outside of emotional need. Atheism and the nonreligious will last as long as reason and skepticism but will likely never achieve a majority because emotion and need insulate reason. The human psyche may need substantial reform, based on where it's gotten us so far. We normally use reason to solve problems and navigate everyday life. We could progress to the point where we use reason alone to solve our problems. Reason might eventually wring a consensus on the key elements governing our existence, the religions and ethics that have ruled us since the beginning. Tom says perhaps, but he's as skeptical as I am.

In practice, all men are
atheists; they deny their faith by
their actions.

Ludwig Feuerbach

Feuerbach was a student of Hegel
but altered Hegel's idealism to
materialism, directly influencing
Marx.

The majority of the species, contrary to its public posture, ignores religion while publicly proclaiming its validity. Actions violating ethics seem far worse than a breach of religious rules. Religious sins, no matter the religion, are often unrelated to ethics. Eating pork and similar religious sins pale in comparison to the slaughter of the species in endless conflicts fueled by religion. The Bible's First Commandment, prohibiting the toleration of other gods, is the clearest example of intolerance parroted by almost all religions. Christians have methodically sought to eradicate those believing in other gods, including the forerunner of and derivation from its own religion, Judaism and Islam. The primary religious commandment is intolerance, which overwhelms the politically ignored commandment that thou shalt not kill. Tom says for once I'm perfectly correct, though, as usual, I've overstated my case.

Atheism is the only means
of ensuring the happiness of the
world, which has been rendered
impossible by the wars brought
about by theologians.

Julien Offray de la Mettrie

De la Mettrie's illnesses
convinced him that psychic
phenomena, such as miracles and
religious experience, originate in
the brain and nervous system; this
resulted in the public burning of
his book *L'Art de Jouir,* earning
him exile from France.

Theologians, to protect themselves, usually support the local
government, no matter its cruelty or corruption. Governments
(excluding historical Marxism) intertwine with the dominant
religion and protect it. Universal atheism wouldn't ensure the
happiness of the world. Only the individual can attain happiness.
But atheism might remove a major part of us-versus-them. Our
divisiveness is largely caused by Catholics versus Protestants,
Christians versus Jews and Muslims, Muslims versus everyone else,
and most every religion against all the others. Equally guilty of the
schisms dividing the species are nationalism and ethnicity, and
sheer greed. Without the excuse of religion for national and ethnic
conflicts, wars and terrorism might wither away and we might
enshrine a single species unencumbered by religion, nationalism,
and ethnic chauvinism, which isn't worth a single human death
under any circumstances. Theologians aren't responsible for war or
terrorism. Politicians, patriots, and similar others share the blame
with religion for the unending slaughter of the species. Tom says
that's pretty much true.

By night an atheist half
believes in God.

Edward Young

Young was known for an almost
10,000-line poem on death

165

inspired by the deaths of his
stepdaughter (1736), her husband
(1740), and Young's wife (1741).

By night a theist half disbelieves in God, often acting out
disbelief during daylight hours. Whether a theist half disbelieves or
an atheist half believes in a god is unimportant. All believers trust
their beliefs as utterly true. Valid beliefs are those probably true;
beliefs only possibly true (since anything is *possibly* true) are
unworthy of consideration. Many reasonable individuals believe in
a god, and many reasonable individuals believe there isn't one. Tom
says he's in the majority, and I say yes and that proves what?

No one has died an atheist.

Plato

No one knows what portion of
Plato's writing reflects his own
ideas and how much, if any, was
thought-up by Socrates, who
published nothing and is
principally known through Plato.

The inevitability of death forms the basis of most Western
religions but doesn't prove their validity. We cling to hope,
admitting no atheist in foxholes, which I studiously avoid. The fact
that most of us hope to avoid death neither proves nor disproves the
efficacy of religion. We're bet-hedgers who grasp at straws when
nothing else is available, an imminently rational reaction. The last-
second-before-death conversion provides solace to the dying and
the surviving religious. It says nothing about the validity of theism
or atheism. Tom says true enough, but he sincerely believes that
religious experience is proof of religious efficacy, and I believe that
for him, this proves it.

The equal toleration of all
religions . . . is the same as
atheism.

Pope Leo XIII

Yet Leo XIII was the first pope to

166

establish extensive diplomatic relations with non-Christian countries.

Intolerance is the first commandment of all religions: Thou shalt have no other gods before our god. Toleration may be an attribute of atheism because many atheists consider ethnic, national, and religious affiliations unimportant labels. The sole yardstick of justice should be the ethics and integrity of the individual, which vary no matter the individual's race, religion, or national origin. Leo XII would have been correct if he meant that no religions should be tolerated and that all religions should be obliterated to facilitate the expungement of hate, intolerance, and pseudo-moralism. Tom says that's extremely intolerant, and he has a point.

There are but two ways, the way of Rome and the way of atheism.

John Henry Newman

Newman preached his last Anglican sermon, entitled "The Parting of Friends," on September 18, 1843, and three weeks later was received into the Roman Catholic Church.

There are several more ways than two between Rome and atheism. If the choice is between religion and its rejection as superstition and a major contributor to conflicts and poverty then atheism is morally preferable. The species shouldn't be relegated to religious wars and the miring of the majority in poverty caused by religious no-nos against contraception and the intolerant uniformity of religious first commandments. Tom says the best way is the way of Rome and that other ways are worse than second best.

The devil divides the world between atheism and superstition.

George Herbert

Of Herbert's writing, Coleridge

said, "Nothing could be more pure, manly, and unaffected," a combination I have difficulty visualizing.

The world is divided every which way based on nationalism and patriotism, religion, ethnicity, race, and other irrelevancies. We're a single species divided too long by trivial differences. Whether we're religious, superstitious, scientific, intellectual, laborer, female, oriental, black, or gypsy, we're human, more closely related than distinguishable on artificial grounds. The only valid distinction should be based on individual ethics, integrity, and honesty. No other distinction is ethically valid. Tom actually agrees.

Atheism, consequently, can only mean the attempt to remove any ultimate concern—to remain unconcerned about the meaning of one's existence. Indifference toward the ultimate question is the only imaginable form of atheism.

Paul Tillich

Though Tillich served as a WWI German army chaplain, he was barred from university teaching in 1933 Germany, calling himself the first non-Jew "to be so honored."

The Tillich quote displays no erudition. Atheists may be more concerned with the ultimate question than the religious who embrace the existence of an unseen and unknowable god. Most religious adopt their forbears' beliefs without examining alternatives. Those with Catholic parents become Catholics, and those with Muslim or Jewish parents become 90 percent affiliated with the religion of their ancestors. Most atheists probably examine alternatives before deciding that gods are derived from the superstitions and fears of our ancestors and likely don't otherwise exist. Atheism expresses the ultimate concern about the ultimate question and is thus the antithesis of unconcern. Our imaginations, whether religious or atheist, are circumscribed by a philosophical mindset for or against religion. There's no middle ground; we must choose between religious superstition or what many religious consider blasphemy. Tom says his personal experience proves religion isn't mere superstition.

> What yesterday was still
> religion is no longer such today;
> and what today is atheism
> tomorrow will be religion.

> Ludwig Feuerbach

> Feuerbach's first book attacked
> the idea of personal immortality,
> arguing that the only possible
> hereafter was the absorption of
> human qualities into nature.

Atheism can't be a religion because it excludes the possibility, requiring proof for beliefs and propositions of faith based on bare hope. Religion is belief without evidence. Because atheism denies the existence of an unevidenced god it can't be a religion, which by definition believes in a god or higher power. Tom says I protest too much.

> Theist and Atheist; The
> fight between them is as to
> whether God shall be called God
> or shall have some other name.

> Samuel Butler

> Butler was so impressed by *The
> Origin of the Species* that he
> renounced Christianity and wrote
> about evolution for the next
> twenty-five years.

Butler assumes the existence of a god. Because semantics are much of the substance in the debate between rationality and superstition, perhaps Butler meant that an alternative, such as science, can become a god for atheists, as it later did for him.

The Benefits of Belief in a God

I admit that the love of God,
if there were a God, would make it
possible for human beings to be
better than is possible in a Godless
world.

Bertrand Russell

Russell was raised by a puritanical
grandmother until age eighteen,
which would be enough to render
most anyone unreligious.

The love of a god hasn't prevented the slaughter of a single soldier in religious wars or the poverty suffered by poor families spooked from birth control by religious dogma. The love of a god is love in its most abstract. An admittedly godless world might aid the species by removing incentives to war and the poverty caused by anti-birth-control mania. Goodness and badness are unrelated to religion but instead depend on our understanding of and obedience to ethics. We're not a naturally ethical species, because our instincts often fantasize the annihilation of those we dislike. Religion, nationalism, and ethnic hatreds, interwoven with natural competitiveness, make the love of a theoretical god at best a featherweight. Love of God is overwhelmed by religious competition and conflict. Tom says that's a bad truth but suggests no solution.

No free man needs a God.

Vladimir Nabokov

Nabokov was always broke,
making money by teaching tennis,
Russian, and English at Cornell
and playing walk-on parts in
movies until he published *Lolita* in
1955.

We likely all need a god but may gain our independence by

170

facing the likelihood that a god's existence is remote. A free man may need no god, nation, race, or other granfalloon of the species. The species is sufficient by itself. Tom says God helps, immeasurably.

> I believe in God, whom I understand as Spirit, as Love, as the Source of all.
>
> Leo Tolstoy

> Tolstoy was excommunicated from the Russian Orthodox Church in 1901.

Tolstoy believed and disbelieved in a god, always examining the possibilities. As far as we know no particular spirit, love, or source seems to have created the universe, though we don't have the foggiest notion what, if anything, did. Our experience of gods prove they tolerate evil together with the priests, cardinals, ministers, and rabbis who relay their mystic messages. A god who would talk to humans is similar to a man who would talk to ants. A rational god wouldn't sacrifice a son or daughter to save ants from death, encourage ants to fight wars against ants believing in other gods, or prohibit ants from practicing birth control unto poverty. Religious explanations for how things work out-fictions science fiction. Tom says I might be a nut case.

> The fundamental symbol of our ultimate concern is God. It is always present in any act of faith, even if the act of faith includes the denial of God.
>
> Paul Tillich

> Tillich rejected the personal god of Christianity but obviously wasn't an atheist because he affirmed the reality of *god,* a word he would have capitalized.

Religious reasoning is circular. We're religious because

we're predestined to be. It's in our genes. Because a god made us, we must commune with that god. Our ultimate concern with any belief, no matter the belief, is a god. If we deny the existence of a god, it's because that god exists. This is heady stuff beyond understanding. Tom says he understands, and I numbly congratulate him.

What Is Heretical?

There is never any fair and thorough discussion of heretical opinions . . . The greatest harm done is to those who are not heretics, and whose whole mental development is cramped and their reason cowed, by the fear of heresy.

John Stuart Mill

At age twenty-four, Mill fell in love with Harriet Taylor, a married woman. He waited twenty years until her husband died, and finally married her; seven years later she died of tuberculosis.

Except among fundamentalist religions, the idea of heresy fled at the tail-end of the twentieth century. Opinions contrary to fundamentalism demand death in fundamentalist cultures. Many religious shun violence, but fundamentalists still seek the assassination of heretics. The discussion of heretical opinions is difficult for everyone because opposition to our ideals may breed murder. We can't discuss religious (and other factually unsupported topics) without taking offense. Without a civil discussion, we can't understand the other person's viewpoint, which solidifies our artificial boundaries. Tom is happy that he and I can civilly discuss things we can't agree on; me, too.

Heretical views arise when the truth is uncertain, and it is only when the truth is uncertain that

censorship is invoked. . . . [I]t is
difficult to find anything really
certain outside the realm of pure
mathematics and facts of history
and geography.

Bertrand Russell

Upon entering Cambridge at age
eighteen, Russell was greatly
influenced by J. S. Mill.

The facts of history are filtered through the biases of
historians on the winning side. Only pure mathematics and
geography hold the potential for absolute certainty. Until we know
a fact for certain, we should only believe in probabilities, avoiding
mere possibilities. Tom says religious experience elevates
possibility into certainty.

For it is a graver matter to
corrupt the faith which quickens
the soul, than to forge money,
which supports temporal life.
Therefore, forgers of money and
other evil-doers are condemned to
death at once by the secular
authority, much more reason is
there for heretics, as soon as they
are convicted of heresy, to be not
only   condemned   to
excommunication but even to be
put to death.

Thomas Aquinas

After twenty years of prodigious
theological output, Aquinas died
at the age of forty-nine at a
monastery on his way from Naples
to Rome to attend the Second
Council of Lyons.

Death was one sentence imposed by Middle Ages religion on

those who disagreed with its premises. Religion has mostly lost the means and authority to execute those disagreeing with religious dogma, though still relishing the means to execute heretics in the Middle East, plus parts of Asia and Africa. Fundamentalist religion can't tolerate inquiry, assuming those who question a religiously decreed fact to be indistinguishable from evil, devils, or "them." Only actions that harm others are sufficiently serious to be physically punished, much less by the death penalty. The species hasn't progressed to the point that speech is everywhere protected from death. Tom says it's okay by him that I ramble on.

> Man gives indifferent names to one and the same thing from the difference of their own passions; as they that approve a private opinion call it opinion; but they that mislike it, heresy; and yet heresy signifies no more than private opinion.
>
> Thomas Hobbes

> The Fire of London and the Great Plague, both in 1666, were seen as the wrath of God stemming from atheism, blamed in part on Hobbes' *Leviathan;* thus the King forbade Hobbes from publishing anything for the rest of his life.

Any belief not based on facts probably true is mere opinion, superstition, religion, or faith. These concepts are synonymous, or at least difficult to distinguish between. Tom agrees, except he levitates religion to probable fact based on personal experience.

> 1. If any man after legall conviction shall have or worship any other god, but the lord god, he shall be put to death. . . . 3. if any person shall Blaspheme the name of god, the father, Sonne or Holie ghost, with direct, expresse, presumptuous or high handed

blasphemie, or shall curse God in
the like manner, he shall be put to
death.

Massachusetts Body of
Liberties, 1641
Anti-heresy statutes in the American colonies were seldom
enforced because few citizens tempted fate by public statement.
However, these statutes set the tone for the fledgling United States
and were similar to laws in many other countries at the time.
Fundamentalist Muslims permit the actions proscribed by the first
quoted statute but persecute actions violating the second, such as
the vendetta against Salmon Rushdie (verbally rescinded in October
1995). Tom says religious intolerance is unreligious, whereas I find
it inherent.

The artist's contribution to
religion must in the nature of
things be heretical.

Karl Shapiro

Shapiro received the 1945 Pulitzer
Prize for poetry.

Though art is outside the scope of religion, Shapiro's analogy
provides a useful comparison. Progress and art represent change;
religion is tradition and stability. Tom's for both.

Heresies are experiments in
man's unsatisfied search for truth.

H.G. Wells

The Wells family was poor with
many children; H.G. heard his
mother praying for no more
children, to no avail, and rejected
the idea of a god.

Debates over religious orthodoxy are a search for truth,
whether they're called heresy or debate. No matter the label,
nothing should impede the search for truth. Until we can agree on

basic truths, assuming they exist, we continue divided. Assuming the species survives that long, Tom and I are both optimistic about conditions ten thousand years from now, a mere drop in time.

> Heresy is the lifeblood of religion. It is faith that makes heretics. In a dead religion there are no longer heresies.
>
> Andre Suares

Suares pined for a Celtic heritage but was Jewish.

Us versus them, or truth versus heresy and untruth, is the lifeblood of the organization, whether religious or other, and a matter of self-defense. The goal of the group sets it apart from the individual and other groups. That goal brands the organization's uniqueness, without which it dies. Faith in an organization's goal requires a belief that the goals of competing organizations are inferior, otherwise we would choose the other one. A religion is an organization like any other but with its goals and dogma founded on the mysterious and unverifiable. Faith in the unverifiable competes with goals of similar organizations, which in a religious context may constitute heresy, though the age of ecumenicalism may deem heresy a petty discrepancy. This is progress for the species but may be the death knell for some religions, such as the Church of England, for one example. Tom says the idea of heresy is archaic, and most religions, excluding their fundamentalist wings, avoid such accusations.

> Many people have to surrender old privileges and everybody has to give up old customs without which life may seem hardly worth living. The old penalty for heretics was dramatic: death. The modern penalty is less drastic: boycott and social ruin.
>
> Ernst Toller

Toller was a pacifist who fled

176

1930s Germany for Hollywood; he became convinced that his writing was passé and committed suicide in a Manhattan hotel room.

We're naturally suspicious of non-mainstream thinkers because they disagree with the majority, who are us. Outside the university, and often within, non-mainstream thinkers are ostracized and socially excluded. The process is a natural one, because minority opinions threaten the security of the majority and the potency of our personal philosophy. We usually believe in a particular philosophy because our parents did and our peers do. No thought is necessary. The non-mainstream thinker threatens our foundations; exclusion, as a matter of self-defense, removes the threat. Tom says this is unfortunate.

The Relation of Creeds and Thought

Christianity: A religious system attributed to Jesus Christ, but really invented by Plato, improved by St. Paul, and finally revised and corrected by the Fathers, the councils, and other interpreters of the church. Since the foundation of this sublime creed, mankind has become better, wiser, and happier than before. From that blessed epoch the world was forever freed from all strife, dissensions, troubles, vices, and evils of every kind; and invincible proof that Christianity is divine, and that it is to be possessed of the very devil himself to dare to commit such a creed or doubt its origin.

Voltaire

Voltaire used as many as 300 pseudonyms, for obvious reasons.

Christianity sprang from Mithraism (based on the primary myths of Judaism, Hinduism, and beyond) through the catalyst of Jesus Christ. Religion has boasted nothing new for millennia. Religion, whether Christianity, Judaism, Hinduism, Mohammedanism, or any other *ism*, pits "us" against "them," often considering others to be the inferior worshipers of false gods deserving death and desolation. Saint Paul shoehorned Christianity into antagonism against other faiths, helping erase tolerance. This foundation of Christianity was bolstered by later Christians, such as Luther, a notorious anti-Semite, and Luther's opponent, the Roman Catholic hierarchy with its crusades and inquisitions. Religion is a synonym for intolerance; if religions were tolerant, they would cease to exist. To tolerate other gods is to devalue one's own. The first commandment of all religions is to tolerate no other gods. Religious history raises the question whether gods are aliases for devils, the epitome of evil, and the antithesis of morality. Tom says balderdash, at least for one particular god.

> The last taboo of mankind, avoiding forbidden and dangerous thoughts, must be removed. There are no illegitimate thoughts.
>
> Theodor Reik

> This protégé of Freud was denied admission to the American Psychoanalytic Association because he wasn't a medical doctor; Freud wrote a famous article defending Reik's right to practice psychotherapy.

Thoughts can't be regulated from without or within, but uncoupled from action, thoughts are uniformly innocuous. Only action lends danger to thoughts. Thoughts can't be controlled, but actions can. There are no illegitimate thoughts; only unethical actions.

> We don't know yet about life, how can we know about death?

Confucius

> Confucius was a self-educated philosopher who became the most educated man of his time, greatly influencing all eastern Asia civilizations with his nonreligious social ethic; his books formed the basis of Chinese education for over two thousand years.

We know enough about life to have serious doubts about the possibility of immortality. Religion promises a life after death that no one has experienced. Though we don't fully understand life, we can easily understand death as the end of life. Religion provides hope for human immortality based on belief, the mechanics of which Confucius hints is less knowable than life and less clear than the regularly observed finality of death, for which no exception has been verified. Confucianism is supremely practical, hardly qualifying as a religion. Confucianism is rationality, common sense, and whatever works, which is how the average person operates, religious or not. The charm of Confucian rationality lies in its refusal to hope for immortality. Tom says that's Confucianism's fatal flaw.

The Rationality of Belief

> Agnosticism, in fact, is not a creed, but a method, the essence of which lies in the rigorous application of a single principle. That principle is of great antiquity; it is as old as Socrates, as old as the writer who said, 'Try all things, hold fast by that which is good'; it is the foundation of the Reformation, which simply illustrated the axiom that every man should be able to give a reason for the faith that is in him; it is the great principle of Descartes; it is the fundamental

179

axiom of modern science. Positively the principle may be expressed: In matters of the intellect, follow your reason as far as it will take you, without regard for any other consideration. And negatively: In matters of the intellect, do not pretend that conclusions are certain which are not demonstrated or demonstrable. That I take to be the agnostic faith, which if a man keep whole and undefiled, he shall not be ashamed to look the universe in the face, whatever the future may have in store for him.

T. H. Huxley

Huxley was Darwin's foremost defender, a position based on his belief that religion is a deadly enemy of science. He coined the term *agnostic*.

Agnosticism takes no position on the merely possible or the unverifiable. Because gods and immortality are unverifiable, agnosticism ignores them while labeling them as improbable. The unverifiable should always be rejected in favor of the verifiable and probabilities always chosen over remote or unverifiable potentialities. Tom says that's perfectly acceptable, having personally verified immortality.

Nothing is so easy as to deceive one's self; for what we wish, we readily believe.

Demosthenes

Demosthenes perfected his oratory in order to successfully sue his guardians, who had squandered his estate before he reached the age of majority.

We believe in religion because it promises rescue from the brick wall of death. Without this promise, Western religion wouldn't exist, because it would hold little or no attraction. A Christian sect sells a bumper sticker that says, "God said it; I believe it, and that settles it." Discussion can't begin when truth is *revealed,* based neither on logic nor evidence. We readily believe a remote possibility because we fervently hope it's true. Tom assures me it is.

> Knowing no God, I have
> made of man my worship.
>
> Jack London

> London was the highest paid writer of his time, though he was always broke. His reputation receded after his death except abroad. In Russia, the 1956 commemorative edition of his works sold out in five hours.

No one knows a god, though many hope or purport to. Gods are unknowable by definition. We should only believe in and hold reverent that which can be verified or is probably true. Limited to these choices, the species ranks high on reverence for illogic. Tom says he's way up there on reverence, and I might add, logic too.

> Personal interest is often the standard of our belief, as well as of our practice.
>
> Edward Gibbon

> Gibbon planned the entire narrative for *Decline and Fall of the Roman Empire* at age fourteen but didn't begin writing his famous tome until age thirty-five.

Personal interest is usually the standard for both belief and action. The widespread belief in Western religion is based on promises of immortality, which is in every individual's presumed self-interest. We lust and hunger to escape death, to achieve the immortality promised by religion based on the visions and traditions of our forefathers, which we wholeheartedly believe, though many may believe in order to hedge bets and attain social acceptance, sustaining religion by lip service. Like government, religion exists on one level to fill its coffers and support its leaders. We hope the claims of religion will result in a self-fulfilling prophecy; if we have sufficient faith and believe hard enough, it will happen; as we believed in childhood about Santa Claus and believe as adults about God, Santa's natural successor. A god promises us life forever, the ultimate present, while Santa Claus brought us presents and our belief dovetailed with our self-interest. Tom says religious belief transcends self-interest.

> In every unbeliever's heart
> there is an uneasy feeling that,
> after all, he may awake after death
> and find himself immortal. This is
> his punishment for his unbelief.
> This is the agnostic's hell.

> H.L. Mencken

Likewise, every believer has the uneasy feeling that he won't awake after death. The believer has more to fear because immortality is a remote possibility while death is a sure thing. Except for religious myth, resurrection lacks verification. No one has avoided death, ever. It's too harsh to say that this truth is the believer's punishment or the believer's hell. No one knows anything in this realm; but there are probabilities and there are exceedingly remote possibilities. Tom says he's banking on revealed truth.

The Egotism of Bare Belief

> Religion, in short, is a
> monumental chapter in the history
> of human egotism.

> William James

James's grandfather emigrated

182

from Ireland in 1789, dying in
1832 worth millions. He molded
James's father into a permissive
parent who shuttled the family
between Europe and the U.S.

Religion reflects human egotism. We believe we're immortal
because creatures as marvelous as ourselves don't deserve to die.
Surely, we must live forever. Except for its atrocities, religion might
be accorded a few sentences in human history, assuming we
negotiate the next million years or so. In order to survive we need
to overcome the intolerance and us-versus-themness of religion,
nationalism, and racial prejudice. Then we might survive as a
species. The species is ego enough. Elevating his gaze, Tom says
there's even more.

Altogether, both the glory
and the tragedy of Israel may be
traced to the singular idea
cherished by its people—the
exalted, conceited, preposterous
idea that they alone were God's
chosen people.

Herbert J. Muller

Muller taught at Cornell, Purdue,
and Indiana University (1959–
1980); served in the Department of
State and on the War Production
Board; and frequently lectured
abroad.

The relative prosperity of the Jews makes them a target for
the have-not majority. The majority of the species adopted the
Jewish god, the basis for Christianity and Islam. The Jews were the
first chosen people, after Hindus and Buddhists, the Egyptian,
Zoroastrian, Mithraic, and other gods having died off. Slaughter
continues like an earthquake zone where religious Jews, Christians,
and Muslims intersect, grinding us into dust for the glory and
tragedy of Judaism and our other infallible religions. Tom says,
now, now.

183

> Even so, oxen, lions and
> horses, if they had hands
> wherewith to grave images, would
> fashion gods after their own
> shapes and give them bodies like
> their own.

Xenophanes of Colophon

> Xenophanes wandered the
> Mediterranean coast from age
> twenty-five until his death at
> ninety-two, attacking the
> immortality of the Greek gods and
> materialism, and was cited by
> Plato and Aristotle.

Modern religious philosophy fashions gods as incorporeal spirits in the image of superman. Fundamentalists believe in a superman god who kicks the butts of other religions, the same as cave men fashioning a god in their own image. Tom says stark but not wholly inaccurate.

The Logic of Immortality

> If there is a sin against life,
> it consists perhaps not so much in
> despairing of life as in hoping for
> another life and in eluding the
> implacable grandeur of this life.

Albert Camus

> As an editorial writer on the *Alger-Republicain,* Camus wrote about
> the social injustice that led to the
> 1954 Algerian War fifteen years
> before it happened.

Religion obscures earthly pleasures by burdening believers with silly sins unrelated to morality. Religion may harm the believer by banning hedonism that harms no one else, teaching intolerance toward the "them" of other religions, and promoting poverty, amply sufficient to obscure the grandeur of life. Tom says pish-posh, but with little gusto.

> That we should cease to exist, that we should live and so profoundly will our existence, only to face annihilation a few years hence, is a thought from which men recoil, not pausing to ask why such simple non-existence should be filled with such dread for them, but dreading it nevertheless. It is from this calamity that religion promises salvation, and upon this promise its strength and appeal entirely rest.

Richard Taylor

Egotists like ourselves suffer grave difficulty wrapping our minds around looming nonexistence. We act as if the world couldn't exist without us, trusting death will blink and give us a bye. We dread nonexistence because it appears obscene for us, individuals too grand to die, ignoring daily obituaries. The idea of immortality began before our Neanderthal days. We buried our dead with tools for the next life and believed in immortality because we saw our deceased relatives in our dreams. They lived on, and we will too. Through religion we believe we'll live forever, though the only evidence is putrefaction. Tom says he'll live forever, and I begrudge him nothing.

> To mourn for the time when one will be no more is just as absurd as it would be to mourn over the time when as yet one was not.

Arthur Schopenhauer

Schopenhauer quarreled with his mother over his frivolous lifestyle, a dispute reaching such

185

proportions in 1814 that he left
Weimar and never saw her again
though she lived another twenty-
five years; he corresponded with
her during the last eight years of
her life.

We don't pity the yet unborn because they'll outlive us. We
pity our own death but not the death of others, though resenting the
death of others as a reminder that we, too, that way go, the only
question being when. Tom says the flesh is weak and particularly
mine.

If anyone pities the dead he
must also pity the yet unborn.

Lucius Annaeus Seneca

Seneca the younger, author of a
dozen philosophical essays and
124 letters on morality, was forced
by Nero to commit suicide.

If we could mourn not yet being born, we might do that too.
Some pity the aborted fetus who has no opportunity to mourn. Tom
says he does too, but then, so do I. But if religions championed birth
control and sex education, abortions would drop to near zero, but
they don't. This is called hypocrisy. Tom sadly nods.

Better to die, and
sleep
The never-waking
sleep, than linger
on
And dare to live
when the soul's
life is gone.

Sophocles

Of Sophocles' 123 plays, only 7
survive; he never came in lower
than second in Greek drama

186

competitions.

Instead of eternity in a wheelchair, religion assumes youthful immortality. Only the mentally impaired would want to prolong life in the condition we usually leave it. The debility leading to death from old age cushions the fall like a golden parachute to oblivion. Tom says he's not going to oblivion.

> From too much love
> of living,
> From hope and fear
> set free,
> We thank with brief
> thanksgiving
> Whatever gods may
> be
> That no life lives
> forever;
> That dead men rise
> up never;
> That even the
> weariest river
> Winds somewhere
> safe to sea.
>
> Algernon Charles
> Swinburne

> Swinburne failed to graduate from Balliol College, Oxford, but met his best buds there: Dante and William Morris.

The end is often relief from illness and confusion. The prolongation of severe trauma has nothing to recommend it. Only youth restored with the wisdom of experience retained would make prolonged life palatable, but no religion reveals the details of life after death, except the canny Muslims. Tom says he's quite optimistic.

> Without knowing what I am and why I am here, life is impossible.

Leo Tolstoy

Tolstoy was a party animal at
Kazan University but was so ugly
that he wore a full beard his entire
life.

Life simply is, being neither impossible nor particularly
difficult, at least in prosperous countries, though myth may
accentuate the adventure. No one knows whether a *why* for life
exists, much less what it might be. Religious theories of the species'
purpose are based on wishful thinking that fits neither common
sense nor probability.

The belief in the
immortality of the human soul is a
dogma which is in hopeless
contradiction with the most solid
empirical truths of modern
science.

Ernst Heinrich Haeckel

Haeckel concluded in 1866 that
the nucleus of cells passed on
inherited traits.

The key rules of religion contradict science, no matter the
religion, whether the concept of the immortality of the soul, taught
by Christianity, Muslims, and some Jews, or the Hindu concept of
reincarnation. Religious dogma skirts the realm of reason and
ethics. For example, the "ethical" rules of religion, such as
prohibiting birth control and supporting whatever government is in
power, are more corrupt than moral. Any scientific discovery that
challenges religious dogma is first considered heretical, then
possibly reconcilable, and lastly, a minor part of religious tradition.
Christian examples include Galileo, Darwin, and Stephen Hawking.
We cling to the marvelous, especially when it suits our fear of death
and dream of immortality. In these circumstances, science and logic
are irrelevant and hateful. Science can't accommodate the
resurrection of a rotted body. Tom says no problem.

How very hard it is to

be a Christian!
... ' 'Tis well
averred, a
scientific faith's
absurd ... '

Robert Browning

Browning was best known for *The Ring and the Book*, which detailed a Roman murder trial in twelve books.

Science and faith are mutually exclusive: Science demands evidence, and faith demands that evidence not exist. With evidence, faith would be unnecessary. An anomaly of religion is its attempt to find evidence proving articles of faith, such as the Shroud of Turin, the resurrection of Christ, miracles, and magical properties of relics. Tom says faith is worthy of its mystery.

Humanism or Religion?

When men can no longer be theists, they must, if they are civilized, become humanists.

Walter Lippmann

Lippmann's newspaper columns ran in 250 U.S. newspapers and twenty-five countries, influencing the attempted establishment of the League of Nations.

The only choice is between theism and humanism. Humanists disbelieve a soul because there's no evidence of its existence, or the existence of any other spirit. The species is a natural phenomenon, apparently evolved from small wiggly things less than supernaturally created. No spirit seems to guide or control the species; witness its intolerant divisions into groups based on religious, national, and ethnic affiliations. The species and its members should instead rely on the power of self and the species as

189

a whole, avoiding those things that splinter us into artificial camps. Tom says largely true but grossly deficient without religion.

> I use the word 'Humanist'
> to mean someone who believes
> that man is just as much a natural
> phenomenon as an animal or a
> plant; that his body, mind or soul
> were not supernaturally created
> but are products of evolution, and
> that he is not under the control or
> guidance of any supernatural
> being, but has to rely on himself
> and his own powers.

> Julian Huxley

> This Huxley was the grandson of
> T.H. and the first director of
> UNESCO, from 1946 to1948.

For the next few hundred years the species will probably consist mostly of theists. If the species could no longer believe in a god it would have nothing to believe in but itself and necessarily be humanist. Tom says that would be a sad day, yet I feel nary a tear.

> The soul of man is
> objectively considered—
> essentially similar to that of all
> other vertebrates; it is the
> physiological action or function of
> the brain.

> Ernst Heinrich Haeckel

> Haeckel was attracted to biology
> by a field trip to the North Sea
> while a student at the University of
> Berlin.

The Haeckel type of soul disappears when the brain dies without oxygen, disintegrating within minutes. Science can't conceive of a resurrection or how the brain could be reconstructed after death. The religious believe in the improbable, based on hope. The brain contains our intelligence or soul, disappearing with death. Tom says I could be shown the way.

> I bow to man because beyond the incarnations of man's reason and imagination, I feel and see nothing in our world. God has been one of man's inventions, just like photography, with the difference that the latter fixes that which really exists, whereas God is a photograph of an idea which man invents, of a being one wishes—and is able—to be omniscient, omnipotent and perfectly just.
>
> Maksim Gorki

> Gorki means "bitter," a name adopted by the Russian novelist and playwright while he was living and writing as a tramp; he died under suspicious circumstances engineered by Stalin.

A god is a fuzzy photograph of a superman based on man's imagination. The concept of a god is indistinguishable from our imagination. The imagination may yearn for a god that combines omniscience, omnipotence, and perfect justice, but reality confirms the hollowness and evil of religion. Tom says religion is our feeble attempt to construct a just world. Then religion gets an F.

What Is a Soul?

> The soul is only the thinking part of the body, and with the body it passes away. When death comes, the farce is over, therefore let us take our pleasure

while we can.

Julien Offray de la Mettrie

When de la Mettrie was forced to
leave Holland (after his exile from
France) in 1748, he was welcomed
by Frederick the Great, made the
court reader, and appointed to the
academy of science.

It can't be bad advice to take pleasure while we can, as long
as we act ethically. We can think and feel, as far as we know, only
while we're alive. The odds of feeling anything after death are
astronomical; the line in Las Vegas is likely a theoretical one
because few truly believe they can collect after death. Betting on
heaven is a poor insurance program, worse than lottery odds. Tom
says he has a winning ticket.

No evil is glorious. But
there are cases of glorious death.
Death therefore is not evil.

Zeno the Stoic

The founder of Stoicism combined
logic, a theory of knowledge,
physics, and ethics, with the last
being central to his philosophy,
though only fragments survive.

Zeno says that glorious deaths aren't evil. Death is never
glorious unless perhaps to protect others from death. Nothingness
and death are otherwise the ultimate personal evil, though healthy
for the species. Tom says we reap our just glory after our demise.

Man is immortal, but not
men.

H.G. Wells

Wells studied under T.H. Huxley
and, after his literary success,

associated with Conrad, James,
Ford, Chesterton, and Shaw.

The species is likely as mortal as the individual. As a species
we're a few thousand years old, an eye blink in the life of the
universe. Whether we survive more thousands of years depends on
our ability to eliminate our artificial differences based on religion,
nationalism, and ethnicity, no matter their label. Tom says religion
is okay, though parts may need polish.

It is also not consistent with
the reality of the soul to admit that
there is anything in the known
universe more divine than men
and women.

Walt Whitman

Whitman's brother was wounded
at Fredericksburg in 1862,
prompting Whitman to spend the
Civil War nursing the wounded.

Women may be divine, but I'm not so sure about men.
Notwithstanding hoity-toity gods, their followers seldom act
divinely, though bits of the species act more ethically and seem
more divine than game-playing gods. Whitman's soul is being,
sensing, feeling, and seeing intimately, tangibly, and with clarity.
Tom says he sees and feels as well as I do, and I can't deny that.

Motherhood is neither a
duty nor a privilege, but simply the
way that humanity can satisfy the
desire for physical immortality
and triumph over the fear of death.

Rebecca West

West bore a son fathered by H.G.
Wells but is best known for her
brilliant reporting on the
Nuremberg Trials.

Literature has enshrined the idea of the immortality of the species. Literature and art, similar to religion, help relieve our fear of death, which gallops onward, no matter unending attempts by literature, motherhood, fatherhood, and religion to rein in our fears. Tom graciously agrees.

> I can do very well without God both in my life and in my painting, but I cannot, suffering as I am, do without something which is greater than I, which is my life, the power to create.
>
> Vincent Van Gogh

> After giving all his earthly goods away, Van Gogh became a missionary in the coal-mining region of southwest Belgium in 1879; he was fired as a missionary for interpreting the Bible too literally.

Perhaps we need a belief in a greater power, whether to escape death, achieve immortality, or bolster creativity. A greater power works for Alcoholics Anonymous, a day at a time, and as an inspiration for intellectuals and artists. Creativity is unfortunately limited to the creative, which excludes many of us. For a higher power, the majority turns to religion. Tom says right on.

> The true God, the all-powerful God, is the God of ideas.
>
> Albert Victor, Comte de Vigny

> Vigny's eight-year affair with the actress Marie Dorval, for whom he created the lead role in his play *Chatterton* (1835), crashed when she had a liaison with George Sand, making Vigny forever bitter over women.

194

For the intellectual minority, ideas are god. For the majority, ideas are a poor substitute for bread, shelter, social standing, and wealth. Ideas are heard by few, grasped by fewer, and trash to many, if not most. Tom says that may unfortunately be true.

> On the whole, I am on the side of the unregenerate who affirm the worth of life as an end in itself, as against the saints who deny it.
>
> Oliver Wendell Holmes

> Holmes was himself an unregenerate who loved burlesque, was loved by his fellow U.S. Supreme Court justices, and said, "I thank God I am a man of low tastes."

Holmes reminds me of Richard Feynman, both unregenerate hedonists attracted to women, and well, why not? Of course, there are saints rightly vilified for preaching ignorance of life. I sat by the Rio de Pontevedra where it meets the sea in Galatia after a month walking the Camino de Santiago de Compostela, sun shining brightly on the mile-wide channel, evergreened cliffs and water-lapped rocks fringed by lush grass, blanketed with utter tranquility, wondering at a saint who could impugn this life in favor of a life experienced by no one. Tom says there's nothing wrong with saints or with this life either.

> It was previously a question of finding out whether or not life had to have a meaning to be lived. It has now become clear, on the contrary, that it will be lived all the better if it has no meaning.
>
> Albert Camus

> Camus was raised in a two-room apartment with his mother, grandmother, and paralyzed uncle

in Algeria in conditions so noxious
that he contracted tuberculosis at
age seventeen.

Religion answers the meaning of life for many, but we don't
know how many religious believe that temporal life has little or no
meaning; I'd guess few. However, a religious belief that temporal
life is meaningless may render poverty, disease, and war bearable,
speeding the faithful to a happier eternity. Nonbelievers are freed
from archaic beliefs and can more easily direct their energies to
improving the only life we know exists. Why life should have a
higher meaning is inexplicable to me. Tom says it's not inexplicable
for him and exudes great meaning.

> The great mystery is not
> that we should have been thrown
> down here at random between the
> profusion of matter and that of the
> stars; it is that from our very prison
> we should draw, from our own
> selves, images powerful enough to
> deny our nothingness.

> André Malraux

> Among other great adventures,
> Malraux joined the Republican
> forces in the Spanish civil war in
> 1936, a colonel in charge of an
> international flying squadron.

Egocentrism is no great mystery. We believed ourselves the
center of the universe until the last few hundred years. Galileo's
discovery that the earth isn't the center of the universe, but is instead
an insignificant particle in a minuscule solar system on the edge of
an average-sized galaxy out of billions of galaxies, allows us to
accurately place ourselves in the context of the universe. Our
grandiose ideas were born from an ignorance that can't be
eradicated until belief based on bare possibility evaporates, which
is likely never. We'll never deny the bare possibility of an immortal
soul and face the likely reality of a short and insignificant life in a
remote corner of the universe. Tom says he's not insignificant and
that unbelievably, I'm not either.

The pleasure and delight of knowledge and learning, it far surpasseth all other in nature. . . . We see in all other pleasures there is satiety, and after they are used their verdure departeth; which showeth well they be but the deceits of pleasure, and not pleasure: and that it was the novelty that pleasured, not the quality.

Francis Bacon

Bacon turned his era on its ear, separating medicine from a literary pursuit largely unrelated to science, separating science from theology, speculation, and superstition.

Knowledge and learning are a delight for many, with maybe half of us able to afford the luxury. Many are inculcated into ignorance by bare belief, which is understandable when education in many countries means memorizing a holy book or attending a religious school. We may never know whether it's more satisfying for an intellectual, such as Francis Bacon, to acquire knowledge than for the average guy to watch football and quaff a few beers, and whatever most women want. Pleasure is subjective, whether derived from learning, family, sports, religion, reason, atheism, and the rest of the dictionary. Tom suggests the answer is religion.

Now the answer . . . is plain, but it is so unpalatable that most men will not face it. There is no reason for life and life has no meaning.

W. Somerset Maugham

Maugham was a realistic cynic with four plays running at the same time in 1908 London; he

served as a secret agent during
World War I.

Asking the reason for life seems a nonquestion. Questions
that don't compute may include the reason for life and why birds
fly. The reason for life is unclear to everyone, including the
religious, who know as much for certain as the nonreligious.
Whether life has a reason makes little or no difference. The meaning
of life is what we make it. We're born and we die. What occurs in
between may be of no more significance than the birth and death of
a trout. Other than wishful thinking, we have no contrary evidence.
Tom says he does.

Life.   Consider   the
alternative.

Marshall McLuhan

McLuhan predicted the potent
force of television, computers, and
media.

Belief in a god is a poor alternative to life. The meaning of
life is to live. The alternative overtakes us sooner than we think, and
almost always before we're ready. The alternative to life may be
nothingness, before and afterwards. Tom says not for him and a
billion or so others.

On the basis of biological,
sociological, and historical
knowledge, we should recognize
that the individual self is subject to
death and decay, but the sum total
of individual achievement, for
better or worse, lives on in the
immortality of the Larger Self;
that to live for the sake of the
species and posterity is religion of
the highest kind; and that those
religious who see a future life
either in Heaven or in the Pure
Land, are selfish religions.

198

Hu Shih

From 1914 until 1949 Hu Shih was
the leading political liberal in
China; he helped reform the
archaic Chinese language in 1922,
spurring literacy.

The immortality of the Larger Self is contained within the
species; nothing else may count, except the individual. The species
is two millionths the age of the universe, a dollop in time, leaving
our ultimate achievement unknown. The only proper religion may
be humanism, based entirely on the value and worth of the species,
whatever that might be, if anything. Religions that wrap us in an
egocentric salvation could be considered selfish for pitting us
against ourselves, plunging many into poverty, and banking on a
future life no one has experienced. Tom says he'll experience it and
is also gung-ho on the species.

But the race remains
immortal.

Virgil

Virgil is the most celebrated
Roman poet, best known for the
twelve books of the Aeneid
celebrating the period from the
settlement of Rome and Troy
through the unification of the
world by Augustus, an epic
unfinished at his death from a
fever contracted on a visit to
Greece.

The species is immortal only if it survives beyond a few
billion years, a limited though nigh unimaginable immortality.
Whether we'll survive that long may depend on removing the parts
of religion, nationalism, racism, and greed that divide us into us-
versus-them. Tom says fair enough, but religion retains
unfathomable value.

In the midst of all the doubts

which we have discussed for four
thousand years in four thousand
ways, the safest course is to do
nothing against one's conscience.
With this secret, we can enjoy life
and have no fear of death.

Voltaire

In 1717 Voltaire landed in the
Bastille for writing a verse
lampooning the government.

The key to a good life may be ethics, removing the fear of
retribution by others and thus lessening our fear of death, on both
the individual and national level. Ethics requires that nothing be
done against individual conscience, which boils down to harming
no one else and performing whatever positive acts strike one as
appropriate. Tom says crude. We'll work on refinement in the
appropriate chapter.

Would We Be Better Off Without Religion?

> This would be the best of all possible worlds, if there were no religion in it.
>
> John Adams

Adams became the first vice president of the United States by coming in second in his race for president against George Washington, 69 to 34 electoral votes.

John Adams would have been more accurate if he had added to his best-of-all-worlds-if-no-religion, "and no racism, nationalism, or greed." The us-versus-them watershed is grounded on religion, nationalism, racism, and greed. Until these disappear the species may neither thrive nor survive. If the species were not divided along these artificial lines, we'd be substantially more civil to each other, likely eradicating war and poverty from the planet, boosting our togetherness to explore the universe. United we will thrive, and divided we will fail. Tom says religion could fix a few things, the same as any unwieldy bureaucracy.

> Supposing a man-hater had desired to render the human race as unhappy as possible, what could he have invented for the purpose better than belief in an incomprehensible being about whom men can never be able to agree?
>
> Denis Diderot

Diderot's early education was by

Jesuits; he moved from
Catholicism to atheism and a
theory of evolution (for which he
was imprisoned three months), a
hundred years before Darwin.

The first commandment of the Christian religion says, "Thou
shalt have no other gods before me." Because no one can agree on
an incomprehensible god, Christian and other religions have battled
since time immemorial, dispatching millions to early graves.
Though Christians share the Jewish and Muslim god, these three
religions terminate each other with abandon because thou shalt not
allow any other gods before the shared god that teaches
commandments resulting in jihads, crusades, inquisitions, the
Middle East, and fundamentalism. Tom says settle down at once.

Anyone who has the power
to make you believe absurdities
has the power to make you commit
injustices.

Voltaire

In his fifties, Voltaire had a
passionate amour with his forty-
year-old niece, Madame Denis, an
affair kept secret for two hundred
years.

Unerring identification of absurdity isn't easy. One person's
absurdity is another's lifeblood. Many agree that tolerance flows
from education while intolerance gushes from those things that
divide us. For Christianity, knowledge was the original forbidden
fruit. Though many embrace religion after extensive education, they
are comparatively few. Some religious believe their members will
live forever if they kill those who believe differently, a unique
concept of justice. It's difficult to draw the line between gods
sufficiently similar for respect and those whose adherents should be
slaughtered. Tom would never slaughter a religious other and
doesn't personally know anyone who would. He doesn't get around
much anymore.

A wise and courageous

prince, with money, troops, and laws, can perfectly well govern men without the aid of religion, which was made only to deceive them; but the stupid people would soon make one for themselves and as long as there are fools and rascals there will be religions. Ours [Christian] is assuredly the most ridiculous, the most absurd, and the most bloody that has ever infected the world.

Voltaire

Madame Denis died in childbirth, bearing neither her husband's nor Voltaire's child but that of Saint Lambert, a dashing minor poet.

As long as the species exists, religion will exist, because we need the promise of deliverance from death and the assurance that we're better than others. The Christian religion may be the bloodiest religion in history but suffers stiff competition from other religions, particularly Islam. Through a self-proclaimed connection with ethics, religion justifies atrocities in most of the world's hot spots. Those not fools or rascals cling to religion as the fountainhead of ethics, love, and immortality, such as my good buddy Tom.

Man is a very strange animal. In much of the world half the children go to bed hungry and we spend a trillion on rubbish— steel, iron, tanks. We are all criminals. There is an old Hungarian poem, 'If you are among brigands and you are silent, you are a brigand yourself.'

Albert Szent-Gyorgyi

Szent-Gyorgyi found and isolated ascorbic acid from plant juices and adrenal gland extracts, helping prove it identical to Vitamin C. The American biochemist was awarded the Nobel Prize in 1937.

The effort to oppose brigands takes enormous personal courage. Many are poor because of religious interdictions that make personal accountability difficult. We spend trillions of dollars on war materials because we're afraid of the "them" who live elsewhere, idolize a different god, wear a darker skin, or suffer under a more egregious government than our own. We're perfectly predictable animals who are often deafeningly silent in the face of brigands. We prefer identification with artificial groups instead of the species. We fancy false karasses and granfalloons over basic human kindness and a refusal to harm others. The species is more alike than different but we fixate on the differences, elevating them into mountains of religion, nationalism, and race (including sexual preference), perpetuating the cannibalism of the species. Silence in the company of brigands may be more self-defense than complicity, but any excuse will do. Tom says he's speechless.

Better contraceptives will control population only if people will use them. A nuclear holocaust can be prevented only if the conditions under which nations make war can be changed. The environment will continue to deteriorate until pollution practices are abandoned. We need to make vast changes in human behavior.

B.F. Skinner

A professor emeritus of psychology at Harvard, Skinner was attracted to psychology by Pavlov's experiments with conditioned reflex and trained animals, accomplishing the implausible, such as teaching pigeons to play table tennis.

Vast changes in human behavior won't happen until the things dividing us are castrated and cauterized. Religion generally forbids contraception, spreading abject poverty among those who actually believe, the uneducated and third world. Religion will have no other gods before its own, sometimes recommending that partisans of other religions be slaughtered in the name of the father, son, and holy ghost. And climate change is similarly divisive, another science-versus-greed-and-nationalism issue. Human behavior can't imagine forsaking the immortality guaranteed by Western religion though shunned in the East. Religion, nationalism, and ethnicity will continue to call the shots and, as a result, the species may not survive. Tom says things aren't that bad, and we toast to him being right.

> Man is destined to live without religion, but the moral law is eternal and absolute. Who would dare today to attack morality?
>
> Pierre Joseph Proudhon
>
> Proudhon, a Socialist and founder of the French labor movement, coined simplistic and grossly misleading phrases such as "Property is theft" and "I am an anarchist," passionately influencing Russian Populists, radical Italian Nationalists, Spanish Federalists, and similar philosophies.

Religion often has only a vocal connection with morality while perpetuating atrocities from abusive priests to religious wars, with religion influencing most wars; we'd be better off without it. Tom says my suggestion may be immorality itself.

> A man may have no religion, and yet be moral.
>
> Napoleon Bonaparte

Napoleon's father abandoned his pro-Corsican stance when the French recognized his claim to nobility, greasing Napoleon's entrance into the French Military Academy at age ten.

The irreligious are as moral as the religious. Religion is unrelated to morality except negatively; its intolerance of others and prohibitions against birth control are the antithesis of morality. Tom would reform the bad parts, whispering that the church should have allowed birth control ages ago.

The chief cause of slavery, then, is sin—that a man should be put in bonds to another; and this happens only by the judgment of God, in whose eyes it is no crime.

Saint Augustine

The Numidian-born Christian convert and bishop of Hippo is famous for his pre-Christian abandon with a mistress and resulting son, praying, "Lord make me pure and chaste but not just yet," though he was monogamous.

Mainstream religion would repudiate Saint Augustine's justification for slavery, but his example reminds us that religion is literalist and supports those in power, no matter their predilections. Tom says religion shouldn't be blind but it must be practical, the same as everyone else.

Color line is a great problem of this century. . . . Back of the problem of race and color lies a greater problem which both obscures and implements it; and that is the fact that so many civilized persons are willing to

live in comfort even if the price of
this is poverty, ignorance and
disease of the majority of their
fellowmen; that to maintain this
privilege men have waged war
until today war tends to become
universal and continuous, and the
excuse for this war continues
largely to be color and race.

W.E.B. DuBois

DuBois co-founded the NAACP
in 1909 with seven white
progressives and flirted with
communism. He became a citizen
pf Ghana in 1963 and was buried
there.

Excuses for war include religion, nationalism, and simple
greed. Poverty, ignorance, and disease stem partly from bans
against birth control which result in poverty caused by unplanned
and often unwanted children. Religion, patriotism, and ethnicity are
an excuse for waging war against other religions, governments, and
ethnic groups. It's difficult to sympathize with those who can't or
won't improve their station in life because they believe the tales of
religion, though Tom says higher things aren't the fault of the poor.
Many are taught by religion that birth control is evil, though it offers
the best hope of escaping poverty. Religion and patriotism venerate
the happenstance of local government. Because many countries
consist of a dominant ethnic group, the us-versus-them is
emphasized within the dominant religion and the government in
power. The three greatest evils are arguably religion, nationalism,
and greed, with nationalism a synonym for racism. If the racism of
religion and traditional racism were eradicated, many if not most of
our problems might vaporize. Poverty could be largely eliminated
by universal education and birth control, alleviating much disease
and boosting the life expectancy of the world's children. Our flaw
is failing to recognize and remove the causes of poverty, ignorance,
and disease. We instead cling to promises of immortality
conditioned on the observance of religious rules unrelated to
morality. We fail to comprehend that religion consists of some nasty
bits. Tom says religion, like all bureaucracies, has its bad parts and

categorically refuses to turn eggplant purple.

Prohibiting Birth Control Causes Poverty

I want nothing to do with any religion concerned with keeping the masses satisfied to live in hunger, filth and ignorance. I want nothing to do with any order, religious or otherwise, which does not teach people that they are capable of becoming happier and more civilized, on this earth, capable of becoming true man, master of his fate and captain of his soul. To attain this I would put priests to work, also, and turn the temples into schools.

Jawaharlal Nehru

Nehru died while prime minister of India. His daughter was prime minister for fifteen years, his grandson for five years, and his sister was the first female president of the U.N. General Assembly.

Nehru speaks heresy to organized religions that preach the necessity of procreation into direst poverty, illustrated in third world countries including India where the population believes more in religion than reality. The three major Western religions by their actions, no matter their contrary lip service, endorse masses content with hunger, filth, and ignorance. The original religious sin was education, eating from the tree of knowledge. No good can spring from those who prefer ignorance to knowledge. The primary virtue of religion is to calm our fear of death, though world poverty seems an unfair trade-off for bare belief in immortality. If temples and churches were converted into schools they would better assist the species, which hasn't exactly been accomplished by madrassas in mosques with a single curriculum, to memorize the Koran. Together, education and birth control are among the most important means of mastering our fate. Religion mandates slavery by prohibiting birth control. Tom agrees that birth control should be actively taught instead of discouraged, but he tries to be a loyal Catholic brother.

> God damn the society that will permit such poverty! God damn the religions that stand for such a putrid system!
>
> Sinclair Lewis
>
> Lewis drank with abandon, his second wife was political columnist Dorothy Thompson, and he was the first American to receive the Nobel Prize for literature.

World population grew by 100 million in 1995 to 5.75 billion people and will hit 8 billion in 2023. According to the Population Institute: "Ninety percent of the growth [is] in poor countries already terribly torn by civil strife and social unrest and where all too many people live in brutal poverty."

There are three risk factors for poverty according to the October 1994 *Atlantic Monthly:* "teenage child-bearing, failure to complete high school, and non-marriage." When all three are present, "then it is all but inevitable that the mother and her child will live in poverty: 79 percent of all children born to mothers with these three risk factors are poor."

Religion can't be considered a bastion of morality when its prohibition against birth control traps many in poverty, bordering on evil if not evil itself. Religious advocacy of death to the infidel pales in comparison to the misery suffered by those believing that their primary duty in life is to produce children for the Christian (using the largest as our guide), Muslim, and Hindu religions, the world's three largest that prohibit birth control, so that they may compete for parishioners while overpopulating the earth. Women are primarily affected by bars against birth control but are more loyal to religion than men, a paradox perhaps explained by women's subordination to men, in the name of religion, since the species realized that men were necessary for propagation. Before that time (about 6,000 B.C.E.), our religions were matriarchal, headlining female goddesses. Since then women have been controlled by religion and society to preserve the integrity of the male lineage. The Christian New Testament prohibits women from speaking in church, reflected by the Christian prohibition (primarily by its largest sect, Roman Catholicism) against the ordination of female priests. Women are subject to male domination in the three biggest religions, which total 73 percent of the world's population, or 5.6 billion out of 7.7 billion in 2019. Of course, sects and many individuals ignore prohibitions against birth control, but the result is still a majority of uneducated poor in the third world. When a god says do "whatever" as interpreted by earthly ministers, it must and shall be done, such as propagating the earth to death. Tom says I caricature the problem. It doesn't help that in 2018, 26 men owned as much wealth as half the world's population, 26 versus 3.7 billion men, women, and children.

> Other circumstances being the same, it may be affirmed that countries are populous according to the quantity of food which they produce or can acquire, and happy according to the liberality with which this food is divided, or the quantity which a day's labor will purchase.
>
> Thomas Robert Malthus

> Darwin credits Malthus's *Essay on the Principle of Population* and the term "struggle for existence" with providing him "a theory by which to work."

Malthus said population could be controlled only through "vice" (which included contraception), "misery," and "self-restraint," concluding that poverty was unavoidable, but since then, birth control methods and their acceptance has greatly improved.

Countries are populous based on the general education level of the citizenry; the more educated ignore the outlawing of birth control by the dominant religion. Population is unrelated to the availability of food. India is populated unto poverty by Hinduism and Islam, similar to the effect of religious taboos against birth control in Bangladesh, Africa, South America, Central America, and much of the world. We're happy according to our ability to purchase food, which requires enough education to acquire a marketable skill and ignore religious embargoes on birth control. Tom says mostly true.

> You must strive to multiply bread so that it suffices for the tables of mankind, and not rather favor an artificial control of birth, which would be irrational in order to diminish the number of guests at the banquet of life.
>
> Pope Paul VI
>
> Paul VI's encyclicals confirming priestly celibacy (1967) and prohibiting birth control (1968) were widely criticized.

Many guests at the banquet of life have insufficient food because of the general religious forbiddance of birth control. Religious leaders who preach the irrationality of birth control decree more misery on the species than the most monstrous criminal. Hitler was a piker, liquidating and starving a few million compared to organized religions that plunge billions into poverty. The individual is a slave if not allowed to determine the number of guests at the dinner table. Tom says, now, now.

Poverty Promotes Crime

A laborer who marries without being able to support a family may in some respects be considered as an enemy of all his fellow-laborers.

Thomas Robert Malthus

Malthus thought mankind could never be happy because population growth seemed geometric, always outrunning increases in the production of food, which he described as arithmetic.

Anyone, male or female, who produces a child without being able to provide basic necessities of clean water, food, medical care, education, and shelter, is irresponsible, an enemy of their children and of the species itself. The excuse of papal and other religious mandates is a crutch for individual irresponsibility. Religion considers this irresponsibility the fulfillment of its god's commandments.

That they [the dogmas of religion] do little harm is not true. Opposition to birth control makes it impossible to solve the population problem and therefore postpones indefinitely all chance of world peace.

Bertrand Russell

Until age thirty-eight, Russell was mostly interested in mathematics, preoccupied with writing *Principia Mathematica* in cahoots

213

with Alfred North Whitehead.

The major religions cause irremediable harm not only by blackballing birth control but also by encouraging and fomenting the religious overtones of almost every war. Religion, in league with racism and nationalism, may indefinitely postpone the possibility of world peace, illustrating the apparent and irremediable evil of the three primal forces that govern us. This triumvirate constitutes society, enforcing its dogma through custom and societal approbation. Religious opposition to birth control may cripple the chances for world peace to an unknowable degree but it certainly plunges many into the misery of poverty, preventing control of their lives and retarding happiness. Tom says I'm overly brutal.

> To bring into the world an unwanted human being is as antisocial an act as murder.

> Gore Vidal

> Vidal's first real writing success came in 1955 with a television screenplay, *Visit to a Small Planet*.

The only act more antisocial than murder is the mass murder of war. To bring an unwanted human being into the world may be less antisocial than either, barely. The religious embargo against birth control and the male's inability to control testosterone are the two main reasons why unwanted human beings are conceived. Religion seems directly and indirectly responsible for most wars and the bringing of unwanted children into the world; shame on religion. Tom says that's the fault of organized religion, not religion. I'm unclear on the distinction.

> The poor man is never free; he serves in every country.

> Voltaire

> Voltaire was relatively poor for three years starting in 1726 when he had a spat with Chevalier de Rohan that exiled him to England

until 1729.

The poor must focus their energies on survival, which may corrode personal responsibility. Many poor are born when religion deems birth control as sin. The rich and middle classes ignore religious restrictions on birth control while the poor and uneducated reap the storm. Freedom belongs to those who ignore religious dogma and practice birth control. Tom says mostly true.

> Poverty is the mother of crime.
>
> Magnus Aurelius Cassiodorus
>
> Cassiodorus completed an encyclopedia of pagan learning and Roman history, which helped to preserve Roman culture and postpone impending barbarism. (Marcus Aurelius said "Poverty is the mother of crime" 350 years before Cassiodorus said the exact same thing.)

Few starve in the first world while many starve or suffer debilitating malnutrition in such countries as Pakistan, India, and Bangladesh. The poor and hungry must concern themselves more with survival than refraining from property crimes, which should be deemed less sinful or unethical when committed for purpose of subsistence. The religious concept of sin often has little connection with ethics but instead serves to immortalize religious dogma. It may be sinful to have other gods before the god of a particular religion, but it's hardly unethical. Ethics at a minimum consists of refusing to harm others; beyond this minimum, ethics is altruism. Crime should be defined by unethical behavior, which may be any action causing harm to the property or person of another. If we aren't free to harm ourselves and our own property then we're not free to be adults. Tom says I've finally sold him on this view of ethics.

> A hungry people does not listen to reason.

Lucius Annaeus Seneca

This leading intellectual of first-
century Rome ended up as Nero's
right-hand man, either condoning
or helping engineer the murder of
Nero's mother, Agrippina.

The noise of a hungry man's stomach may overpower reason
and civility. But survival of the fittest works. The poor who move
up the social and economic ladder through talent and hard work
survive to provide the next generation's middle and upper classes,
at least in the first world. However, government and religion are
reluctant to allow equal opportunity for advancement of the fittest.
Without the religious taboo against birth control a higher percentage
of the poor would improve their economic lot by limiting their
number of children. The poor, unburdened by restrictions on birth
control, could hold the key to the economic future of the species.
Tom says that's obtusely optimistic.

A generous and noble spirit
cannot be expected to dwell in the
breasts of men who are struggling
for their daily bread.

Dionysius of Halicarnassus

Dionysius' history of Rome in
twenty volumes (ten of which
survive) is the most valuable
source for the period between
Rom's founding and the First
Punic War, an attempt to justify
the Romans to the Greeks.

Poverty has this defect; it
prompts a man to evil deeds.

Euripides

This youngest of the three great
Greek tragedians wrote ninety-two

plays—only nineteen of which survive—taking heroic figures of ancient legends and transforming them into ordinary people of his time.

A generous and noble spirit resides in the majority of those struggling for their daily bread. However, a struggle for daily bread should be distinguished from struggles where no bread can be earned. When local economics mires a majority below the subsistence level no matter their effort, the fight is impossible. Violence sometimes springs from the impossibility of improving one's lot or securing sufficient food. If daily bread can easily be earned by most of the population there's no excuse for not earning it. No able-bodied person is entitled to a free ride. Tom quite agrees.

Hunger persuades to evil.

Virgil

Virgil's first major work was a collection of ten pastoral poems envisioning local tranquility and world peace resulting from the benevolent rule of Augustus.

Hunger persuades us to eat though the food may belong to another. Society and government should be structured to allow equal opportunity for everyone, which might result in provision for most everyone, annihilating much poverty if we deep-sixed the religious opposition to birth control. Hunger is an inherent evil presenting a dilemma to the hungry, whether to continue hungry or enjoy food or property taken from another (or getting a job, says Tom). Taking food or property from another is inexcusable for the voluntary slacker (a small portion of the poor) but less morally reprehensible for those who are involuntarily hungry. Tom says hunger is exaggerated.

World peace is difficult until the three main world religions, Hinduism, Christianity, and Islam, promote birth control, which could drop the abortion rate near zero. Religion preaches unlimited population growth and, together with ethnic pride and patriotism, divides the world into camps of "us" versus "them." We should focus on the single identity of the species. Evil results from the violence caused by one camp seeking superiority over another camp, whether identified by race, nationality, or religion, typified by ethnic cleansing, religious war, and regular war. The primary goal of the species should be the abolition of harm to others.

> All men then would be necessarily equal, if they were without needs. It is the poverty connected with our species which subordinates one man to another. It is not the inequality which is the real misfortune, it is the dependence.
>
> Voltaire

> Voltaire believed his physical father was a little-known poet named Roquebrune or Rochebrune, who Voltaire regarded as far more intelligent than his legal father.

Dependence on another person means being under their control. Control, no matter its benevolence, is impertinent except over children. Adults should never be controlled, whether by religion, government, or society, unless necessary to prevent (or obtain restitution for) harm caused to another. Tom says maybe, though dependence on religion seems entirely benevolent to him.

> Poverty is the mother of crime.
>
> Marcus Aurelius Antonius

> This philosopher-emperor wrote his great stoic work, *Meditations*, in snatches between battles on the Roman frontier, based on conversations with Epictetus, a former slave.

Poverty never justifies harm to another, whether the poverty is voluntary or involuntary. The involuntary poor should be provided for by society, whether family, religion, or government. To jump-start self-sufficiency, the involuntary poor should be provided with a vocation. Poverty in Western democracies has been profitable for all but the poor, mostly aiding government employees who administer poverty programs and the few voluntary poor who would rather receive government benefits than work. Uneducated single women with children constitute the largest class of the involuntary poor, no matter the government or economic system. These mothers are seldom perpetuators of crime but are the mothers of crime because their children, who may live in misery and hunger, are excluded from the fruits of society, relegated to its dregs. Poor mothers can't support their children because the education of women is denigrated by most religions and societies. Women are instead encouraged to bear children and avoid birth control for the greater glory of religion. These are called Handmaidens or Stepford Wives. The result is poverty for almost half of the earth's population, single mothers and their children. Tom says I surely exaggerate.

> The praise of poverty need once to be boldly sung. We have grown literally afraid to be poor. We despise anyone who elects to be poor in order to simplify and save his inner life. . . . We have lost the power even of imagining what the ancient idealization of poverty could have meant: the liberation from material attachments, the unbribed soul, the manlier indifference, the paying our way by what we are or do and not by what we have, the right to fling away our life at any moment irresponsibly, the more athletic trim, in short, the moral fighting shape.
>
> William James

James was a contrarian, a manic-depressive whose cousin's death

in 1870 shocked him into
recognizing the nothingness of his
egotistical fury.

The choice of a subsistence existence by those who could be
relatively rich, such as members of the middle class who drop out
of the rat race to pursue other goals, is no deprivation at all
compared to those forced into involuntary poverty, and has
probably never exceeded a tiny percentage of the population. A
substantial portion of the world is fiercely glued to the religious bar
against birth control, stuck in certain poverty without enough to eat,
inadequate shelter, and little, if any, education, deprivations
suffered by few in the thirty or so affluent countries out of our
almost two hundred. Voluntary poverty, independent from society,
government and religion, requires separation from material
attachments, and may constitute an unbridled soul in moral fighting
shape though I don't know what that means. For some, complete
independence is happiness. Poverty often grinds the mind to
inactive placidity or opportunistic criminality. The portions of
religion and government that oppose the eradication of poverty, by
opposing birth control, should themselves be eradicated. Voluntary
poverty to achieve independence is unrelated to the poverty
described by philosophers other than William James.

There is no virtue that
poverty destroyeth not.

John Florio

Florio's father was a Protestant
refugee from Tuscany; Florio
wrote the definitive Italian-
English dictionary.

Excluding voluntary and independent poverty, involuntary
poverty destroys the human spirit with hopelessness, misery, and
death for those who must drink contaminated water resulting in
diarrhea, dehydration, malaria, and neonatal diseases, the world's
leading causes of death for children under five years old. Voluntary
poverty, excluding that chosen for independence with an otherwise
adequate means of financial support, may erode the virtues of self-
reliance and responsibility which are difficult to sustain in the face
of insufficient food, shelter, or potable water. Involuntary poverty

erodes other virtues, but the vast majority of the poor wouldn't harm another person, though unending poverty may warp the character, producing deviant children in a small percentage of offspring, resulting in the destruction of virtue or a tendency toward criminality. Tom says that's no excuse, and I agree.

> Starvation, and not sin, is
> the parent of modern crime.

> Oscar Wilde

Wilde was caught in an affair with Lord Alfred Douglas by Douglas's father, the Marquess of Queensbury, whom Wilde sued for libel. He lost not only the lawsuit but also his health, his reputation, and his fortune.

Prisons are stuffed with the poor. Few convicts come from the rich or middle classes, no matter the dominant religion. Assuming poverty is related to unprotected sex, resistance to birth control resides mainly with organized religion, the sex shame of which has become part of the social fabric. Religion opposes the teaching of birth control to the young, preventing sex education from being taught in schools controlled by the social and religious power structure, which in turn breeds crime. Tom says that's a glib over-simplification.

> Day by day we lower
>   sink, and lower,
> Till the God-like soul
>   within
> Falls   crushed
>   beneath   the
>   fearful   demon
>   power
> Of poverty and sin.

> Lady Jane Francesca Wilde

Oscar's mother was fluent in French, German, Italian, and

221

ancient Greek and had an active
imagination, fantasizing a family
tie to Dante, among others.

Poverty has many defects including misery, pain, cold,
hunger, premature death, exploitation, and humbling of the spirit.
Poverty seldom results in evil deeds except for a small minority.
Most poor endure silently. Poverty might almost be eradicated if
birth control were championed by society. The impoverished should
live so long. Tom says some truth resides here.

Birth   control,   family
planning and population limitation
are most important in any effort to
bring real peace into the world.

Margaret Sanger

The   founder   of   the   Planned
Parenthood Federation originated
the term *birth control* and, upon
opening the first U.S. birth control
clinic, in Brooklyn in 1916, was
arrested as a "public nuisance,"
serving   thirty   days   in   the
hoosegow.

The number of poor people can't be regulated by government
as if they're inferior aliens. Instead, society and religion should
embrace birth control so the poor aren't led to believe that a
diminutive family is a sinful family. A smaller family enables a
higher per capita standard of living, which helps the poor escape
poverty by their own efforts. If everyone had equal economic
opportunity, then everyone, except for those mentally or physically
unable, would be able to obtain a subsistence income. Economic
elevation of the poor can't begin until society believes in birth
control and careful family planning, which can occur only when
religiously inspired sex shame is eradicated and the use of birth
control is the norm when another child cannot be financially
supported. Only we can prevent poverty by avoiding parenthood
when we can't support our children. Perhaps government could help
by appropriate sloganeering: "Want a Porsche. Use a condom."

> Anticipate charity by preventing poverty.
>
> Maimonides
>
> This greatest of medieval Jewish philosophers escaped execution at the hands of Egyptian Muslims by proving he'd never been a Muslim; he was therefore allowed to practice Judaism without persecution.

Poverty can only be prevented by us. Many can't prevent their own poverty without being allowed to control family size and seize the opportunity to earn a living. Religion, racism, and nationalism hamper the eradication of poverty. Perhaps all poverty can't be finally expunged, but we might be able to get rid of most by identifying the causes of poverty and removing them. The primary cause of poverty may be the religious barricade against birth control, contributed to by the divisiveness emanating from religion, racism, and government allegiances cementing "us"—our religion (the only true and infallible religion); our country (right or wrong); and our race, tribe, or ethnicity—against "them." To prevent most poverty these boundaries should be removed.

> Deeds of violence in our society are performed largely by those trying to establish their self-esteem, to defend their self-image, and to demonstrate that they, too, are significant. . . . Violence arises not out of superfluity of power but out of powerlessness.
>
> Rollo May
>
> May studied under Adler in Vienna and under Tillich in New York City, finally giving up the ministry and becoming one of the most influential psychologists in the U.S.

Violence is inexcusable except in self-defense. Acts of violence may arise from powerlessness, lack of self-esteem, and in defense of self-image, but they're eternally inexcusable. The urge to prove our individual significance subdivides the species into religions, ethnic groups, and mother countries. Still, our significance resides in the individual, not in our groups. Recognizing the individual and the species as the two primary entities would remove powerlessness from the individual, no matter the artificial group into which we're born, whether Catholic, Jewish, Muslim, Chinese, Indian, Mexican, white, black, yellow, or any other potential adversarial group in our near endless groups of contending religions, races, and countries. The elimination of group categories might unite us into a collective realization of our individuality and oneness. Tom says that sounds pretty high fallutin' but what does it really mean and why are families almost an afterthought? Because emphasis on the family obscures the species.

> I must say to myself that I
> ruined myself, and that nobody
> great or small can be ruined except
> by his own hand.

> Oscar Wilde

> In the final analysis Wilde was a
> realist.

We're culpable for injury to ourselves. Those suffering harm from another are responsible to the extent that they placed themselves in circumstances risking harm. This doesn't excuse violent or harmful actions by others, who are likewise responsible for their actions and should be prepared to suffer the penalty for harming others. No one can be ruined except by his or her own complicity. Tom says I exaggerate.

> Becky Sharpe's acute
> remark that it is not difficult to be
> virtuous on 10,000 Pounds a year
> has its application to nations and it
> is futile to expect a hungry and
> squalid population to be anything
> but violent and gross.

Thomas Henry Huxley

> Huxley wrote one hundred essays,
> two hundred scientific papers, and
> twenty books, enjoying three
> famous grandsons.

Nations are unrelated to virtue; only individuals can be virtuous. Nations, other groups, and individuals act in their own best interest as they see it, actions only coincidentally virtuous. Those with an income equivalent to last century's ten thousand pounds a year have no need to physically harm others except in defense of their loot. It's preposterous to expect a small percentage of a hungry and squalid population to be other than violent. When the choice is survival or violence, self-defense wins every time. Few first worlders have to make a choice between eating or violence though the conflict is common in the third world. It's easy to be virtuous when unearned money avoids effort and conflict with others. Grossness is no business of government or ethics so long as it harms no one else. Tom says yakkety yak.

> It is a truth which admits not
> a doubt, that the comforts and
> well-being of the poor cannot be
> permanently secured without
> some regard on their part, or some
> effort on the part of the legislature,
> to regulate the increase of their
> numbers, and to render less
> frequent among them early and
> improvident marriages.

> David Ricardo

> Ricardo was originally a Dutch
> Jew, but at age twenty-one, he
> broke with his rich father over
> religion, becoming a Unitarian,
> marrying a Quaker, and
> establishing the first unified
> system of economics.

Character is always more important than economic class. The

rich and middle classes display the same character as the poor, though character often means conforming to the societal, religious, and political status quos dominated by the middle and upper classes. Religion renders unto caesars, shahs, and ayatollahs, it mattering not who holds power so long as it's administered as an instrument of the majority religion. Tom says there might be a grain of truth in there somewhere.

> We come inevitably to the fundamental question. What are people for? What is living for? If the answer is a life of dignity, decency and opportunity, then every increase in population means a decrease in all three. The crowd is a threat to every single being.

> Marya Mannes

> Mannes' parents, grandfather, and uncles were noted musicians. Besides writing biting satire, she was an editor of *Vogue*.

Dignity, decency, and opportunity require an above-subsistence income. Poverty is caused by a growing and unproductive population, which inevitably results from taboos against birth control. The religious prohibition against birth control is a threat to everyone. Tom tends to agree but trusts we won't tell the pope, who might yank Tom's brotherhood.

> It is cruel crime thoughtlessly to bring more children into existence than can be properly taken care of.

> Rabindranath Tagore

> Tagore was a gifted poet, short story writer, novelist, composer, playwright, essayist, and painter who melded Western and Indian

thought.

Most people in the middle of sex aren't deliberating about children. Children are thoughtlessly brought into existence because society and religion believe birth control is a sin, preaching sex shame except to have children for the greater glory of whichever god. We mysteriously revere religions that impose misery on the species by their prohibitions against birth control, an utterly cruel crime. We literally worship our religions, governments, and ethnic groups. Tom says maybe we shouldn't but there's no appropriate substitutes. I suggest the species.

> Yes, we will do anything
> for the poor man, anything but get
> off his back.
>
> Leo Tolstoy

> In 1862 Tolstoy set up a school for
> peasant children, but because of
> his ill health the school lasted a
> single year.

Centuries of indiscriminate do-goodism have resulted in the dependency of the poor on government and religion. We'd do better to get off the backs of the poor, at a minimum providing an education, vocational or otherwise, so that everyone who wishes can make a decent living. Tom agrees completely.

> The implications of
> evolutionary humanism are clear.
> If the full development of human
> possibilities are the overriding
> aims of our evolution, then any
> overpopulation which brings
> malnutrition and misery, or which
> erodes the world's material
> resources or its resources of
> beauty or intellectual satisfaction
> are evil.
>
> Julian Huxley

This grandson of T.H. Huxley worked several years at the Rice Institute in Houston, Texas; he returned to London as secretary of the Zoological Society, transformed Regent's Park Zoo, and was knighted in 1958.

Organized religion is uninterested in the full development of the species, instead prohibiting birth control, which results in overpopulation, malnutrition, misery, and the erosion of the world's material, intellectual, and aesthetic resources. Religion promises immortality in exchange for unprotected sex and divides the species into armed camps, which is despicably evil. The ethics and spirituality claimed by religion do little to salvage its integrity. Religious ethics are societal ethics that exist independent of religion. Spirituality is difficult to distinguish from mumbo jumbo and incapable of definition other than anti-materialism, to which I subscribe unreservedly. Perhaps spiritualism is simply being kind to others, which religion isn't to religious others. Tom says religion is the supreme good because it erases our sins and guarantees immortality.

There is no exception to the rule that every organic being naturally increases at so high a rate, that, if not destroyed, the earth would soon be covered by the progeny of a single pair. Even slow-breeding man has doubled in 25 years, and at this rate, in less than a thousand years, there would literally be no standing room for his progeny.

Charles Darwin

Darwin entered Cambridge University in 1827 to prepare for the clergy but disliked the curriculum because he thought the Bible was literally true; the university disagreed.

Religion deserves most of the credit for overpopulation. The bulk of the species is prohibited from limiting family size or bearing only those children it can afford to clothe, feed, and educate. Instead, religion teaches us to overpopulate the earth. However, even were the religious and societal prohibitions against birth control overcome, many might continue to bear children they can't support because, in many societies, children are the equivalent of immortality, virility, and prestige. Though our intelligence is blind in sundry areas, such as bearing children we can't afford to support, the better educated generally limit child bearing. Good idea, says Tom.

>Suffering does not ennoble,
it degrades.
>
>W. Somerset Maugham

Maugham's modest success with his first novel, about an obstetrician not unlike himself, allowed him to quit medicine and write full time.

If suffering ennobled, then our highest ideal would be masochism. The forbiddance of birth control degrades us by imposing the sufferings of poverty on an uneducated majority. Tom says this part of religion should be fixed but can't hazard a guess when this might occur.

Religious Intolerance Foments War

> Of all religions, Christianity is without doubt the one that should inspire tolerance most, although, up to now, the Christians have been the most intolerant of men.
>
> Voltaire

> Voltaire's lampoons of the Regency and religious opinion offended many (if not most) of his countrymen.

Christianity has been the dominant religion, but Muslims have surged, with the two soon to be neck and neck and Islam (which allows up to four wives and unlimited children) projected to take the lead by 2030. Christianity was the most intolerant because it was the most fundamentalist, until recently, shamed into moderation by the Crusades and Inquisitions, far from limited to Roman Catholics. Though Christian fundamentalism prospers in the United States, it's been eclipsed by Muslim fundamentalism. The foremost filmmaker in the Arab world, Youssef Chahine, produced *All Mouhager (The Immigrant)* in 1994 and it played for weeks to sold-out audiences in Cairo. A character bearing a distant resemblance to the biblical Joseph, son of the prophet Jacob, suggested reconciliation between differing religions. Fundamentalists labeled it heresy and filed suit to stop its exhibition. Fundamentalism is a synonym for intolerance; religion is often a near synonym, similar to nationalism and racism. Tom is against religious intolerance, though he knows there's only one true religion out of the world's thousands.

> The sectaries of a religion, which preaches, in appearance, nothing but charity, concord, and

peace, have proved themselves more ferocious than cannibals or savages, whenever their divines excited them to destroy their brethren. There is no crime which men have not committed under the idea of pleasing the Divinity or appeasing his wrath.

Paul-Henri Thiry, Baron d'Holbach

D'Holbach's writing wasn't always logical or consistent; he derived many opinions from those he knew, such as Voltaire, who disliked D'Holbach.

All wars are either religious wars or supported on both sides by the majority religions of the country or countries involved. Always and without fail countries go to war with religious ceremony and encouragement. Religious charity, concord, and peace often translate to cannibalism, savagery, and murder of our brethren. No crime seems unjustified when committed under the banner of religion, illustrated by every war everywhere. The United States has been at war an average of once a year since its founding. Few countries can match this record, though Russia, in second place, has been at war an average of seventy-five years in each century. The European, Asian, Arab, African, and other countries have similar records, though this changed in the late twentieth-century, with most wars becoming "civil." We're a warlike species, spurred by the universal belief that our particular religion, country, and race is superior to every other. We aim to please our respective gods by slaying our neighbors and brethren. Tom says he'd like to deny this but can't.

Religions, particularly the Christian, have attempted the destruction of religious others, including sects within Christianity. According to Adolph Hitler, he killed six million Jews for the glory of the Christian god. The Christian Crusaders slaughtered Jews as they marched to liberate the Holy Land, also holy to Muslims and Jews. The Middle East, the Balkans, Russia, Asia, and Africa are crammed with armed camps divided by religion, race, and ancient hatreds based on religion and race. The daily Sarajevo newspaper

231

L'illjan said that "Differences between Muslims and non-Muslims [Christians] are so glaring that we must advise the coming generations not to marry people who don't think as they do. In this way, we will build a society free of trauma." The leader of the Islamic community in Sarajevo responded, "For us, the rapes [of Muslim women by Serbian militiamen] are horrible and incomprehensible. But they are less painful and easier to accept than all these mixed marriages [with Christians] and all these children born of mixed marriages."

> I decline Christianity because it is Jewish, because it is international, and because in cowardly fashion, it preaches peace on Earth.
>
> Eric von Ludendorff

> During the last years of WWI Ludendorff ran Germany in partnership with Hindenburg and supported Hitler in his rise to power in the 1920s but was ignored when he warned against the tyranny of Hitler in the 1930s.

General Ludendorff should have embraced Christianity for encouraging war by its first commandment that no other gods be allowed in the same room with its god, promoting armed camps between "us" and "them." Christianity is a history of anti-Semitism and was vehemently anti-Jewish until the Holocaust. Peace on earth is the opposite of cowardliness, taking considerably more gumption than the knee-jerk reaction of trying to destroy those we consider different from ourselves. Tom agrees completely. Boring old Tom.

> There is no wild beast so ferocious as Christians who differ concerning their faith.
>
> William Edward Hartpole Lecky

> Lecky wrote histories of

Rationalism (1865), of European
morals (two volumes, 1869), and
of England (twelve volumes by
1892).

Lecky's position has been illustrated all over the world,
beginning with the various Christian Inquisitions about 1000 C.E.
(after 600 years of dark ages perpetuated by Christian prohibitions
against medicine, sanitation, and knowledge and a Bible possessed
only by priests), not officially ending until 1918, though the bulk of
Christian human sacrifice occurred several hundred years earlier.
The Jews were expelled from many European countries by
Christians, mostly from Spain and its colonies, but generally
throughout Europe. The Catholics killed Protestants and vice versa,
and everyone killed Jews. The battle lines were drawn between
Christians and Muslims, enduring in Africa and the Middle East.
Muslims, Hindus, and Sikhs battle in India, Pakistan, and
Bangladesh. Religion dominates the war biz, with Christians the
first big guns. Tom says mea culpa.

> Christians   have
> burned each other
> quite persuaded
> That all the Apostles
> would have done
> as they did.

> Lord Byron

> Byron was the Elvis of his time but
> far outdid Elvis in debauchery,
> with both men and women,
> including his half-sister. By age
> twenty-one he suffered raging
> bouts of syphilis and gonorrhea.

If the Apostles had armies, they might have forcibly
converted the populace. Founders of religions and countries,
notwithstanding mellowing over time, are seldom saints. The
French know that Napoleon was a saint and perhaps a god; every
country and religion similarly glorifies its antecedents, ignoring the
blood-and-guts viciousness of reality, from Alexander and Genghis
Khan to today. Tom says Christ wasn't so bad. But Christ has the

tiniest connection to the practice of Christianity.

> Gospel: Signifies good news. The good news that the gospel of the Christians came to announce to them is that their God is a God of wrath, that he has predestined the far greater number of them to hell-fire, that their happiness depends on their pious imbecility, their holy credulity, their sacred ravings, on the evil they do to one another through hatred of one for another . . . and on their antipathy for and persecution of all who do not agree with them or resemble them.
>
> Voltaire

> While exiled to England from 1726 to 1729, Voltaire met Alexander Pope and Jonathan Swift and first read John Locke and Isaac Newton.

Christians try to balance a gospel of wrath and hellfire with a god of love who incidentally hates other religions to death. See Commandment No. 1. Those killing the greatest number of enemy others are entitled to front-row seats around the throne of their god, no matter the god. Most religion renounces a god of hellfire, assuring the masses that the bulk are saved, even atheists, continuing pious imbecility, holy credulity, and sacred ravings. The evils of religion, pitting the species against itself and blocking birth control unto poverty, will likely last forever. Tom hopes religion lasts forever though he agrees it has some small room for improvement.

> The mob that would die for a belief seldom hesitates to inflict death upon any opposing heretical group.

Ellen Glasgow

Glasgow was a Southern belle and
intensely serious novelist who
won a Pulitzer Prize for literature
in 1942.

Heresy is a suggestion that disagrees in any part with the
dogma of our thousands of religions. Every religion is heretical to
all others. Christians burned those at the stake who failed to believe
the politically correct version of conflicting Biblical texts or
believed in another religion or no religion at all. Religion seems to
sponsor the cruelest ethical systems imaginable. Whether religion
can stop the slaughter of the species by elevating a message of love
above its First Commandment is problematical. For one religion to
survive and prosper and win the battle for numbers, other religions
must wither and die. Survival of the fittest includes religious battles
to the death. The losers are ourselves, individuals crushed in the
cogs of belief. Tom says God is God, no matter whose, though I'm
guessing he'll give Allah a miss.

Bear witness, O
Thou wrong and
merciful One,
That earth's most
hateful crimes
have in Thy name
been done.

John Greenleaf Whittier

Whittier was portrayed by various
biographers as a "Quaker
militant," a "bard of freedom," and
a "friend of man." Many of his
poems became church hymns.

Crediting a particular god with a hateful crime tarnishes its
followers and the idea of gods. We can justify anything, no matter
its morality or logic. The idea of a god ordering harm to the believer
in another religion is barbarous. Tom quite agrees.

Religion, oh, how it

235

comeddles with policy! The first
bloodshed in the world happened
about religion.

John Webster

Webster's life roughly paralleled
Shakespeare's; Webster wrote
tragedies similar to Macbeth, and
was an actor who became a
playwright.

Bloodshed swirls around religion. The larger the religion, the
more bloodthirsty its history. Christians rank first in the bloodshed
sweepstakes, Muslims second, Hindus third. Everyone used to kill
the Jews, who are now beating up on the Palestinians, and vice
versa. Tom says thou shalt not kill. Yes, unless some god or
government tells you to.

It is forbidden to decry
other sects; the true believer gives
honor to whatever in them is
worthy of honor.

Asoka

Asoka single-handedly spread
Buddhism throughout India and
was the most benevolent of
emperors.

Religion preaches love while delivering hatred by exhorting
the extermination or conversion of those believing differently. This
result is inevitable in any group, whether religious, racial, or
political, because groups necessarily pit themselves against other
similar groups to prove their own superiority. Insisting that my god
can whip your god is juvenile.

Once the apostle Paul had
laid down universal love between
all men as the foundation of his
Christian community, the
inevitable consequence in

236

Christianity was the utmost intolerance towards all who remained outside of it.

Sigmund Freud

Freud suffered from intolerance most of his life; when he entered the University of Vienna at age seventeen, he was expected to feel inferior because he was Jewish.

A possible explanation of this behavior was given by Sultan Shanin, a Muslim, in *Hindustan Times* (May 29, 1995), which could possibly be biased: "Muslims suffer from an acute inferiority complex, which causes them to go to great lengths to prove their superiority over others. Thus, the less a Muslim believes in his religion, the more he feels compelled to demonstrate to the world his unshakable faith." We couldn't commit cruel prosecutions and intolerance for less reason. Tom says we could and have, conceding the main point.

We have just enough religion to make us hate, but not enough to make us love one another.

Jonathan Swift

Gulliver's Travels was the only one of Swift's many works for which he received payment; he began it in 1721 and published it to instant acclaim in 1725.

Intolerance isn't the inevitable product of a doctrine preaching universal love, though sarcasm can be illustrative. Christianity learned early, upon becoming the official religion of the Roman empire, that religion dominates more through power than love. Intolerance naturally follows from the religious requirement of converting those who believe in other religions. Because no religion can tolerate another religion thumbing its nose at the only true god, the religious trademark becomes intolerance resulting in massacre, war, and miscellaneous bloodshed. Those outside our religion, race, or country are "them," foreigners unworthy of basic human courtesy. The best way to eradicate racism is to remove the idea of sub-groups of the species, personified by the intolerant aspects of religion. Tom says chopping out two of the three would suffice, but doesn't know how that could be done.

> Cruel persecutions and intolerance are not accidents, but grow out of the very essence of religion, namely, its absolute claims.

> Morris Raphael Cohen

> Born in Minsk, Russia, Cohen emigrated to the U.S. with his parents at age twelve and became a friend of Einstein.

The near universal claims of religious infallibility render differing beliefs of other religions heretical, or at least bogus. Religions often consider bogus others better erased lest they contaminate the singular true beliefs based on revealed and infallible truth.   Trading life for bare belief places the ultimate premium on conjecture, notably for those believing in the immortality pioneered before the Dark Ages and passed to us through *modern* religion. Charting life based on probabilities is rational; risking life for the bare possibility of immortality, experienced by no one, is the height of folly and absurdity, except to hedge bets. Those who'd die for bare belief would butcher for bare belief. Tom wouldn't kill unless in self-defense and says he'd probably bungle that.

Guns or Butter?

> Every gun that is made, every warship launched, every rocket fired, signifies in the final sense a theft from those who hunger and are not fed, those who

are cold and are not clothed. The world in arms is not spending money alone. It is spending the sweat of its scientists, the houses of its children.

Dwight D. Eisenhower

Eisenhower failed to distinguish himself at West Point, but out of 164 graduates his class of 1915 produced a remarkable 59 generals.

The us-versus-them mentality of religion, racism, and nationalism are the primary causes of worldwide conflicts unto war. War not only means the slaughter of noncombatants and naive combatants but a massive diversion of resources from food and housing production to food and housing destruction. Every cent in every arms budget is money that could otherwise be used for the benefit of the species instead of its destruction. However, the diversion of government budgets from arms to social programs is at best a temporary respite for the hungry who aren't fed or the cold who aren't clothed, and who mostly need education and jobs. Eisenhower was likely correct, though indirectly, that every gun, tank, warship, and bomber takes food from the mouth of the hungry and strips them naked.

Many would protest that national defense is the first business of government, but it isn't. Costa Rica has no military yet no other country would embarrass itself by invading Costa Rica. If no country had a military there'd be an identical balance of power the same as if every country had a nuclear arsenal. The removal of the reasons we fear and hate each other would be more fruitful than the billions of dollars spent on modern armaments. By removing the reasons we hate each other, trillions of dollars could be saved in the defense of the worlds' arbitrarily drawn borders.

There are three main reasons we fear and hate each other: first is government itself, illustrated by the wars and conflicts created by nationalism and patriotism; second is racism (ethnicity or tribe), and third is religion. These set us apart from others and make us feel superior. Our religion, race, and country are best. Others are inferior. We can't let those from other countries cross our borders, except temporarily on visas, because they'd contaminate the country, race, and religion we know to be superior, or they might compete with us for jobs, women, and wealth, or live off whatever safety net the country provides. An armed world spends its future, retarding progress by killing its young in war, generation after generation, and diverting enormous resources from those who need them most.

> You can't dig coal with bayonets.
>
> John L. Lewis
>
> The American labor leader was the son of Welch mining immigrants, leaving school in the seventh grade to work in the mines.

The choice between guns and butter is a partially valid analogy. Money spent for one can't be spent for the other except to the extent that companies manufacturing arms pay salaries to employees who spend them on butter. Arms are a costly waste of resources when unused, and when used, a horrific waste of human resources. Whether we should allocate resources to buy bayonets or produce energy depends on our level of paranoia and fear of others. Some fears are valid; most aren't but are instead invented by politicians to reward campaign contributors and consolidate power. Us-versus-them isn't a healthy attitude for the species. Tom entirely agrees, but he sure as heck wouldn't cut the defense budget.

War or Education?

> Probably no nation is rich enough to pay for both war and education.
>
> Abraham Flexner
>
> As the first director of the Institute for Advanced Study at Princeton, Flexner hired Einstein, in 1933.

The cost of war readiness outweighs the cost of education in every nation on earth save Costa Rica and a few others. Buying both justifies government growth and increased taxes together with lowered production and efficiency. Tom's not much interested in the obvious.

> Were half the power
>   that   fills   the
>   world with terror,
> Were half the wealth
>   bestowed   on
>   camps and courts,
> Given to redeem the
>   human mind from
>   error,
> There were no need
>   of   arsenals   or
>   forts.
>
> Henry Wadsworth
> Longfellow

Longfellow first tried travel writing, which didn't work, so he turned to poetry, becoming the most popular poet of nineteenth-century America. He also presided over the Harvard modern languages program for eighteen years.

Education, whether through travel that reveals the commonality of the species or through the statics of book learning, nurtures tolerance by lessening the influence of nationalism, patriotism, religion, and other racist divisions of the species into "us" versus "them." The big problem is agreeing on what constitutes error. What I see as error is embraced by others as universal truth. Error consists at a minimum of any doctrine that makes one portion of the species believe that another portion, identified by nationality, religion, or race, is inferior or worthy of snuffing. Tom boringly agrees.

All Wars Are Civil Wars

> All wars are civil wars, because all men are brothers. . . . Each one owes infinitely more to the human race than to the particular country in which he was born.
>
> Francois de Salignac de la Mothe-Fenelon
>
> This Catholic archbishop preached the forcible conversion of Protestants after Louis XIV revoked the Edict of Nantes' toleration of Protestants in 1865, later changing his mind and offending Louis XIV.

All wars are civil wars. Our accidental countries of birth cripple us more than any cause other than religion. No species except ours is caged within invisible lines arbitrarily drawn. Skunks can freely cross the Mexican border but Mexicans can't, the same as Mexico theoretically prohibits Guatemalans from crossing Mexico's southern border while skunks prance saucily across. Every country (excluding those in the European Union) militarizes invisible borders, requiring little colored stickers so foreigners may cross. If visas and passports were no longer necessary, we might come to understand that we're all siblings, owing more to the species than accidents of geography. The only restriction on travel should be based on character, not one's accidental country of birth, to which nothing is owed. Borders are racist lines based on the bizarre idea that those outside our invisible borders are inherently inferior and can't cross. A major impediment to a borderless planet is that many countries provide welfare and other benefits, thus encouraging benefit shopping for the voluntarily unemployed, who are a tiny percentage of potential immigrants. Tom is bored with agreement and therefore disagrees.

The Immigration Backlash

Give me your tired,
    your poor,
Your huddled masses
    yearning   to
    breathe free,
The wretched refuse
    of your teeming
    shore,
Send   these,   the
    homeless,
    tempest-tossed,
    to me;
I lift my lamp beside
    the golden door.

Emma Lazarus

Lazarus was raised in a cultured
family of Sephardic (Spanish)
Jews. "The New Colossus"
expressed her faith in the U.S. as a
refuge for all the world's
oppressed, particularly persecuted
Jews.

This famous line on the Statue of Liberty has been amended to exclude those unable to fit within the quotas assigned to their country of origin, skill set, or political beliefs, a clear definition of racism. Those with no resources except their brains and brawn are barred because equality of opportunity is observed nowhere. All countries, races, and religions discriminate against their counterparts. As stated by Paul J. Smith in *The International Herald Tribune* (February 14, 1996), 1995 "was the year in which the backlash against immigrants . . . went global. . . . Any honest discussion of the problem must recognize that nativism and xenophobia are characteristics found in abundance throughout the world."

And it has proceeded apace, threatening to tear the EU asunder and polarizing the politics in many countries, including the U.S. Removing the causes of political and economic repression—

the us-versus-them mentality inherent in all organizations and particularly in the monoliths of race, nationalism, and religion— would similarly remove much of the impetus for migration. Masses would no longer huddle but would breathe free everywhere, free from the racism inherent in nationalism and religion. Every shore is a golden door when it provides unhindered, free, and open opportunity for all. Except for me, everyone shudders, including Tom.

In 1994 California adopted Proposition 187, aimed at illegal aliens from Mexico, where immigration laws are far more stringent than in the United States. Propositions and laws are inapplicable to markets for capital and labor. People go where they wish, notwithstanding barbed wire and Berlin walls. Mounting machine guns on borders will never stop immigration. Nothing will. The idea of limiting immigration is racist.

As stated by Bob Sutcliffe in *Index on Censorship,* a London-based human-rights bimonthly, "Much of the opposition to immigration is based on irrational prejudice that expresses itself in xenophobia, racism, and the erroneous fear that immigration brings unemployment, and increase in crime, and homelessness . . . those with fewer immigrants tend to have more unemployment"—why emigrate where jobs are unavailable?

> ". . . [P]art of the problem is the almost universal failure to regard the freedom to move as a basic human right. If there existed a country in which various ethnic groups lived and in which the richest and the most powerful group divided the country into ethnic areas and forbade the poorer less powerful groups to enter the privileged groups' areas, then there is a good chance that it would be declared a pariah by other nations for its denial of human rights. Such a country did, until very recently, exist: South Africa under apartheid. And it was universally condemned. Yet viewed as a whole, the world is worse in these respects than South

Africa under apartheid. The freedom to migrate would be an essential plank in an anti-apartheid movement for the world."

In an article published in the *Atlantic Monthly,* Matthew Connelly and Paul Kennedy observed that the twenty-first century promises a world with "a relatively small number of rich, sated, demographically stagnant societies and a large number of poverty-stricken, resource-depleted nations whose populations are doubling every twenty-five years or less":

> "It is difficult to believe that Switzerland, with an annual average per capita income of about $35,000, and Mali, with an average per capita income of less the $300, are on the same planet. . . . [V]irtually all the factors of production—capital, assembly, knowledge, management—have become globalized, moving across national boundaries in the form of investments, consulting expertise, new plants, patents, and so on. . . . [O]ne factor of production has been similarly liberated: labor. . . .95 percent of the twofold increase in the world's population expected before the middle of the next century will occur in poor countries. . . . Europe and North America, which contained more than 22 percent of the world's population in 1950, will contain less than 10 percent by 2025."

If free immigration isn't allowed across national borders, it occurs anyway, explosively. Much of the population increase of the poor is attributable to religion. Back in the fray, Tom says nonsense. As far as income inequality, it's undeniably gotten much worse; 26 individuals, by 2018, owned the same amount of assets as half the

245

world's population, or 26 with the wealth of 3.7 billion individuals.

The conservative think tank Cato Institute concluded that the effects of immigration are primarily beneficial or neutral. "Immigrants do not increase the rate of unemployment among native-born Americans," observed A.M. Rosenthal in a 1995 editorial published in the *International Herald Tribune*. "Total per capita government expenditures on immigrants are much lower than those for the native born." Rosenthal further pointed out that all major religions teach that we should "take in the stranger, care for him." and that "one-third of all U.S. Nobel winners are foreign-born and judging by mathematical doctorates, science degrees, patents, prizes, and publications, one-third of American geniuses are foreign-born." Whether altruistic, based on religious "morality," or practical, based on a need for over-achieving geniuses, open immigration makes good sense. Racism doesn't make good sense. Tom says we're becoming a nation of mongrels, and I say we're a species of mongrels within artificial national boundaries.

> To understand all makes
> one tolerant.
>
> Madame de Stael
>
> The Swiss-born French novelist (1766–1817) hosted the leading intellectuals of her time and helped begin the movement to Romanticism.

No one has ever understood all. Only a god could understand everything, and gods probably don't exist, though Tom believes in one (or three). We can understand as much as possible by putting aside religious and political biases, which philosophers have sought to do with mixed success. Their bottom line appears to be that religion is a fraud, subjecting the species to more evil than any other human institution, followed closely by nationalism and racism in the devastation derby. So, what do evil and good consist of? This may be best answered by first examining what ethics isn't.

The Ethics of Christianity

> The Christian ideal has not
> been tried and found wanting. It
> has been found difficult, and left
> untried.

Gilbert Keith Chesterton

The British essayist and novelist
(1874-1936) was known for his
exuberance, rotundity, support for
redistribution of land, literary
criticism, fiction, and converting
from Anglican to Roman
Catholicism.

The Christian ideal suggests we love others as ourselves,
which is eminently laudable though appearing impossible and
observed nowhere. Christianity defeats its own ideal by helping
divide the world into religious camps. We can't love those who
believe their god is better than our god. Our god must win every
contest (as must theirs), which seems to require the stomping of
those believing in a god other than our one true god. The Christian
ideal is internally inconsistent and impossible to implement,
canceled by the First Commandment that other gods, and those
believing in them, must not be tolerated. This is not ethics. Tom
agrees.

> The Christian churches
> would not recognize Christianity
> if they saw it.

Lincoln Steffens

Steffens was a leading figure
among those writers Teddy
Roosevelt called "muckrakers,"
specializing in uncovering
political corruption.

Christianity is a tonic hawked by the Christian churches with little connection to the moral teachings of Jesus Christ, who unbelievably suggested that everyone should be loved instead of being destroyed for believing in other gods, converted, or shunned. If Christianity had followed the teachings of Jesus Christ it would've died in its infancy. The actual Jesus Christ—if there was such a person—was an admirable being worthy of an emulation never achieved by any portion of Christianity except perhaps the Quakers and similar pacifists. Christian leaders support whatever war is decreed by government, advocating wholesale slaughter of the species by the species for whatever ephemeral goal nationalism decrees. Jesus Christ tacitly approved by suggesting that Caesar's coin be rendered unto Caesar. Until enemy soldiers are first tried by Western concepts of due process, justice, and fairness, their deaths are no more than murder. No one should be deprived of life without a trial, especially the 90 percent of innocent noncombatants killed in twenty-first-century wars. Jesus Christ would never have approved such slaughter under any circumstances, notwithstanding his rendering unto Caesar. Christianity approves war even when both sides are "Christian." This isn't ethics, and Tom again agrees, wholeheartedly.

> If Christ should appear on earth he would on all hands be denounced as a mistaken, misguided man, insane and crazed.
>
> Henry David Thoreau
>
> Thoreau was jailed for refusing to pay a poll tax to support the U.S. war against Mexico; Emerson visited and asked why Thoreau was in jail and Thoreau replied by asking why Emerson was not.

The theology of Jesus Christ is unworkable. Far less than 1 percent of us are capable of giving all of our belongings to the poor, mimicking communism, or of loving everyone else. Practical ethics must be workable. Our philosophers have identified basic ethical rules, which may provide a foundation for ethical behavior. Christ was utopian but hardly insane or crazed, except perhaps to the extent that he believed his father was a god. The New Testament traces Christ's lineage through Joseph, which makes little sense if his mother was a virgin and his father was a god. Tom says I border on the heretical.

> The moral idea of Christian love is like a pillar of flaming light extending from earth to heaven, but the supernatural religion of freedom, solace, and joy that should have evolved from it was choked and poisoned. The successors of Christ, from St. Paul down to the censors, obscurantists, and tyrants of today have done their conscientious worst to hide the light from men.
>
> William Pepperell
> Montague

> This future professor of philosophy at Berkeley, Barnard, and Columbia failed to take college seriously until he was suspended from Harvard in his sophomore year.

The moral idea that Christians should love everyone is eclipsed by the command that other gods, and those believing in them, should never be tolerated. Religious ecumenicalism tries to overcome the First Commandment, but with little success. We hide the light of universal love by dividing ourselves into groups we believe superior to groups indistinguishable from our own. This is unethical nonsense. Tom quite agrees though he suspects that Roman Catholics have a leg up in the immortality race.

> I can see how sincere, how passionately proletarian a religious prophet may be, that is the fate which sooner or later befalls him in a competitive society—to be a founder of an organization of fools, conducted

by knaves, for the benefit of
wolves. That fate befell Buddha
and Jesus, it befell Ignatius Loyola
and Francis of Assisi, John Fox,
and John Calvin, and John
Wesley.

Upton Sinclair

Sinclair's exposé of immigrant
working conditions at the Chicago
stockyards aroused the public's
indignation at unsanitary meat
processing, causing Sinclair to
remark that "I aimed at the
public's heart and by accident I hit
it in the stomach."

Religious ethics degenerate into the bureaucracy required to
run any large organization. Ethics and the competitive regimen
needed to run a large bureaucracy are constantly at odds,
particularly Christian ethics that instruct us to love religious
competitors and other heretics. Large organizations are often run by
knaves who supervise fools for the benefit of wolves. Religious
bureaucracies erode religious ethics in favor of pragmatism. No
question, says Tom.

But the churchmen
    fain would kill
    their Church,
As the churches have
    killed   their
    Christ.

Alfred Lord Tennyson

When Tennyson was twenty-two
his closest friend died suddenly.
Seventeen years later, this event
resulted in an epic poem that
influenced Queen Victoria to
appoint Tennyson as poet laureate.

The church is the bread and butter of its leaders. Without the church they'd be left to other employment without the mysticism of a direct pipeline to a god. Only a fool would kill the fountain of his hope and daily bread.

> Many people have looked upon Jesus as a true theist, whose religion has been by degrees corrupted. Indeed, in the books which contain the law which is attributed to him, there is no mention either of worship, or of priests, or of sacrifices, or of sufferings, or of the greater part of the doctrines of actual Christianity, which has become the most prejudicial of all the superstitions of the earth.
>
> Denis Diderot

> Diderot revered Socrates, wearing a ring with an inscribed picture of Socrates, which he used to seal his letters.

The Christian church plunges many into poverty by outlawing birth control. Such success is a counterproductive revolution. However, Jesus's teaching that individuals and races are equally worthy was an early milestone of the species though almost entirely ignored. Unfortunately, most religions derived from Jesus are more bloodthirsty than pacifist, and none venerate the unity of the species. This is not ethics. Tom agrees, though he says religion doesn't plunge people into poverty, deeming the rhythm method adequate. Come on, Tom. You don't really believe that. You're just trying to butter up the pope.

> First, that the blood of so many hundred thousand souls of Protestants and Papists, spilt in the wars of present and former ages for their respective consciences, is not required by Jesus Christ the

Prince of Peace.

Roger Williams

Williams founded Rhode Island as
a haven for religious tolerance, a
unique exception among the
American colonies.

The ethics of religious founders disappears after a few
generations. Roger Williams founded the Baptist Christian sect that
split into American, Southern, and other Baptists unable to agree on
doctrine. My Baptist upbringing didn't exactly take, but I have clear
memories of Baptist ministers denigrating the Catholics, Southern
Baptists (we were American Baptists), and other Protestants.
Muslims and Jews were so far beyond the kin as to be
unmentionable, perhaps because there were none in rural Colorado.
The spirit of armed camps continues unabated within most
organized religion, and this too is not ethics. Tom says that's true
and asks my solution, as if he didn't know.

The essential teachings of
Jesus . . . were   literally
revolutionary, and will always
remain so if they are taken
literally.

Herbert J. Muller

Muller was an eminent historian
who published 67 influential
books and 508 publications in
three languages.

Jesus Christ prescribed an ethical system as the means to a
worthy life and had no apparent intent to found a religion. He
believed in a Jewish god, the same as Christians and Muslims. The
Jewish, Christian, and Muslim gods command that thou shalt not
kill, but invisible ink provides the exception "unless the government
says so," and then religion will provide the trumpets. War burnishes
the greater glory of religion, whether Jewish, Christian, Muslim,
Hindu, or other, with minor exceptions such as Quakers and a few
Buddhists. The Christian New Testament nowhere mentions

worship, priests, sacrifices, sufferings, popes, ministers, birth control, murder of combatants or noncombatants, celibacy, abortion, or education, but it does condemn public prayer and women speaking in church. What would we expect from the ethics of religions concocted before the Dark Ages? Christianity marks other religions for exclusion, religiously following the First Commandment. Religious dogma is a surrealistic horror movie, not to be taken seriously and scarcely to be emulated. The mainstream religious prohibition against birth control sinks millions into poverty. Religion, racism, and nationalism are the big three predators. Racism and nationalism are grounded on fear and the building of empires, exploiting our innately racist us- versus-them mentality. This is not ethics. Tom says true religion, apart from the organized kind, isn't horrible but instead deserves serious consideration and emulation; the bad parts can be fixed; and so I ask when and how, and what exactly is the unorganized kind?

> It is a mistake to say that it is doubtful whether there is a God or not. It is not in the least doubtful, but the most certain thing in the world, nay, the foundation of all other certainty—the only solid absolute objectivity—that there is a moral government of the world.
>
> Johann Gottlieb Fichte
>
> Though obviously a theist, Fichte resigned from the faculty of the University of Jena after being accused of atheism but ended up as the first rector of the new University of Berlin.

Neither the idea of a god nor the question whether a god exists is necessarily connected to morality. Gods, or the ideas of gods, have mired us in the ultimate immorality of war, murder, mayhem, intolerance, and the plunging of billions into poverty. Morality, at a minimum, is a refusal to harm others, which is unrelated to vestments, communions, baptisms, nunneries, absolutions, censorships, or crucifixions. The facade of organized religion has no connection with ethics, the same as its core commandment prohibiting the toleration of those believing in other gods. Tom says morality is rooted in God, without which there'd be no morality, notwithstanding simplistic theorizing.

> I believe in the fundamental Truth of all the great religions of the world. I believe that they are all God-given. . . . I came to the conclusion long ago . . . that all religions were true, and also that all had some error in them.
>
> Mohandas Karamchand Gandhi

> Gandhi took a vow of celibacy with his wife's consent because he felt that service to the world meant he "could not live with both the flesh and the spirit."

Equally believably, all religions are false but contain practical and beneficial ideas. Or are all religions equally true? Christianity teaches love but practices intolerance unto war. Muslims teach tolerance but pursue jihads against others as Sunnis bash Shi'ites, and vice versa, with the Jews open season for all, but now Israel has the bomb. The fundamental truth of all religion is that we should revere the species by loving everyone. Few, if any, put fundamental truth into practice. As a matter of probability, no religion harbors a god. Tom disagrees with me but agrees with Gandhi. Gandhi has the rep.

> Morality is simply the attitude we adopt toward people whom we personally dislike.
>
> Oscar Wilde

> It's unclear whether Wilde died from cerebral meningitis, an ear infection, or syphilis.

Holier-than-thou is the attitude most commonly adopted toward those belonging to a different religion, nationality, or ethnic group. Because they're different, we dislike them or believe they fail to bathe. We're no better or worse than those different from us because of their religion, ethnicity, or nationality. We belong to the same species with the same desires and fears, represented by religions often promising immortality, our greatest desire, and avoidance of our greatest fear, death. These are unrelated to morality. Tom quite agrees.

> Wherever morality is based on theology, wherever right is made dependent on divine authority, the most immoral, unjust, infamous things can be justified and established.
>
> Ludwig Feuerbach

> Feuerbach believed that God was a projection of man and had no independent existence.

Belief in an amorphous god justifies anything and is thus unrelated to morality. Religion requires the conversion, shunning, or elimination of those believing in other religions that only differ on the means of achieving immortality or nirvana. If the other's god were a true god, then our ticket in the immortality sweepstakes might be a loser, which is intolerable. War and poverty are properly laid at the doorstep of religion, no matter which of our thousands of denominations, whether Christian, Muslim, Hindu, or a hundred others. Religion generally prohibits birth control and foments conflicts within and between its sects. Religion is arguably evil and the antithesis of ethics. Tom says no way.

Society and the Individual

> The struggle is always between the individual and his sacred right to express himself . . . and . . . the power structure that seeks conformity, suppression and obedience.
>
> William O. Douglas
>
> This star defender of civil liberties and individualism contracted polio as a child; his doctor prescribed a strict physical regimen which fashioned Douglas into a lifelong outdoorsman.

The power structure sits on our heads, restricting our actions to those allowed by our representatives elected through political action committees or subject to the arbitrary antics of a dictator or oligarchy of the elite, no matter the political party. Religion rules with an equally iron hand, trusting that its teaching of love and charity will obscure support for interminable conflicts and the impoverishment of the populace through bans on birth control. We find free expression only through choices unrestricted by religion and government. Conformity produces robots, quelling our innovative intelligence by forced obedience to the arbitrary laws of government and ancient religions. Neither are necessarily related to ethics. Tom says religion is ethics, but otherwise agrees. Or Tom agrees that government is unrelated to ethics, otherwise disagreeing.

> Whoso would be a man, must be a nonconformist. He who would gather immortal palms must not be hindered by the name of goodness, but must explore if it be goodness. Nothing is at last sacred but the integrity of your own mind. . . . A man is to carry

himself in the presence of all opposition as if everything were titular and ephemeral but he. I am ashamed to think how easily we capitulate to badges and names, to large societies and dead institutions.

Ralph Waldo Emerson

Emerson led the American renaissance, preaching the ethics of self-reliance and the need to express oneself.

After our terrible twos the vast majority naturally conforms through socialization, forced into a mold by the opinion of others. Groups tend to ridicule, overtly or covertly, those different from themselves. Minor differences in mannerism, dress, or decoration may excite ridicule as readily as philosophical, ethnic, or religious divergences. Those differing a whit from the majority may be treated as unacceptable lepers or "others." The majority is often unable to accord basic human courtesy to those different in any way, though they harm no one else. Nonconformists may be facially tolerated though often treated as social outcasts. Only individuals are ethical; society has no capacity to act ethically toward nonconformists or anyone who's different, no matter the breadth of the difference.

We bow to large societies and dead institutions, including Emerson, who asked why Thoreau was in prison for failing to pay a poll tax to support a war against Mexico. We must personally discover the sacred (if such there is) for ourselves, instead of passively accepting ideas of sanctity dictated by religion, government, and kindred dead institutions. Government and religion stifle us, crushing nonconformity to sameness while masquerading as purity. The good resides solely in the individual, not in institutions of religion and government, or in any group, no matter how or why constituted. Religion adds nothing to basic ethics beyond that central to the species and its social fabric. Tom rather disagrees, with Emerson too.

Both [church and state] have the same principle as their

point of departure: that of the natural wickedness of man, which can be vanquished, according to the Church, only by divine grace and the death of the natural man in God; and according to the State, only by law and the immolation of the individual upon the altar of the State. Both strive to transform men, the one into a saint, the other into a citizen. But the natural man must die, for the religions of the Church and of the State unanimously pronounce his sentence.

Mikhail A. Bakunin

Bakunin was the leading nineteenth-century revolutionary; his quarrel with Marx may have further forced Bakunin's anarchism into the antithesis of Marxism.

The power structure consists principally of government and religion, melded into society while eternally seeking our conformity, suppression, and obedience. One basic philosophical question is when the individual or the power structure should be the boss. The sacred right of expression should be guaranteed for individual acts that harm no one else, rigidly limiting the power structure. If government militaries and nonessential services (what is essential in government?) were shrunk to their ideal size and religion confined to preaching that we should harm no one else, society would blossom from mere conformity, suppression, and obedience, spurring individual creativity and more closely realizing the potential of the species.

Except as its clown and jester, society does not encourage individuality, and the State abhors it.

Bernard Berenson

Berenson emigrated to Boston from Lithuania, graduated from Harvard, and became the foremost authority on Renaissance art. He was later a buddy of Ray Bradbury.

Individuality is revered in the arts and technology but is otherwise deplored. The individual threatens ideas of conformity, challenging the norm, causing severe discomfort to the average conforming person and the leaders of government, society, and religion, who overlap. Though some societal norms are extremely valuable, perhaps countable on one hand, blanket enforcement of the norm smothers ingenuity. The state dislikes idiosyncrasy because it threatens millions of laws that apply to all without exception, excluding the rulers and the rich, who can buy their way out of most any scrape and often consider themselves the only true and deserving individualists. Tom quite reluctantly agrees, individualist that he is.

The individual is the true reality of life. A cosmos in himself, he does not exist for the State, nor for that abstraction called 'society,' or the 'nation,' which is only a collection of individuals.

Emma Goldman

Goldman spent a year in prison for inciting a riot in 1893 New York City and two years in prison for obstructing the military draft in 1917.

The idea of "society" is substanceless, existing as a fuzzy cloud. Only individuals exist. No one agrees precisely what societal norms are or should be, even when codified in government law, religious dogma, and custom. A collection of individuals, no matter why or how collected, is conscienceless and without sufficient knowledge of individual circumstances and necessities to make proper decisions for the individual. Governments, religions, and other bureaucracies lay down broad rules to control our behavior, deriving these rules from tradition or decisions by "representatives" and others who have no conception of or concern for those who fail to make large campaign contributions or tithe. Society treats the individual as if our purpose in life is to be governed by the state, religion, and society. Adults exist to govern themselves, not to be governed by others, no matter how benevolent. Tom says he can go along with that, up to the point that the individual impinges on the liberty of another. I fear we agree too much.

Religion and government sentence us to conformity with ancient ideas of right, many of which have deteriorated into wrong, particularly the unswerving placement of individuals into camps of us versus them and the designation of mores deemed wrong before the Dark Ages. A tiny minority of the species is naturally wicked, tending to harm others. The vast majority would refuse to stone a heretic, except when caught up in the fervor of patriotism, racism, or religion. The apparatus of the state and religion force us into a single mold and blind conformity, no matter the inherent goodness of the majority. Religion and government teach us to harm others upon the commandment of government or religion. Individualism literally dies under religion and government, which often encourages us to inflict massive harm on each other. Tom slightly agrees.

> The Christian who wants to live his faith in political action conceived as service cannot, without contradicting himself, adhere to ideological systems that are radically, or in substantial points, opposed to his faith and the concepts of man—neither to the ideology of Marxism, its atheistic materialism, its dialectics of violence and the way it absorbs any transcendental character of man and his personal and collective history; nor to the ideology of liberalism, which tends to exalt individual freedom without any limitation.

260

Pope Paul VI

Paul VI's father was a middle-
class lawyer, journalist, and
politician who, because Paul VI
was frail, home-schooled him.

Violence is utterly intolerable to ethics. Atheism is rational
when defined as the refusal to believe in a god without any evidence
that one exists, faith being difficult, if not impossible, to distinguish
from superstition. Materialism is the fodder of capitalism, its harm
depending on individual susceptibility. Individual freedom should
be exalted without limitation save one, a refusal to harm others.
Tom says no to atheism, but I sometimes think he's tempted.

When will the world learn
that a million men are of no
importance compared with one
Man?

Henry David Thoreau

Upon his graduation from Harvard
at age twenty, Thoreau began
keeping a journal and continued
for the rest of his life.

Only the species and the individual are important. Everything
in between is balderdash, particularly groups of any flavor. Even
veneration of the family obscures the primacy of the species.
Metaphorically, a million men are of no importance compared to
the individual. But a million individuals, acting individually, are on
average a million times more important than a single individual. A
million men acting in concert are a menace and of Lilliputian ethical
or other importance. Tom says he's speechless; family is all. We
never argue irritably though we sometimes snipe.

Liberty of speech inviteth
and provoketh liberty to be used
again, and so bringeth much to a
man's knowledge.

Francis Bacon

261

Bacon grew up as a favorite of
Elizabeth I, who called him her
little Lord keeper until he entered
Cambridge at age twelve.

Civilization advances through freedom of expression by
encouraging criticism of government, religion, and other
bureaucratic institutions. Religion and government may retard
civilization except when government bankrolls science to further
military aims that incidentally benefit civilians. Religion and
government preserve the status quo, which often perpetuates error.
Only individuals independent of government and religion combat
error and challenge staid orthodoxy. Individual liberty to search for
truth by criticism of government and religion should never be
fettered, but liberty of expression will always be shackled, overtly
or covertly, because government and religion detest criticism. Tom
says almost everyone and every organization hates criticism.

But the peculiar evil of
silencing the expression of an
opinion is, that it is robbing the
human race; posterity as well as
the existing generation; those who
dissent from the opinion, still more
than those who hold it. If the
opinion is right, they are deprived
of the opportunity of exchanging
error for truth; if wrong, they lose,
what is always as great a benefit,
the clearer perception and livelier
impression of truth, produced by
its collision with error.

John Stuart Mill

Mills's only instructor was his
father James Mill, author,
historian of British India, and a
friend and disciple of Jeremy
Bentham.

Fair exchange of opinions should be sacrosanct, though we
see how frighteningly fast it deteriorates on social media. Editorial

pages seldom reflect all sides of an issue, which always number more than two and which should be made available to the public, though most of the public couldn't care less. As a result, truth is often more susceptible to suppression than error, but truth will eventually out if we last long enough. Individual freedom hinges on freedom of speech, a precondition for the growth of knowledge. Without free speech knowledge shrinks and individual freedom evaporates. Neither government nor religion are inherently sympathetic to freedoms of speech or action. Tom agrees but says religion is improving. He may have forgotten about the fundamentalists of every persuasion.

> The Framers [of the Constitution] knew that free speech is the friend of change and revolution. But they also knew that it is always the deadliest enemy of tyranny.
>
> Hugo L. Black

> Justice Black mostly dissented until the 1960s, when his philosophy gained a majority on the Supreme Court; he helped strike down school prayer, make attorneys available to criminal defendants, and upheld the *New York Times* publication of the Pentagon Papers.

Absence of dissent foreshadows *Stepford Wives* and any boring or controlled existence. Uniform agreement is dry and lifeless. The juices of life demand dissent and lively debate. Prevailing mores are the conservative status quo. Change is the spice necessary to improve the species. Society, government, and religion are symptoms of grave illness because they consider criticism as heresy or revolution, often resulting in bloodshed, continuing in Venezuela, Nicaragua, Iran, Syria, and other parts of the Middle East, in Asia and Africa. Government means management, oversight, regulation, supervision, command, control, domination, rules, administration, dictation, direction, reign, and possible tyranny. No one deserves governance, management, oversight, regulation, supervision, command, control, domination, rule, administration, dictation or direction, except children and miscreants harming others, though control is the primary role of government, negating individual responsibility by demanding submission and suppressing dissent. Tom is glad he's not an anarchist like some big mouths, as he smiles like the Cheshire cat.

> Those who begin coercive elimination of dissent soon find themselves exterminating dissenters. Compulsory unification of opinion achieves only a unanimity of the graveyard.
>
> Robert Houghwout Jackson
>
> As general counsel for the IRS, Jackson successfully prosecuted Andrew Mellon for tax evasion; while on the Supreme Court, he helped strike down a California law forbidding entry to "emigrants" from Oklahoma.

Dissent hardens when dissenters are hushed. Extermination of dissenters elevates them to martyrdom and hero status. Opinion can't be compulsorily unified because even the individual is unable to control thought and opinion. Threats buy at most a facade of accord. Dissenters can be silenced but dissent can never be, though religion and government never stop trying.

> Fear of serious injury cannot alone justify oppression of free speech and assembly. Men feared witches and burnt women. It is the function of speech to free men from the bondage of irrational fears.
>
> Louis D. Brandeis
>
> Brandeis was confirmed to the Supreme Court by the U.S. Senate

over vigorous opposition of business and anti-Semites, becoming the first Jew to serve on the court.

The only speech justifiably oppressed is falsely shouting "Fire!" in a crowded theater, almost guaranteeing serious injury. The line between fear of serious injury and near certainty of serious injury determines when speech can be suppressed. Disputing the existence of a particular god or the efficacy of a particular government should never justify the suppression of free speech, but good luck to us against the Stalins of the world. Fear alone is groundless; only the immediate threat of physical harm justifies the suppression or punishment of speech. Allowing all speech, with the single exception of that threatening serious and immediate physical injury, should free us from fear, particularly that engendered by religion and government. Tom agrees.

> When men can freely communicate their thoughts and their sufferings, real or imaginary, their passions spend themselves in air, like gunpowder scattered on the surface—but pent up by terrors, they work unseen, burst forth in a moment, and destroy everything in their course. Let reason be opposed to reason and argument to argument, and every good government will be safe.
>
> Thomas Erskine

Erskine defended the most controversial cases of his time including Thomas Paine, whistleblowers, Queen Charlotte for adultery against George IV, booksellers, and the would-be assassin of George III.

The banning of a political party insures its survival, similar to forbidding a child to fulfill his heart's desire. When freedom is

265

granted unconditionally, except to prevent harm to others, little harm results because tensions and aggravations are defused. The most closely reasoned thought remains coarse until tested by the fire of debate. We owe ourselves and others the right to freely communicate our thoughts. Because all governments are administered by the imperfect, no government is safe under the spotlight of unbridled debate, which all government knows only too well. Tom says this isn't complicated stuff.

> Long experience has taught us that it is dangerous in the interest of truth to suppress opinions and ideas; it has further taught us that it is foolish to imagine that we can do so. It is far easier to meet an evil in the open and defeat it in fair combat in people's minds, than to drive it underground and have no hold on it or proper approach to it. Evil flourishes far more in the shadows than in the light of day.

> Jawaharlal Nehru

> Nehru was first imprisoned by the British in 1921 and then eight times thereafter, the longest for three years ending June 1945; his imprisonments totaled over nine years during India's fight for independence.

Truth is established more through debate than imposed by government or divinely revealed religion. Evil and inherent wrong dry up when subjected to full and unbiased debate. The weaknesses of government and religion are buried by omission from our history courses. The excesses of government and religion are discoverable only by independent research, never in school textbooks. Tom says each protects its own.

> Freedom of expression is the well-spring of our

civilization. . . . The history of civilization is in considerable measure the displacement of error which once held sway as official truth by beliefs which in turn have yielded to other truths. Therefore, the liberty of man to search for truth ought not to be fettered, no matter what orthodoxies he may challenge. Liberty of thought soon shrivels without freedom of expression. Nor can truth be pursued in an atmosphere hostile to the endeavor or under dangers which are hazarded only by heroes.

Felix Frankfurter

The U.S. Supreme Court justice was born in Vienna. He advised President Wilson at the 1919 Paris Peace Conference and helped found the ACLU in 1920.

Though we disapprove of an opinion, we should, in fairness, allow its expression, the same as its author should allow a reasoned response. Those denying freedom of speech harm themselves and others. No one should have to defend freedom of speech to the death. Those who believe they live forever may be less tolerant of speech than those who don't. The species should defend to its death the right to express any opinion. Sticks and stones are far more serious than words, though many can't handle words.

The history of intellectual growth and discovery clearly demonstrates the need for unfettered freedom, the right to think the unthinkable, discuss the unmentionable, and challenge the unchallengeable. To curtail free expression strikes twice at intellectual freedom, for whoever

deprives another of the right to
state unpopular views necessarily
deprives others of the right to
listen to those views.

C. Vann Woodward

Woodward was a leading
interpreter of the post-Civil War
history of the American South,
concluding that the South wasn't
segregated until 1890, twenty-five
years after the war's end, receiving
a Pulitzer Prize for history.

Nothing is unthinkable, because no one can control thought. The unmentionable and unchallengeable are labeled by society, government, and religion, not by those seeking truth. Progress requires those who wield unfettered expression to withstand unfettered opinion. Speakers and listeners are essential to complete freedom of expression, our lone opportunity to fine tune truth. Tom shrugs. This really is old hat to most first worlders.

If liberty means anything at
all, it means the right to tell people
what they do not want to hear.

George Orwell

Orwell's experience in the
Spanish Civil War, narrowly
escaping torture at Communist
hands by hiding in a coal bin
infested with giant rats, molded his
work, similar to the real Soviet
poster encouraging completion of
a Five-year Plan in four years that
headlined the formula: $2 + 2 = 5$.

We don't want to hear contrary viewpoints, particularly those related to ethics and religion. While no one should be forced to listen to an unwanted opinion, everyone should be allowed to express and listen to every range of contrary opinion. Religion and ethics are often sculpted to fit the biases of those in power and aped by the public, topics particularly appropriate for unbounded discussion.

> Mere unorthodoxy or dissent from the prevailing mores is not to be condemned. The absence of such voices would be a symptom of grave illness in our society.
>
> Earl Warren

> The Warren Court concluded that "separate educational facilities are inherently unequal" and "legislators represent people, not acres or trees," and decided the *Miranda* decision.

Change and bloodless revolution are essential to human progress. Without change, we vegetate. Even the best government grows mold when innovation is suppressed. Government is eminently inclined to a rut because it defines and protects the status quo. Free speech is an enemy of organized religion because unbounded by concepts of fidelity or heresy. Tom says any government or religion fearing free speech is unworthy of trust or fidelity.

> Whatever crushes individuality is despotism.
>
> John Stuart Mill

> Mill was greatly influenced by his father's close friend, Jeremy Bentham, and particularly Bentham's "Greatest Happiness" principle.

Crushing individuality smashes creativity. Every law expands the scope of government and purports to limit individual action. Customs of a particular racial, ethnic, or social group keep us on the narrow paths trodden by our ancestors, restricted by government and religion to the way things have always been done and will be done as long as government and religion are mindlessly revered. All well-established groups pretend to interpret the long-forgotten intent of their founders while stifling the individual and acting despotically. The state insists on controlling everyone within an arbitrary physical boundary formed by economic, religious, and ethnic interests. Religion and ethnicity insist on similar controls. Government, religion, and race are the ultimate despots, intent on crushing the individual in favor of an amorphous concept of society. Tom says I must feel put upon and suggests benevolent therapy. Tom and I are prone to sarcasm.

> I disapprove of what you say, but I will defend to the death your right to say it.
>
> S.G. Tallentyre (pen name, E. Beatrice Hall)

> Replying to the question whether she or Voltaire was the author of this world-famous quotation, Miss Hall wrote attorney Harry Weinberger of New York City, July 20, 1935: "I believe I did use the description of Voltaire's attitude. . . . l did not intend to imply that Voltaire used these words verbatim." She preferred turning a phrase to marriage.

> Printers are educated in the belief, that when men differ in opinion, both sides ought equally to have the advantage of being heard by the pubic; and that when truth and error have fair play, the former is always an over-match for the latter.
>
> Benjamin Franklin

In 1776 Franklin foreshadowed
Jerry Lewis, charming the French
as an unsophisticated noble from
the New World.

Suppression of opinion slanders knowledge, dignity, and progress. Exposure to other opinion begets knowledge, though attended by stress, while possibly improving the lot of the species. Holding fast to popular opinion may guarantee error, except for the perfect individual, society, or god. Mill comes as close to perfection as the species is likely to achieve. Tom says except for good religious types, of whom I must agree there have been several.

A free society cherishes
non-conformity. It knows that
from a non-conformist, from the
eccentric, have come many of the
great ideas of freedom. Free
society must fertilize the soil in
which non-conformity and dissent
and individualism can grow.

Henry Steele Commager

Commager co-authored the most
successful textbook of American
history in the first half of the
twentieth century and wrote
masterfully on social problems.

Most of the great ideas of freedom have come from nonconformist eccentrics. Nonconformity is our salvation. Without nonconformity, we'd neither evolve nor progress, because conformity regresses. Individual freedom is the means to nonconformity. This freedom requires the least interference from government and no interference from religion or those insisting on the superiority of a particular race, religion, government, or ethnic group. The best means of insuring the production of nonconformists and the progress of the species may be to limit government to its smallest necessary size and to exclude ideas of religious, ethnic, and racial superiority from education and social acceptance. Tom agrees except for the part excluding religion.

The only true and natural
foundation of society are the wants
and fears of individuals.

Sir William Blackstone

Blackstone was a classic example
of those lawyers who can't do, so
instead they teach, which he did
superbly.

The individual filtered through society, government, race,
and religion is part of a mob. Two people can attempt
communication but can't think. Only the individual can think. Thus,
only the wants and fears of individuals should define the free and
ideal society and government. The wants and fears of the individual
are suppressed by religion, which allows no individuality on matters
of faith, murder of "others" in war, birth control, or education.
Insofar as government and religion direct the individual, except to
prevent harm to others, they're expendable. The destruction and
impoverishment caused by wars and proscriptions against birth
control are the primary fruits of religion and government in their
giddy support of each other. Any governmental or religious policy
that harms the individual should be scuttled, particularly those
encouraging war or repressing birth control to generate more
members of us than can properly be supported. Tom says thou shalt
not kill and concedes, for the umpteenth time, the cruelty of
forbidding birth control.

If all mankind minus one
were of one opinion, and only one
person were of the contrary
opinion, mankind would be no
more justified in silencing that one
person, than he, if he had the
power, would be justified in
silencing mankind.

John Stuart Mill

Mill began working for East India
House at age seventeen and for the
next thirty-five years published

political philosophy on the side.

Society, religion and government shouldn't merely tolerate but should actively encourage the expression of contrary opinions. No individual or group can corral absolute truth, and none has a right to pretend otherwise, notwithstanding the inherent contrary proclivities of most every group, particularly government and religion. Tom says Mill likely can't be improved on.

> Whoever degrades another
> degrades me.
>
> Walt Whitman

> The first thin edition of *Leaves of Grass* was published in 1855 with only the author's picture: Whitman in workingman's clothes with a beard and broad-brimmed hat.

The species is a single unit. Demeaning one of us reflects on our collective ethics and on the species. Until we can agree on a universal rock bottom ethic, we have none. Tom says religion invented ethics, so we'll always have plenty, even though I know he knows it's not true, that such as the golden rule predates every religion.

> We hold these truths to be sacred and undeniable; that all men are created equal and independent, that from that equal creation they derive rights inherent and inalienable, among which are the preservation of life and liberty, and the pursuit of happiness.
>
> Thomas Jefferson

> Among other talents, Jefferson was an architect, designing the U.S. Capitol building, the University of Virginia, and

Monticello.

We should be guaranteed equality of opportunity. Entitlement to life, liberty, and the pursuit of happiness necessarily includes equal opportunity and the right to be left alone, unharmed by others. Happiness should include individual independence, though not appearing in the final form of the Declaration. Tom says I'm a hopeless idealist.

> They who have reasoned
> ignorantly, or who have aimed at
> effecting their personal ends by
> flattering the popular feeling, have
> boldly affirmed that 'one man is as
> good as another'; a maxim that is
> true in neither nature, revealed
> morals, nor political theory.
>
> James Fennimore Cooper
>
> Cooper attended Yale from 1803
> to 1805 and was its best Latin
> scholar, but he was expelled for a
> prank in his junior year.

Cooper is ever the prankster. In political and economic theory, for purposes of opportunity and protection against harm, one man should be weighed as good as another. On the other hand, we're each different in ability and ethics, no matter our race, religion, or country of origin. Cooper confounds by semantics, which trap the credulous. Perhaps he should have said, "One individual is as good as another for purposes of economic opportunity and protection against physical or property harm but disparate in morals and abilities." Yes, but he didn't, says Tom.

> All animals are equal, but
> some animals are more equal than
> others.
>
> George Orwell
>
> Orwell graduated as a talented
> scholar at Eton and perversely ran

off to become an imperial policeman in Burma, a dishwasher in Paris, a tramp in London, and a volunteer in the Spanish Civil War, finally abandoning literary London for a remote Scottish island where he died of tuberculosis at the height of his literary triumph, at age forty-six.

A utopian state, where everyone is accorded equal opportunity, will likely never exist, because the rulers, the rich, and the powerful of every state, no matter the system of government, naturally receive special privileges. This will likely never change; some will always be more equal than others.

Every great advance in natural knowledge has involved the absolute rejection of authority.

Thomas Henry Huxley

Huxley was the seventh child in a poor family of eight children— poor because in 1835 his father was dismissed as a teacher from Ealing School for reasons still unknown.

Every advance in knowledge, no matter the field, has required the rejection of tradition and the status quo upon which previous authority rested. Authority, usually in the form of government and religion, lays waste to innovation, creativity, and some individual happiness, though creating happiness for many others. We shouldn't be cowed by authority but should remain true to self so long as no one else is harmed. Our progress depends on the absolute rejection of authority in favor of the ethical. Tom says religious authority is a legitimate sovereign over the individual. Each different religion of the 4,300 on the planet?

Why does it [government] not cherish its wise minority? Why does it cry and resist before it is hurt? Why does it not encourage its citizens to be on the alert to point out its faults, and do better than it would have them? Why does it always crucify Christ, and excommunicate Copernicus and Luther, and pronounce Washington and Franklin rebels?

Henry David Thoreau

Thoreau resigned his first teaching post in protest against student whippings, returning to work in his father's pencil factory.

The majority considers no minority wise. To the majority, the minority is "them," creating the usual scenario. The majority naturally considers the minority an enemy because the minority usually seeks to change the status quo, through which the majority obtained and retains power. Christ, Copernicus, Luther, Washington, and Franklin were rebels, foreshadowing future majorities while leading a minority in competition for power, naturally on the blacklist of the powers that then were. We're unfair to the viewpoints and ideas of others, considering them enemies of our status quo, usurpers who threaten to upset our applecart, which is precisely who they are. Fairness to competitors, no matter the competition, is drastically difficult.

The spirit of resistance to government is so valuable on certain occasions that I wish it to be always kept alive. It will often be exercised when wrong, but better so than not to be exercised at all.

Thomas Jefferson

Jefferson was born of a wealthy privileged family, receiving the best tutors and private schools.

Resistance to government has seldom been wielded wrongly; government is wrong more often than the ethical individual. Bureaucrats running any government always try to expand its scope in order to obtain a raise or promotion, at least based on my experience as an assistant attorney general for seventeen years. The natural result is generous government growth. The spirit of resistance to government ranks among the loftiest. It's seldom, if ever, wrongly exercised. Tom agrees when the resistors believe generally as he does.

> The degree of non-conformity present—and tolerated—in a society might be looked upon as a symptom of its state of health.

> Ben Shahn

> Shahn's first major work was a series of paintings of the Sacco and Vanzetti trial; he also painted works related to Prohibition for the Bronx post office.

Only the individual is moral. Two of us tend to a mob, losing our sense of vulnerability, combining to form an us-versus-them against outsiders. Any group considers those outside it as less honorable. Us-versus-them dictates most group action. Our natural inclination to associate is beneficial or harmless so long as the resulting group doesn't seek to exterminate, malign, or undermine those belonging to competitive groups, which is seldom. A state of war may result when a government or religion disapproves of or feels superior to another government or religion, which is practically always. Government and religion work in tandem, restricting nonharmful actions of the governed or the religious congregation, weakening individual integrity and equality. The individual is smothered, inducted into a state of perpetual conflict against governments and religions other than his own. East (Muslims, Hindus, Buddhists, Taoists, Confucianists) versus West (Christians, Muslims, and Jews), with much straddling of the line, are natural opponents, with constant friction because we're made up of different religions, governments, and ethnic groups. We propagate the idea of us as superior and them as inferior on the basis of arbitrary political boundaries. Each of us is a citizen of a single government and religion, and we are taught early to consider others inferior, even as they consider us. Conflict often proceeds apace.

> As soon as man enters into a state of society, he loses the sense of his weakness; equality ceases, and then commences the state of war.
>
> Charles de Secondat, Baron de la Brede et de Montesquieu

> Montesquieu wrote a decent travel book based on his three years in Austria, Hungary, Italy, Germany, The Netherlands, and England from 1729 to 1731.

Though we haven't discovered a better form of government to preserve individual rights than a representative, democratic, and constitutional republic, no government is fair to all its citizens even some of the time, and noncitizens must duck for cover. A democracy chooses leaders who share the passions and vices of their constituents, often taking advantage of their office and prestige to treat minorities unfairly. The fact that a democratic form of government may be the fairest doesn't mean it's fair. No form of government has been devised that parcels out benefits strictly according to need, or which limits itself to the smallest necessary size. Government and those running it are naturally greedy, the same as their constituents, who are us. Limiting the human appetite for power is as impossible as limiting government, no matter its form. Tom nods sadly.

> A government by the passions of the multitude, or, no less correctly, according to the vices and ambitions of their leaders, is a democracy. We have heard so long of the indefeasible sovereignty of the people, and have admitted so many specious theories of the nature and

experience, that few will dread all, and fewer still will dread as they ought, the evils of an American democracy.

Fisher Ames

This American statesman declined the presidency of Harvard in 1796 and strongly opposed Jeffersonian democracy, believing Jefferson's 1800 election would lead to anarchy.

Groups are senseless, relying on emotion instead of individual thought (except perhaps that of a dictator) to make decisions for the oversight of others. Anyone presuming to know what's best for another adult is misguided if not moronic. Because groups, particularly government and religion, assume to make infallible decisions for the individual, their decisions are inherently untrustworthy. Individuals are better off making decisions for themselves instead of relying on decree by committee of which they're the tiniest imaginable part. Tom says religion has much wisdom to impart.

The pretense of collective wisdom is the most palpable of all impostures.

William Godwin

This English minister, reformer, and philosopher laid the foundation for both anarchy and its antithesis, communism. His daughter was Mary Wollstonecraft Shelley.

Collective wisdom is an oxymoron. Only the individual is capable of wisdom sufficient to fairly and conscientiously govern the individual. Government would be wiser to leave the vast majority of us alone, leaving us better off and wiser for it. Yet we worship the collective wisdom of government and religion, which is a great pretense, because it's impossible for 4,300 completely different religions and 193 differently structured governments to be the infallible creatures we make them out to be. The religious worship thousands of unverifiable superstitions while patriots worship oppressive governments, rendering suspect our claim that we're the smartest species on the planet. Tom agrees concerning all those other religions and every one of our governments.

> In individuals insanity is
> rare, but in groups, parties, nations
> and epochs it is the rule.
>
> Friedrich Nietzsche
>
> The great love of Nietzsche's life
> was Lou Andress Salome, Rilke's
> mistress, who was a groupie of
> Freud's.

We're a social species, most of us preferring company to solitude. The solitary individual is called a hermit or witch and perhaps considered insane though bothering no one except those threatened by an individual who prefers to avoid social interaction. Social action is often more wicked than individual action, because only the individual has a conscience or moral sense, and social action is aimed at controlling others, instead of ourselves.

> Every man has a mob self
> and an individual self, in varying
> proportions.
>
> David Herbert Lawrence
>
> Lawrence eloped with Frieda
> Weakley, sister of the German
> aviator von Richthofen and wife of
> a Nottingham professor, marrying
> her two years later when she
> finally obtained a divorce.

The goal of society should be to encourage the individual while discouraging the mob self. Society instead encourages the mob in the form of government granting nonprofit status and tax exemptions to religion. Because it's easier to rely on the guidance of others, many if not most of us are ruled by the mob or social self. Social approbation gilds this natural process.

> We are more wicked together than separately. If you are forced to be in a crowd, then most of all you should withdraw into yourself.

Lucius Annaeus Seneca

Seneca got crosswise of Caligula for having an adulterous affair with Caligula's niece; Caligula spared his life on Seneca's argument that his life would likely be short anyway, exiling Seneca to Corsica for years of productive penmanship.

Crowds can easily turn into lynch mobs because they constitute a body with very little brain that can rapidly deteriorate into none at all.

> The majority never had right on its side. Never, I say. Intelligent men must wage war. Who is it that constitutes the majority of the population of the country? Is it the wise folk or the fools? . . . The stupid people are an overwhelming majority all over the world. The majority has *might* on its side-unfortunately; but *right* it has not. . . . The minority is always in the right.

Henrik Ibsen

Ibsen's plays replaced Norway's threadbare repertoire of Norse legends with such as *Peer Gynt*

(1867), *A Doll's House* (1879),
and *Hedda Gabler* (1890).

The majority is often correct but never entirely in the right. The majority blindly serves and venerates government and religion, worshiping them as beacons of law, order, and ethics. The uneducated are the majority but are sufficiently intelligent to ethically govern themselves. The concept of stupidity is subjective. Half the population has an IQ below 100, the median by definition, which isn't a particularly adequate IQ but is often unrelated to moral sensibility. Until a few hundred years ago, Western religion retained the power of imposing the death sentence on unbelievers and misbelievers. The fundamentalists of Islam and a few other religions retain this power. All governments retain the "right" to impose the death penalty for the betrayal of government and numerous other reasons. Government controls unnecessary to protect the person and property of its citizens may deserve betrayal.

> Nor should we listen to those who say 'The voice of the people is the voice of God,' for the turbulence of the mob is always close to insanity.
>
> Alcuin of York

Alcuin was appointed the head of the Palatine School in Aachen by Charlemagne, bringing Anglo-Saxon humanism to Western Europe.

The voice of a god has never been objectively verified. The voice of a mob rooting for a particular religion often demands that those believing in other gods be shunned or liquidated. The turbulence of a mob has no time to balance the competing demands of "others," approaching insanity and always acting unfairly toward a minority. Tom says he can recognize the voice of God.

> ... that government of the people, by the people, for the people, shall not perish from the earth."

282

Abraham Lincoln

After Lincoln was elected
president but before his
inauguration, South Carolina
proclaimed its withdrawal from
the Union; a month after his
inauguration, the Confederate
States opened fire on Fort Sumter.

Government of, by, and for the people is impossible.
Government more closely tracks mob demands than individual
conscience. The implementation of a constitutional and democratic
government seeks to remedy this defect by reserving individual
rights inviolate from government action. Unfortunately,
constitutional safeguards are easily eroded by semantics, hard cases,
the heat of a crisis, and special interests. Tom says no question about
that.

Democracy is the recurrent
suspicion that more than half of
the people are right more than half
of the time.

E.B. White

White spent his entire career with
The New Yorker, writing three
classic children's books, including
Charlotte's Web and *The Elements
of Style* (with William Strunk).

The majority, which is to say more than half the people,
constitute a mob similar to, but ostensibly more morally correct
than, the individual. The majority can't properly judge individual
circumstances and needs before the fact. Democracy can only
approximate justice for the individual, though this approximation
may be fairer than any other form of government. The weakness of
government lies in its insistence on governing when no governance
is needed.

In political speculations
'the tyranny of the majority' is

now generally included among the evils against which society requires to be on its guard.

John Stuart Mill

The poetry of William Wordsworth rescued Mill from deep depression at age twenty.

The majority mindlessly stifles the minority. Only the tiny minority who harm others should be stifled. The balance should be left alone. Any group is mindless. Only the individual is capable of thought. We perversely approve of an unthinking entity such as government to control us, though we increasingly disapprove of nondemocratic governments. The tyranny of the majority may be realistically defined as any action by two or more, altering the action of another. Such collective action is an illegitimate intervention, whether by religion, government, or any group including society itself, except to punish or prevent harm to another. But it's impossible for any group to be on guard against itself. Group checks and balances can't be erected to prevent improper interference with the individual. Any group is inherently tyrannical. Only the individual is potentially just or can properly dispense justice, which doesn't mean that we're always just, seldom just, or sometimes just. Group dispensation of true justice is accidental. The individual is inherently more just than a group, a fact ignored by those who cede authority to groups on the supposition that the group knows better than we do, or is necessary for fairness and justice in society. Mill would have done better to say, "The tyranny of the group, two or more individuals, is a primary evil against which the individual should constantly guard."

What is a minority? The chosen heroes of this earth have been a minority. There is not a social, political, or religious privilege that you enjoy today that was not brought for you by the blood and tears and patient suffering of the minority. . . . It is the minority that have . . . achieved all that is noble

284

in the history of the world.

John Bartholomew Gough

Gough was such a hopeless drunk
in 1841 that his wife and infant
child died of neglect, but by 1843
he was the leading temperance
lecturer in the U.S.; during his
long career he gave over 10,000
lectures, collected 140,000
sobriety pledges, and sold 100,000
copies of his autobiography and a
million copies of his lectures. A
dazzled surveyor named Gough
Street in San Francisco after him.

Insofar as the minority is the thinking individual and the
majority is the mob, the minority has achieved all that is noble and
progressive in our history. The majority is satisfied with and
defends the status quo, which is similar to defending stagnation. The
freedoms of speech, assembly, and the right to privacy, or to be left
alone, weren't conjured up by government or religion, but by those
who opposed the smothering influence of government and religion.
Tom says yep.

To despise legitimate
authority, no matter in whom it is
invested, is unlawful, it is
rebellion against God's will.

Pope Leo XIII

Leo XIII brought a new spirit to
the papacy, effecting a
conciliatory attitude toward civil
governments and making sure the
church supported scientific
progress.

Authority over other than the harmful individual is
illegitimate. No authority is legitimate except in defense of the
individual or his property. Leo XIII inadvertently stumbles upon the

truth when he tempers his statement by insisting on "legitimate" authority. Since no legitimate authority can exist beyond the individual (except to prevent or punish physical or property harm to the individual), there can be no rebellion against a god, whether it exists or not. Though acting against governmental authority is unlawful, despising it isn't, and unlawfulness is often unrelated to ethics. Tom says that's too amorphous for comment.

Men may commit theft as
well as adultery with the eye.

Xenocrates of Chalcedon

This pupil of Plato and later head
of Plato's Academy divided
philosophy into logic, physics, and
ethics, with ethics the most
important.

Thought crimes harm no one (except possibly the individual thinking them) and can't be considered criminal. Neither theft nor adultery may be committed only with the eye; instead, an overt act harming another is required for criminality or a breach of ethics. Tom tends to agreement.

United we stand, divided
we fall.

Aesop

A half dozen stories, none in
agreement, speculate on who
Aesop was, whether a slave, an
adviser to King Croesus, or a
Babylonian adviser to King
Lycurgus, among other
suppositions, assuming he actually
existed.

Aesop's wholesome-sounding admonition could be considered false and immoral, or wholesome. Divided into individuals, we prosper and grow, while united we wage wars against other governments, religions, and ethnic groups. We are only capable of waging war when we unite against others on the basis of race, religion, or nationalism. If no one united with another to impact others, or took up arms, there'd be no war and a golden age of the individual would dawn. On the other hand, if we were united as a species instead of divided into false karasses (thank you, Kurt Vonnegut) based on religion, nationality, and race, there'd also be no war. We could logically conclude that "Divided we stand as sovereign individuals; united we fall as contentious groups based on religion, government, and race." Tom says that's real catchy.

> Neutral men are the devil's
> allies.
>
> Edwin Hubbell Chapin
>
> Besides being a clergyman, Chapin was a poet who wrote *Burial at Sea*, the basis for the folk song *Bury Me Not on the Lone Prairie*.

Neutral men are their own allies. Our bane is the choosing up of sides for an us-versus-them contest based on religion, race, nationalism, or some combination thereof. Protestants and Catholics violently opposed each other in Northern Ireland until 1994, pitting differing ideas of religion and government while sharing an identical ethnicity. Hindus oppose Muslims in India, seeking separate governments composed of similar religious groups. The variations are multiple, but the components always include a division between opposing governments and either religious or ethnic groups. They refuse to choose sides who have concluded that the only race is the human race, the only religion is superstition, and the only government is that necessary to prevent or punish violence among individuals. The devil's allies are those committed to religion, nationalism, or other racist opinions that foment conflict unto war. Chapin should have said that "Neutral men are the allies of morality and ethics. Committed men are the devil's allies; those committed to a religion, government or ethnic group." Tom says commitment to religion doesn't have to be nasty stuff.

> Give me a dozen healthy
> infants … and I'll guarantee to

take any one of them at random and train him to become any type of specialist I might select—doctor, lawyer, even beggar man and thief, regardless of his talents, penchants, tendencies, abilities, vocations and race of his ancestors.

John Broadus Watson

Watson codified behaviorist psychology and was the first to study infants, abruptly abandoning his academic career for one in advertising after the sensationalism surrounding the divorce from his first wife.

A dozen healthy infants could similarly be trained to become the champion of any religion, country, or ethnic group regardless of their talents, penchants, tendencies, abilities, vocations, or ancestry, which government schools do very well. Government education trains us to venerate our government, religion, and society, no matter how mindless or racist. Tom says religion is worthy of veneration.

God said: All men must behave as brothers toward one another; this sublime principle contains everything that is divine in the Christian religion.

Claude Henri de Rouvroy,
Comte de Saint-Simon

This founder of French socialism claimed descent from Charlemagne and joined the U.S. fight for independence in 1781 at Yorktown as a captain of the artillery.

This proposition contains everything outside of religion, because few religions, perhaps only a few isolated Buddhists, realistically consider the followers of other religions as brothers, though Buddhists in Myanmar and Sri Lanka have recently slaughtered hundreds of thousands of religious others. The command of a particular god is worthless unless the god's followers act on the directive instead of only giving it lip service. The ethical directives of religion are independent of religion because they're as closely observed by the nonreligious as the religious. Saint-Simon should have more accurately said, "All men should behave as brothers toward each other, but they do not because of religion, nationalism, and similar racist beliefs." Tom says those could be fighting words.

> Adam was deceived by Eve,
> not Eve by Adam. . . . it is right
> that he whom that woman induced
> to sin should assume the role of
> guide lest he fall again through
> feminine instability.
>
> Saint Ambrose
>
> In 388, as bishop of Milan,
> Ambrose rebuked the emperor
> Theodosius for punishing a bishop
> who burned a Jewish synagogue;
> Ambrose baptized Saint
> Augustine.

If there were such a thing as sin, the female would be no more responsible than the male. Because most males have an inherent weakness for the female, females have been blamed for the ills of society through religious superstition. No one has the right to guide or control another adult, whether male or female, and neither is inherently less stable than the other. Tom says he's not so sure about that but recognizes a trend when he sees it.

> As long as woman regards
> the Bible as the charter of her
> rights, she will be the slave of
> man. The Bible was not written by
> a woman. Within its leaves there is

nothing but humiliation and shame
for her.

Robert Green Ingersoll

This son of a Congregationalist
minister earned up to $3,500 a
night, which was a ton of money
back then ($80,000 in 2019
dollars), for expounding on the
contradictions and superstitions of
religion.

No holy book was written by a woman. The major and minor religions were created by men—not only the Bible but also the Koran for Muslims, the Old Testament for Jews, and similarly anti-female books for Hindus, Sikhs, Buddhists, and all the religious others. Women are the dog food of religion, the religious enemy and corrupter of the male. In reality, females are entitled to equal opportunities with men, though religion deems them inferior. Anomalously, women are the heartiest supporters of religion, though it be their warden. Women are seduced by the imaginary ethical core of religion, swallowing the swill of their own inferiority, humiliation, and shame as part of religious ethics. Tom says that's rather strongly put. I did my best.

The Bible and the Church
have been the greatest stumbling
blocks in the way of women's
emancipation.

Elizabeth Cady Stanton

Stanton's father was a lawyer, a
congressman, and a judge on the
New York Supreme Court; she
learned   about   the   law's
discriminatory effect on women
while working in his law office.

Religion, society, and government operate as a single unit responsible for the subjugation of women. The majority religion almost always supports the reigning government in every country.

290

Religion and government form a partnership preventing the emancipation of women. Only women themselves have been successful in loosening their bonds, through political and religious activism, which requires consorting with the enemy. If you can't lick 'em, join 'em, which women have done in droves. Tom says women are essential to organized religion. No question about that.

> Religion sanctions woman's self-love; it gives her the guide, father, lover, divine guardian she longs for nostalgically; it feeds her day-dreams; it fills her empty hours. But, above all, it confirms the social order, it justifies her resignation, by giving her the hope of a better future in a sexless heaven. This is why women today are still a powerful trump in the hand of the Church; it is why the Church is notably hostile to all measures liable to help in women's emancipation. There must be religion for women; and there must be women, 'true women,' to perpetuate religion.

> Simone de Beauvoir

> Beauvoir wrote classics on aging, feminism, and equality between men and women.

Religion confirms the social order, justifying the resignation of women to the status quo and their enslavement by patriarchal religion. Religion is universally hostile to the emancipation of women or the ordination of female priests, rabbis, and ministers. The emancipation of women would liberate many from the confines of religion and religious service, without which religion would wither away more rapidly than it already is. The large-scale ordination of women, or the dawn of "true women," would likely change religion completely, making it more humane and perhaps less susceptible to an us-versus-them mentality. Tom says perhaps, thinking about something.

> We hold these truths to be
> self-evident: that all men and
> women are created equal.
>
> The Women's Rights
> Convention, 1948

Nothing can fruitfully be added to the truth that men and women are entitled to equal opportunity and rights though their talents may differ and women seem generally more humane than men. Citing a couple of nuns he knows, Tom's not so sure about the last part.

> Love, friendship, respect,
> do not unite people as much as a
> common hatred of something.
>
> Anton Chekhov

> Because of terrible translations,
> shoddy publishing, and the fact
> that what he didn't say was often
> more important than what he said,
> Chekhov gained no international
> recognition until long after his
> death.

Love, friendship, and respect are difficult to cultivate when the parties believe in differing religions, live in different countries, or spring from different ethnic groups. The us-versus-them of nationalism, religion, and race indelibly isolate us. Those isolated from others can't easily cultivate love, respect, or friendship with others. Others are seen as unlike us, as different, as boogeymen. The primary common hatreds are based on religion, national origin, and race. Hatreds unite us within by isolating them without, whether the boundary is drawn by religion, country, race, or a combination thereof. The hatred or fear of others bonds the religious against other religions, patriots against other countries, and racists against other ethnic groups to a far greater degree than intrareligious, patriotic, and racist feelings of love, friendship, and respect based on the fact of a common religion, country, or ethnic group. Tom says Chekhov said it better.

Us Versus Them

Everyone loves his own country, customs, language, wife, children, not because they are the best in the world, but because they are his established property, and he loves in them himself, and the labor he has bestowed on them.

Johann Gottfried von
Herder

Herder became estranged from Kant and Goethe because his competitive nature refused to accept their larger body of work.

We love our own country, customs, language, and family because they're familiar and part of ourselves, which other countries, customs, languages, and families aren't. Our lack of love for others identical to ourselves has been our downfall, resulting in unending conflicts and wars justified by religion, nationalism, and ethnicity. Tom quite agrees, un-Christian-like, I think.

The struggle between the two worlds [fascism and democracy] can permit of no compromises. It's either Us or Them.

Benito Mussolini

Mussolini became Italy's youngest prime minister in 1922 at age twenty-seven, appointed by King Victor Immanuel III and confirmed in the massive ballot fraud of the 1924 elections.

293

Competition among religions, nationalisms, and races admits of no easy compromise. Our three primary motivators demand an us-versus-them mentality, best summarized as racist. We're who we are by accident, where our mom happened to be when we were born, unrelated to inherent inferiority or superiority. One system of government may be better than another, but the folks under the thumb of all governments are everywhere the same. Suggesting one such person is better than another is indistinguishable from racism, thus making Mussolini correct. It's either us or them when it comes to systems of governments, religions, and races. Tom says that's rather pessimistic.

> Hatred is the most clearsighted, next to genius.
>
> Claude Bernard

A literary critic suggested that Bernard try medicine instead of writing plays, and Bernard did; both the critic and Bernard were elected to the French Academy, and Bernard received the first national funeral accorded a French scientist. That probably made him feel all warm inside.

Like clockwork, our hatred and fear of the other slide us unto wars and mutual destruction. We're never more certain than when we hate, particularly when hatred is based on religion, nationalism, or ethnicity. Genius recognizes these boundaries as ephemeral and meaningless, based instead on superstition and geographical accidents of birth. Tom says yes sirree.

> Politics divides us, but humanity unites us.
>
> Fidel Castro

Born the second child of five from his wealthy father's liaison with the family cook/laundrywoman, Castro developed an obsession with his virility after being condemned as a "bastard" loser.

Politics, religion, and race sever more than humanity unites, making us lose sight of the big picture. The only entity fit for veneration is the species. Our warring subdivisions are pathetic remnants of the infancy to which the species ferociously clings. Tom says hatred is childish, except perhaps for that resulting from harm suffered, and then we should forgive and turn the other cheek. We don't really know if Christianity would work since it has never been tried, but most still reject giving all you own to the poor, i.e. communism.

> A nation is a historical group of men of recognizable cohesion, held together by a common enemy.
>
> Theodore Herzl

> Herzl was convinced by the Dreyfus affair that Jews must have their own state; his efforts were instrumental in creating Israel, forty-five years after his death.

Whether our enemies are real, imagined, or made up, they seem essential to many governments and necessary to the mental health of politicians the world over. Those without enemies may lose focus and meaning in life, the same as nations when cold wars end and other excuses must be conjured for billowing military budgets. We seldom learn from our enemies, except to justify war readiness. Only after our enemies become friends do we learn what regular guys they are and presumably always were. Otherwise, we paint them as satans and ayatollahs. Enemies may be as psychologically necessary as friends, which is a pathetic commentary on the species and a mortal enemy of morality.

> We should support whatever the enemy opposes and oppose whatever the enemy supports.

Mao Zedong

This superauthoritarian figure
rebelled against authority and his
father early, running away from
home at the age of ten.

Blindly espousing us-versus-them is the only explanation for
Mao's support of whatever the enemy opposes and opposition to
whatever the enemy supports. We're a species divided artificially
by religion, race, and nationality, the other of which constitutes our
primary enemies. Tom says religion's okay, though it may be
somewhat divisive.

Nations hate other nations
for the evil which is in themselves.

George W. Russell

This Irish poet, artist, and essayist
was primarily interested in the
origins of religion and mystical
experience.

Nations are inanimate objects incapable of hatred. Only
individuals can hate. Nations collectivize citizen opinion, often
focusing on destructive competition with other nations. The result
is a collective slander of other nationals who, consisting of diverse
individuals, can't properly be generalized, positively or negatively.
We often fail to distinguish between a foreign government and its
oppressed citizens, muttering such as "those damn Russians," when
it's a government decision we object to instead of millions of
ordinary Russians. These stereotypical portrayals are often
negative, generating loathing in accord with national or religious
policy. Resulting hatreds may mirror the foibles of the originating
nation, embittered by reciprocal name-calling. Thus, nations may in
fact generate hate for other nations based on the evil in themselves.

I need my enemy in my
community. He keeps me alert,
vital. . . . But beyond what we
specifically learn from our
enemies, we need them

296

emotionally; our psychic economy cannot get along well without them. . . . [O]ur enemy is as necessary for us as our friend. Both together are part of authentic community.

Rollo May

May became an ordained Congregationalist minister, but after two years of preaching, he decided he'd be better at psychology, a field in which he became well-known by the late 1970s.

We have met the enemy, and he is us. The nation is an artificial entity, barring individuals of other nations from crossing its borders without an unending bureaucracy of visa, passports, and long lines at borders, though skunks and rattlesnakes may freely prance across. Why a group historically connected by race or religion should bar groups more similar to themselves than skunks and rattlesnakes is beyond understanding, likely mine alone. Similar others are the enemy though their common traits are far more akin to our own than those exhibited by lower animals that remain uncontrolled at all national borders (without a fence). Tom says I'm borderline committable.

The division of mankind threatens it with destruction. Civilization is imperiled by a universal thermonuclear war, catastrophic hunger for most of mankind, stupefaction from the narcotic of 'mass culture' and bureaucratized dogmatism, a spreading mass of myths that put entire peoples and continents under the power of cruel and treacherous demagogues.

Andrei Dimitrijevic

Sakharov

Sakharov helped develop the
USSR's hydrogen bomb but was
an outspoken advocate of human
rights, civil liberties, and reform of
the USSR, receiving the Nobel
Prize for Peace in 1975.

Our division into religions, ethnic groups, and nationalities threatens and apparently will always threaten us. Until a common enemy unites us, as in *The War of the Worlds,* we appear doomed to immortalize the internecine warfare justified by religion, ethnicity, and patriotism. Thermonuclear and hydrogen warfare still threaten, though the Cold War has supposedly ended. Every nation not having the bomb, slobbers for it, knowing it necessary for international prestige and to join the relatively exclusive nuclear club. A crackpot more insane than the run-of-the-mill dictator will eventually get the bomb, and the threat may become reality. If Khaddaffi, Amin, Hitler, Stalin, or Hussein had had the bomb, they might have used it. The United States used the bomb with arguable justification, which is in the eye of the bombardier. Catastrophic dysentery and AIDS threaten the poor more than hunger, but hunger occupies a spacious dwelling. Stupefaction of the masses by "mass culture" is gaining traction and has exacerbated the divisions among us, becoming one of our favorite narcotics. Myth contributes to the downfall of the species, reflecting our caveman days in the form of superstitious religion, our us-versus-themness, and the impoverishment of the public by religious sexual taboos deterring birth control and sex education. The demagoguery of religion and government are escapable only through an unbiased education, which both uniformly oppose. Barbara Spinelli, the European affairs columnist for *La Stampa* newspaper, compared the attitude of many Europeans toward the pope and the church to their feeling about authoritarian government: "One flees the grip of the church as one flees the grip of the state."

God and Satan alike are
essentially human figures, the one
a projection of ourselves, the other
of our enemies.

Bertrand Russell

298

Russell was fired from Trinity College, Cambridge, in 1916 for his pacifism. He was immediately offered a position at Harvard but couldn't accept because the British government vindictively refused to issue him a passport.

Russell illustrates the arbitrariness of us-versus-them based on religion, which applies equally to country and race. We act as if our side is the equivalent of God. Our god, country, and race bravely oppose the multiple other races, religions, and countries, who are "them," treated as enemies because of three adolescent differences. Our innermost feelings may depend on whether we belong to the Rotary or Lions Club, root for the Bulls or the Knicks, attended Podunk High School, or Timbuktu State, but are mostly dependent on our feelings toward those from other religions, countries, and races, our apparent natural enemies in a projection of Satan vis-a-vis our own natural godliness. Tom says this may unfortunately be true.

Lions do not fight with one another, serpents do not attack serpents, nor do the wild monsters of the deep rage against their like. But most of the calamities of man are caused by his fellow-man.

Pliny the Elder

Pliny the Elder (23-79 C.E.) was a Roman naturalist and Stoic whose *Natural History* filled thirty-seven books. Based on the study of over two thousand works by 473 authors, it occupied all of his working hours from midnight to evening.

Male animals often fight sexual rivals. Still, animals resist division into groups of opposing religious or geographical units, seldom treating each other according to the shade of their pelts, presumably because of their lower intelligence. Religions and superstitions, countries and governments, races and ethnic groups, are the principal causes of intra-species atrocities. Without their eradication, which is highly unlikely, the species may never live in peace. The three primary reasons we fight, attack, and rage against ourselves are nationalism, religion, and race, pitting our clans, tribes, and ethnic groups against each other. Tom says government is necessary, to some extent, that racial hatreds must be overcome, and that religion is the solution.

"Inferior" animals, snails, dumb fish, and fleas under few circumstances slaughter their own, while we commit speciecide without intermission, justified by religion, patriotism, and ethnic groups. We decline to recognize the universal individual rights of equal dignity, opportunity, and treatment, and the most basic human right to remain unharmed as long as we harm no one else. We believe we are harmed when our religion, country, or race is criticized, wearing the three principal badges of our identity as chips on our shoulders. Woe to the other who dares to criticize our religion, race, or country of birth. Of course, offense may rightly be taken, since criticism of a faceless multitude is substanceless. Tom says he doesn't feel that strongly and suspects that few do. To Tom I say, ho, ho, ho.

The Mob has many Heads,
but no Brains.

Thomas Fuller

Fuller (1654–1734) was an English cleric and philosopher whose family grew rich through iron-smelting.

Only the individual has a brain. Any group of two or more tends to a mob, brainless in direct proportion to its numbers. Most mobs have a single fortuitous head but no brain whatsoever. Mobs appear not only at lynchings but in the guise of legislatures and other governmental, religious, and social organizations. A mob reacts emotionally to its leadership, short-circuiting individual brains in the white heat of the moment. Government is helpless to stop individual acts of violence, illustrated in government prisons where drugs are easily procurable though inmates live in the ultimate controlled and freedomless society with walls, bars, razor wire, and machine guns. The heat of the moment justifies any governmental action, over time inexorably withering individual freedoms. The individual brain serves at the pleasure of governmental, religious, and ethnic mobism. Tom says he's impressed by the enthusiasm if not the erudition.

> A group [translatable as "crowd" or "mass"] is extraordinarily credulous and open to influence, it has no critical faculty, and the improbable does not exist for it. It thinks in images. . . . Since a group is in no doubt as to what constitutes truth or error, and is conscious moreover, of its own great strength, it is as intolerant as it is obedient to authority. It respects force and can only be slightly influenced by kindness, which it regards as a form of weakness. What it demands of its heroes is strength, or even violence. It wants to be ruled and oppressed and to fear its masters. Fundamentally it is entirely conservative, and it has a deep aversion from all innovations and advances and an unbounded respect for tradition. . . . In order to make a correct judgment upon the morals of crowds, one must take into consideration the fact that when individuals come together in a group all their individual inhibitions fall away and all the cruel, brutal, and destructive instincts, which lie dormant in individuals as relics of a primitive epoch, are stirred up to find free gratification.

> Sigmund Freud

In order to escape anti-Semitism,
Freud's family, when he was age
three, moved to Vienna, the anti-
Semitic capital of the world.

Religious, governmental, and ethnic groups are inappropriate
to determine individual conduct because they're incapable of moral
judgment. Groups can hypothesize how general actions should be
treated in the future, but have no capacity to anticipate all the factual
circumstances of potential individual action. We implicitly trust the
administrators of our religious, ethnic, governmental, and social
institutions to define right from wrong when no one other than the
individual can possibly know the full circumstances necessary to
determine the proper moral course. Some individuals may be bereft
of judgment and thus unable to morally analyze personal action;
these individuals may be appropriate for group supervision. The
group implicitly trusts its members (birds of a feather), so that a
course determined in the heat of emotion is almost automatically
seconded. Inhibitions shatter when suggestions are supported by
friends and associates. Woe to the minority, individuals outside the
group or those marginally different from ourselves. Because groups
have no critical faculty, they assume a single set of operative facts
when legislating for masses of individuals, though all individuals
are subtly different. Groups are easily influenced by prettily spoken
words, lacking the capacity to anticipate nuances of reality, which
are infinitely complex and daily encompass the improbable. Truth
and error are black and white for groups and mobs, admitting no
shades of gray except accidentally. Because groups govern
individual behavior, they feel power coursing through their veins,
breeding recklessness and feelings of omnipotence. The authority
of the group tolerates no other authority, particularly that asserted
by the mere individual. Kindness or tolerance shown by an outside
individual toward the group is seen as groveling. The group values
strength and violence, particularly its own societally sanctioned
violence. The group, collective, or mob, also known as legislature,
Curia, Ku Klux Klan, or similar, is cruel, brutal, and destructive
toward the individual, gratifying our collective primitive selves.
Tom says he sees structure in my ravings, some of which (those
unrelated to religion) he partially agrees with.

He who speaks of the
people, speaks of a madman; for
the people is a monster full of

confusion and mistakes; and the opinions of the people are as far removed from the truth as, according to Ptolemy, The Indies are from Spain.

Francesco Guicciardini

This quote is from the most important early history of Italy, written by a political philosopher even more radical, or perhaps realistic, than his friend Machiavelli.

Any plural of the individual lacks common sense, though labeling them madmen may be an exaggeration. The people, excluding organized interest groups, are usually well-meaning, which may translate into insanity, confusion, and mistake when applied to individual circumstances. Truth is often irrelevant to groups and too complicated for comprehension. The truth is sufficiently tangled for the individual, who is also often wrong when subjectively judging its validity. Tom says I often miss the mark, and I do, in good company.

Men are cruel, but man is kind.

Rabindranath Tagore

When the British wreaked the 1919 Amritsar Massacre, Tagore repudiated the knighthood he had been awarded upon receipt of the 1913 Nobel Prize.

The group is cruel through intention or neglect, its primal aim always to solidify power. Most individuals, when not overly influenced by a governmental, religious, or ethnic group, are kind. We're individually a warm species; as a group, our cruelty is often unbounded. Tom says organized religion may fit this description, occasionally.

Nor is it you alone
who know what it
is to be evil,
I am he who knew
what it is to be
evil,
I too knitted the old
knot   of
contrariety,
Blabb'd,   blush'd,
resented,   lied,
stole, grudg'd,
Had   guile,   anger,
lust, hot wishes I
dared not speak,
Was wayward, vain,
greedy,   shallow,
sly,   cowardly,
malignant,
The wolf, the snake,
the   hog,   not
wanting in me,
The cheating look,
the   frivolous
word,   the
adulterous wish,
not wanting,
Refusals,   hates,
postponements,
meanness,
laziness, none of
these wanting,
Was one with the
rest, the days and
haps   of   the
rest . . .

Walt Whitman, Leaves of
Grass

While becoming the first great
American poet, Whitman worked
among a jumble of jobs as a

printer's assistant, teacher, journalist, land speculator, and nurse.

The seeds of pettiness live in everyone, flowering to evil in many, though *many* is a tiny percentage of the species. An examination of Whitman's adjectives, adverbs, and verbs illustrates the power of semantics.

- Contrariety may be the same as strength of character.
- Blabbing may represent honesty.
- Blushing can signify modesty.
- Resentfulness or a grudge may be justified by evils previously suffered.
- Lying may be justified to deceive a deceiver or spare the feelings of others.
- Stealing may be vindicated by hunger.
- The guile and slyness of the snake may be necessary for survival.
- Anger and even hate may be justified by serious harm done to a loved one or friend.
- Lust, the cheating look, and the adulterous wish may be inconsequential unless acted upon, nonconsensual, or resulting in harm to another.
- Unspoken hot wishes may harm no one, though they're usually better unspoken.
- Waywardness is in the eye of the beholder, reprehensible only when harming another.
- Vanity in extremis may be harmful, but most of us naturally harbor an amount sufficient for self-respect.
- The greediness of the pig on behalf of a deserving cause is of small consequence when not carried to the point of harming another.
- Shallowness is a character trait difficult if not impossible to cure.
- Cowardliness may be the better part of valor.
- Malignancy and meanness are nigh inexcusable.
- The frivolous word is easily ignored, usually harming no one except the eggshell plaintiff.
- Refusals and postponements may be necessary for self-protection.

- Occasional laziness may be exquisite.

Every equation has at least two sides and often more. Whether we're evil or weak may depend on the circumstances, which we can easily misjudge. We're poor, weak creatures who often resort to whatever it takes for gain and always for survival; some find the distinction illusive. Tom doesn't.

> He who hates vice hates mankind.
>
> Publius Clodius Thrasea Paetus

> Paetus was famous for opposing Nero, walking out of the Senate when it congratulated Nero on the death of his mother in 59 C.E. He finally retired in disgust at Nero's immoralities, but Nero ordered his death nevertheless, two years after his retirement.

If vice is defined as that which harms someone else, then few act excessively and most, not at all. Vice as harm to others is usually generated by groups and less frequently by individuals, and then by a tiny number of individuals. He who hates vice probably tolerates the overwhelming majority of individuals but should beware of groups, collectives, bureaucracies, and committees, no matter how constituted. Tom says religious groups are mostly okay, depending on their essence.

> I fear the Greeks though bearing gifts.
>
> Virgil

> Virgil died of a fever contracted on a visit to Greece.

Ethnic groups are peopled entirely by individuals differing in character and morality, no matter their ethnicity. There are good Greeks and bad Greeks, the same as in any ethnic or national group.

Fear, however, is a reaction of all groups to the outsider, or other. A group bearing an unearned gift is likely up to no good. Tom says except for a few kings and wise men.

> Because the sword is a very great benefit and necessary to the whole world, to preserve peace, to punish sin, and to prevent evil.
>
> Martin Luther

> The sword Luther championed against the peasants in the 1524 Peasants' War handsomely served the aristocracy.

The sword protects the interests of accidental geographic entities called nations and their religions, which often try to punish the evil or sins attributed to other religions and governments. The sword seldom preserves peace, though it could theoretically be used defensively. The peace has already been broken when swords are drawn. The threat of the sword may temporarily preserve peace but usually intensifies tussles instead of avoiding them. If an act is a sin, it should be exclusively punished by the god decreeing the act sinful. No individual, no matter how pompous and titled, has the right to punish another individual for a "sin." More evil is committed than prevented by the sword. Tom says I sound like buckshot.

> The death sentence is a necessary and efficacious means for the Church to attain its ends when rebels against it disturb the ecclesiastical unity, especially obstinate heretics who cannot be restrained by any other penalty from continuing to disturb ecclesiastical order.
>
> Pope Leo XIII

> Leo XIII was the longest-living pope, lasting until age ninety-

three; he championed workers'
rights to a fair wage, safe working
conditions, and the formation of
labor unions.

Those believing in a different god, religion, or in no religion
at all disturb ecclesiastical unity. Any religion executing "others"
would destroy the majority of the species, because no religion can
claim anywhere near a majority of the world's population.
Christians are the largest religion but only comprise about 33
percent of the world population, projected to be eclipsed by Islam
in the 2030s. Heresy is an archaic religious term, retaining vibrancy
only for fundamentalists. It's utterly astounding that a twentieth-
century pope would suggest death to dissenters. Modern
Catholicism knows it's better to ignore dissenters instead of
demanding retraction. Tom says dissenters may also eventually find
the path.

In these four things, opinion
of ghosts, ignorance of second
causes, devotion towards what
men fear, and taking of things
casual for prognostics, consisteth
the natural seed of religion; which
by reason of the different fancies,
judgments, and passions of several
men, hath grown up into
ceremonies so different, that those
which are used by one man, are for
the most part ridiculous to another.

Thomas Hobbes

Hobbes disliked religion because
he thought it diluted the
sovereignty of the state, which he
felt was entitled to absolute
obedience.

Aside from an amorphous feeling that we should act
ethically, there's no single belief common to all religions. Buddhists
and Taoists don't believe in a god though most other religions
believe in one or more. Even the generally claimed ethical

308

orientation of religion agrees on nothing specific, except perhaps that we shouldn't kill each other, which is observed in the breach, with minor exceptions, such as Quakers and a few pacifist sects. Every religion, save their own, appears ridiculous to the vast majority of the species. Tom says his religion is okay.

> Those who are convinced they have a monopoly on The Truth always feel that they are only saving the world when they slaughter the heretics.

> Arthur M. Schlesinger, Jr.

> Schlesinger wrote a sympathetic history of the New Deal, advised Adlai Stevenson and John F. Kennedy, and received a Pulitzer Prize for *The Age of Jackson* in 1946.

Two-thirds of the world's population are technical heretics to the tenets of the largest religion, some members of which consider fellow Christian sects heretical, and the numbers spiral downward for other religions. No one knows the truth about religion, but we can tell the difference between probabilities and bare possibilities, and the practical results of various beliefs. Because no unsubstantiated belief has or can have a monopoly on truth, dying for bare belief is fanatical, and killing for it is maniacal. Neither advance the species. We'd be better off if the beliefs that cause wars and poverty were educated out of our vocabularies. They're not only unrelated to ethics, but antithetical to ethics. Tom quite agrees, knowing I couldn't possibly be talking about him and his.

> The greater the truth the greater the libel.

> William Murray, First Earl of Mansfield

> Mansfield was so remarkably fair that he acquitted Lord George Gordon, who in 1780 led an anti-

Catholic mob of fifty thousand in
an invasion of Parliament and the
burning of Mansfield's house and
library.

If religion were declared evil because it fosters war and
poverty, and false because of its superstitious and unverifiable
foundations, these two truths would be regarded as the greatest
libels in history. Truth can't be libelous, though it may invade
privacy. Western jurisprudence regards truth as an absolute defense
to accusations of libel and slander. The fact that truth may startle,
upset, confound, enrage, and encourage murder is unrelated to its
validity. The greater a truth, the less it's believed and the more it
enrages. Tom says he's feeling quite put out about now, but it must
be happy hour somewhere.

Controversy is only dreaded
by the advocates of error.

Benjamin Rush

Rush, an American physician and
a signer of the Declaration of
Independence,   prescribed
bloodletting for most physical
maladies, with predictable results,
but he fared better treating mental
illness and wrote the leading text
in 1812, which was used for many
years.

Controversy is the catalyst of truth. Most defer to the strongly
spoken opinions of others, no matter the subject matter, having
neither the clarity of thought nor gumption to disagree. The lies and
mistakes of our ancestors are thus bequeathed to us. Discussing
religion and ethics with others often results in one of two reactions:
complete agreement because of the listener's lack of analytical
ability or energy, or a frozen refusal to respond. Few tolerate
controversy or discussion beyond the state of the weather, except
on social media. Those seen as advocates of error may be only lazy
or afraid of losing their temper. Tom says let 'er rip and he'll
respond in kind. Love that Tom. Prost.

A heretic is a man who sees
with his own eyes.

Gotthold Ephraim Lessing

Lessing applied for the post of
royal librarian for Berlin, but
because he had quarreled with
Voltaire, a favorite of Frederick
the Great, Lessing was denied the
post and eventually died a pauper.

All of us are heretics to the other 4,300 religions of the world.
A heretic is one who disagrees with a particular religion,
unsurprising when all religions harbor belief without objective
foundation. A heretic sees with his own eyes, whether right or
wrong. Almost no one, if anyone, truly sees with his or her own
eyes. Our eyes and thoughts are largely determined by our national,
religious, and ethnic origins. Those realizing this fact may see better
with their own eyes. Tom says he sees with his own eyes, obviously
affected by his favorite religion.

There is no method of
reasoning more common, and yet
more blamable, than, in
philosophical disputes, to
endeavor the refutation of any
hypothesis, by a pretense of its
dangerous consequences to
religion and morality.

David Hume

Hume considered philosophy an
inductive experimental science of
human nature, applying the
scientific method of Newton and
the epistemology of John Locke.

If religion is the antithesis of morality and ethics, then the
indefinite survival of religion suggests dangerous consequences for
morality and the species. Morality and ethics should be founded on
a far firmer foundation than that occupied by religion, no matter

311

which of our thousands. Tom says doubtful.

> The true faith compels us to believe there is one holy Catholic Apostolic Church and this we firmly believe and plainly confess. And outside of her there is no salvation or remission from sins. . . . Now, therefore, we declare, say, determine and pronounce that for every human creature it is necessary for salvation to be subject to the authority of the Roman pontiff.
>
> Pope Boniface VIII

> This Roman pontiff engineered the murder of a predecessor and was installed as pope by the Crescentii, an unscrupulous Roman family, who summoned him from Constantinople, where he'd absconded with the church treasury and was finally himself murdered by an irate Roman mob.

Those not for us are against us, labeled "other." Others, outsiders, foreigners, and those not identical to us in nationality, ethnicity, and religion are often accorded special misery. Sins unrelated to morality are artificial. No entity, individual, or god can absolve us from ethical violations. Salvation, in the sense of immortality, is improbable because the idea rests on unverifiable superstition. The overwhelming majority who reside outside the one holy Catholic Apostolic Church have no need of either salvation or remission from sins, except sins of immorality that harm another individual. The authority of the Roman pontiff resides in the mind of the supplicant and nowhere else. Modem Roman Catholicism rejects Boniface VIII, suggesting instead that all individuals are saved, including atheists and those belonging to other religions. Tom says I'm one lucky dog.

> The   Catholic   Church

claims, not only to judge infallibly on religious questions, but to animadvert on opinions in secular matters which bear on religion, on matters of philosophy, of science, of literature, of history, and it demands our submission to our claims.

John Henry Newman

Newman's eloquent books revived the emphasis on the dogmatic authority of the Church of England just before his conversion to Roman Catholicism. The Catholic religious center is named the Newman Center on every college and university campus I've been on.

Groups feel internally infallible, whether governmental, religious, or other. Religion is always decades behind science, philosophy, literature, and history. Any group can demand submission to its claims while we can either ignore or submit to those claims. The chaff of religion should be liberated from its few pearls of wisdom, which should be freely acknowledged. Tom says thanks loads for that.

You have got our country, but are not satisfied; you want to force your religion upon us. . . . Brother, you say there is but one way to worship and serve the Great Spirit. If there is but one religion, why do you white people differ so much about it?

Sagoyewatha

The Seneca chief Sagoyewatha was called Red Jacket because he wore a British coat in the

Revolutionary War, double-dealing against his own people when the Americans eventually prevailed.

Assuming the Great Spirit is something other than the indomitable ethos of the species, it likely doesn't exist. The nature of unseeable undefinable entities makes agreement impossible. No major religion agrees with the core beliefs of any other religion. Religions disagree on whether a Great Spirit exists, whether immortality is granted by a Great Spirit, and what marks the proper path to righteousness and morality. All religion contains facial inconsistencies and absurdities. Tom says yes, but one could be entirely correct. Which one, pray tell?

Race involves the inheritance of similar physical variations by large groups of mankind, but its psychological and cultural connotations, if they exist, have not been ascertained to science. . . . The terms 'Aryan' and 'Semitic' have no racial significance whatsoever. They simply denote linguistic families. . . . Anthropology provides no scientific basis for discrimination against any people on the ground of racial inferiority, religious affiliation, or linguistic heritage.

Resolution by the
American Anthropological
Association (1938)

No important differences exist between races or ethnic groups, nor has any ever existed. We're a single species with an inherent weakness for the evil of arbitrarily dividing ourselves into beliefs, superstitions, and religions; into governments, nations, and flags; into races, tribes, and ethnic groups. Flags should be universally burned while distinctions based on skin color, language, ethnic origin, language, and religion scrapped as juvenile and grossly racist. Tom says he can't see doing away with religious truth

314

or the Stars and Stripes Forever.

> Aryans, Jews, Italians are not races. Aryans are people who speak Indo-European, 'Aryan' languages. . . . As Hitler uses it, the term has no meaning, racial, linguistic or otherwise. . . . Jews are people who practice the Jewish religion. They are of all races, Negro and Mongolian. European Jews are of many different biological types; physically they resemble the populations among whom they live.

> Ruth Benedict and Gene Wiltfish

> Benedict (1887–1948) and Wiltfish (1902–1980) were American anthropologists. Benedict's biography was written by Margaret Mead.

The Israeli Supreme Court ruled in the mid-1960s that Judaism is a religion and not a race. Suggesting that someone looks or acts Jewish implicates the practice of a religion and not membership in a race. There are Jews of every nationality, race, and ethnic group because a Jew practices a particular religion, which varies enormously among Jewish sects. The human race is a single species with common characteristics distinguished only by a shading of individual traits. Tom says he's unique too.

> To me an ethnologist who speaks of Aryan race, Aryan blood, Aryan eyes and hair, is as great a sinner as a linguist who speaks of a dolichocephalic dictionary or a brachycephalic grammar.

> Max Muller

Muller was an English philologist and philosopher whose greatest achievement was the editing of *Sacred Books of the East*, a fifty-one volume collection that stimulated wide interest in linguistics, mythology, and religion.

Sin can only be defined in terms of a particular religion. Attributing individual characteristics based on race, religion, or nationality is racist. We differ only according to our morality and beliefs but are substantially identical in desires, fears, and aspirations, for such as the basic luxuries of life. We're identical in our need for others' respect, protection of privacy, and safety from harm in our person and property. Tom nods numbly.

Purity of race does not exist. Europe is a continent of energetic mongrels.

H. A. L. Fisher

While a member of the British Parliament, Fisher was responsible for a 1918 law requiring school attendance until age fourteen.

Purity of race is meaningless, an oxymoron without substance. We're all more or less energetic mongrels, whether residing in Europe or elsewhere. Because race can't be quantified, it can neither be pure nor impure. There's no such thing as race because "race" has no objective meaning; there is only racism. Tom says quite so.

Truths for a new day:
1. The oneness of mankind.
2. The foundation of all religion is one.
3. Religion must be in accord with science and reason.

Baha'u'llah

Baha'u'llah founded the Baha'i
faith, which advocates the union of
all religions, rejects ritual, and
seeks the abolition of race, class,
and religious prejudice.

Our species is a single entity. Artificial divisions detracting
from our oneness have been enormously destructive, vividly
illustrated by nationalist and religious wars, elements of all war. The
foundation of religion is one: superstition based on our fear of death
and ritualistic hope for a better world. Religion can't exist in accord
with science and reason, because religion is based solely on faith
with no factual foundation or analytic anchor. Religion is based on
fear of the inevitable, a hypnotic search to engineer an escape from
reality similar to any recreational drug or entertainment. Tom says,
come, come.

We decree and order that
from now on, and for all time,
Christians shall not eat or drink
with Jews, nor admit them to
feasts, nor cohabit with them, nor
bathe with them. . . . Christians
shall not allow Jews to hold civil
honors over Christians, or to
exercise public offices in the state.

Pope Eugenius IV

The Greek and Roman Churches
were briefly reunited under
Eugenius IV, thanks to the Plague,
which decimated a rival faction in
Basel.

The keystone of most religion is intolerance toward other
religions. Acceptance of other religions is destructive to any
religion, undermining its authority and infallibility. Religion
presumes its infallibility, though few religions other than Roman
Catholics have formally announced it. Any religion other than our
own is heretical, because it presents another god in the presence of

317

the one true god, acting, for example, in violation of the First Christian Commandment. The largest Christian sect, Roman Catholicism, refused to recognize Israel's existence until 1994. The cut-throat competition between Christians and Jews (anti-Semitism is a history of Christianity), mostly Christians cutting Jewish throats, has continued since the Dark Ages. The Middle East cauldron boils with the unending feud between Muslims and Jews, while Christians and Muslims act no better toward each other. The Jews, because of a tight-knit community, ancient customs, and economic success achieved through hard work, have been a natural target for their generally less educated and less economically successful religious rivals, mostly Christian and Muslim. Attitudes denigrating other races, religions, and nationalities are racism per se. Attitudes are us.

> The Jews are the most miserable people on earth. They are plagued everywhere, and scattered about all countries, having no certain resting place. They sit as on a wheelbarrow, without a country, people or government . . . but they are rightly served, for seeing they refused to have Christ and his gospel, instead of freedom they must have servitude.
>
> Martin Luther

> Luther claimed to be anti-philosophical, calling himself the barbarian from the north, while sounding like Adolf Hitler.

Christians and Muslims have plagued the Jews, insuring their suffering as the most miserable people on earth. Besides envy, Christians persecute Jews (as did Hitler on a Christian pretext) because Jews refuse to recognize the one true god, the Christian god, which the Christians adopted from the Jews. Religious cruelty toward individuals believing in other religions is indistinguishable from evil and is mind-boggling stupidity; I trust I didn't soften that too much. No religion has a monopoly on morality, or any morality

318

at all in dealings with and attitudes toward other religions, or even sects within the same religion. Tom says salvation is available through any religion or no religion at all, throwing me a shriveled carrot.

> Christ cannot possibly have been a Jew. I don't have to prove that scientifically. It is a fact.
>
> Paul Joseph Goebbels

> The Nazi propaganda minister learned his anti-Semitism late. His favorite high school teachers were Jews, and he was engaged to a girl who was half-Jewish—whatever that means, since Judaism, as defined by the Israeli Supreme Court, is a religion.

Denial of the achievements of "others" is used by bigots, racists, and those who believe that one religion, nationality, or ethnic group is superior to every other, an assembly that likely includes almost everyone on the planet. An individual may be morally or intellectually superior to another individual, but groups are a no-show in the superiority sweepstakes. Only individuals have clearly identifiable and quantifiable characteristics; religious, national, and ethnic groups do not and cannot, because they're composed of individuals infinitely variable by honesty, ability, and other characteristics. Tom says some groups are quantifiably better than others because the ideals of some groups are superior to others.

> Such is the debt which Christianity owes to Judaism! Not Jesus merely, not the Bible, the Church and the Sunday, but the whole substance of Christian teaching! . . . We find here an explanation at least, and a very important one, of why the Christians dislike and persecute the Jews. They hate them and would get rid of them because they

are heavily indebted to them. This
is a very simple law of
psychology.

John Haynes Holmes

Holmes helped found the NAACP
in 1909 and the ACLU in 1920 and
served as the chairman of the
ACLU board of directors from
1939 to 1949. He idolized Gandhi.

Christians have no reason to feel indebted to Jews, because
Jews claim no credit for Christianity, likely feeling condemnation
more fitting than credit. Christians dislike the Jews for the same
reasons they resent those who believe that any religion other than
Christianity is the one true religion, a simple law of psychology.
Those believing in another god challenge the one true god's power
and authority to provide immortality, thus threatening believers in
the true god with death and loss of immortality. Few threats could
be more serious. We dislike, hate, resent, and wish to destroy those
who threaten us with death or loss of immortality even though they
have never intentionally made such a threat. The threat is inherent
in the fact that two true gods can't coexist. Hating those who
threaten us with death is a simple law of psychology. Tom says
maybe so.

Racialism is a universal,
anti-Semitism an exclusively
Christian disease.

R. H. S. Crossman

Crossman served in Parliament
beginning in 1945 and became the
leader of the House of Commons
in 1966.

Anti-Semitism is equally a fundamental disease of Islam.
Still, the Jews have suffered more from official Christian sanction
than from any other source. The Jews were tolerated by most
Muslims until the twentieth century. The fundamentalists of any
religion are intolerant bigots. Racialism, in the sense of racism,

nationalism, and religion, is universal. Probably 99-plus percent of the world's population believes that their particular religion, nationality, and ethnic group are superior to all others. The world is almost universally racist. Tom says sadly yes, refusing to exclude either of us.

> Through Christ and in Christ we are the spiritual descendants of Abraham. No, it is not possible for Christians to participate in anti-Semitism.
>
> Pope Pius XI
>
> Pius XI was a learned humanist who established the Vatican as a separate state.

It shouldn't be possible for Christians to participate in anti-Semitism, but the overwhelming majority do so, consciously or unconsciously. Unconscious anti-Semitism infects most non-Jews, because it's cultural. My closest friend in law school was an Orthodox Jew. We studied together, went back and forth from classes together, and were as close as those from two different cultures can be. However, I once used the phrase "Jew them down" in his company, unthinking, it being something I'd heard in my non-Jewish environment (rural Colorado) since childhood. My friend was pole-axed, and I can't blame him. Though this happened in 1968, I've felt badly about it ever since, knowing that I harbor the unconscious cultural biases that I condemn. Tom says heavy.

> I love humanity but I hate people.
>
> Edna St. Vincent Millay,
> *Aria da Capo*
>
> A poem Millay published at age twenty procured her a benefactor who paid her way through Vassar.

The species may be more lovable than the individual because we can't help seeing the species, "us," in a relatively positive light, though we know with assurance that every individual has character defects. The species has its own defects, principally the almost universal tendency to believe in superstition and religion, now about 84 percent; the tendency to nationalism and the 100 percent belief that one's nation is superior to all others; and a majority belief that one's ethnic group is superior to all others. Tom says one point for me.

> For the biologist there are no classes—only individuals.
>
> Jean Rostand
>
> This noted French biologist, moralist, and writer was never as famous as his father who, among other things, wrote *Cyrano de Bergerac.*

Any generalization characterizing individuals as a group is inherently irresponsible, because individuals can't accurately be lumped together. No accurate classes exist for the individual, whether stodgy accountant, uneducated janitor, or brilliant CEO. General classifications are always erroneous stereotypes, perhaps including this one. The characteristics of a single individual are too numerous to allow the proper grouping of one with another, except based on generalities of race, religion, and nationality. It may be accurate to say that A and B are criminals because they have violently harmed others without justification, but it is never accurate to say that because individuals A and B belong to a particular religion, nationality, or ethnic group that they are criminals, lazy, or deserving of approbation or congratulations. Tom says I'm an impractical idealist because stereotypes are necessary to deal with people in general. Tom didn't really say that.

> I have a dream that my four little children will one day live in a nation when they will not be judged by the color of their skin, but by the content of their character.
>
> Martin Luther King, Jr.

King's famous speech was given
at the largest peaceful
demonstration in U.S. history and
led to the passage of the 1964 Civil
Rights Act.

No individual can be accurately judged by the color of his or
her skin, racial or ethnic antecedents, religion, or nationality.
Because these are unrelated to character, they're unimportant for
any purpose other than curiosity and granfalloons. All ideas of
racial, ethnic, religious, and national superiority are substanceless
and racist. The only valid means for judging the integrity and
morality of the individual is based on actions only and never on
race, ethnicity, religion, or nationality. Tom says correct, not just
politically but ethically.

The difference of race is
one of the reasons why I fear that
war will always exist; because
race implies differences,
difference implies superiority, and
superiority leads to predominance.

Benjamin Disraeli

The most fortuitous event in
Disraeli's young life was his
father's quarrel with the family
rabbi, resulting in the children's
baptism as Christians, opening up
the possibility of a political career
for Disraeli.

Race and ethnicity, religion, and nationality, not only imply
differences but cause and mandate differences, demanding
superiority and dominance. Because all groups, whether religious,
ethnic, or national, believe their group is superior to all others, they
likewise consciously or unconsciously believe that they deserve to
control and rule these inferior others. The result is conflict, war, and
unending slaughter of the species by the species for no rational
reason. War will exist as long as differing religions, ethnic groups,
and nationalities exist. Until we're considered one species without
distinctions based on nationality, religion, and race, war will out.

Members of a religion believing in an unseeable, never seen, intangible, incomprehensible, and unknowable god have scant reason to believe themselves superior to others who believe in a different never seen, unseeable, intangible, incomprehensible, and unknowable god. The only rational reason for war, though obviously unjustifiable, is to covet and to take something of value owned by another nation, such as land or natural resources. Plain greed is understandable; superstition and racism are not similarly rational. Tom says they're all irrational.   But Tom, does that include the invisible-friend part?

> A new peace will make Germany master of the globe, a peace not hanging on the palm fronds of pacifist womenfolk, but established by the victorious sword of a master-race that takes over the world.

> Alfred Rosenberg

> Rosenberg helped form the Nazi party in 1919, along with Hitler, Hess, and Rohm; recruited Quisling; and ordered the removal of French artwork to Germany.

Nationalism, tinged with a weird bit of racism based on an Aryan or German race, justified two world wars in less than thirty years. Whether based on ethnicity, nationality, or religion, the main reasons for war are racist. Rosenberg is a racist the same as anyone espousing the superiority of a particular religion, nationality, or ethnic group. Such racism implicates approximately 100 percent of us. Most, if not all, feel superior to beggars in India, among an almost endless list of those we feel superior to. Tom asks what follows from that? We should fix it, which can only be accomplished by erasing the boundaries among all groups. Tom says radical, and definitely anti-organized religion.

> Race hatred is the cheapest and basest of all national passions, and it is the nature of hatred, as it is the nature of love, to change us

into the likeness of that which we contemplate. We grow nobly like what we adore, and ignobly like what we hate. . . . All hatreds long persisted in bringing us to every baseness for which we hated others.

George W. Russell

Russell attended the Dublin Metropolitan School of Art, where he befriended W.B. Yeats.

Race hatred is no cheaper or baser than hatred based on religion or nationalism. The hatred of others is a transparent attempt to hoist esteem by our own petard. We deem others inferior, magically making us superior beings. We despise similar attitudes in others, considering them silly and slanderous. The Japanese, Mexicans, Argentinians, and every other nationality consider themselves superior to those living elsewhere. The basis for this sincere belief is firmly grounded in culture, religion, and folklore. Folks in poorer countries believe themselves superior to the rich countries because of their emphasis on family, tradition, and founding heroes. When we believe that our religion or ethnic group is superior, as we almost all do, we declare others inferior. This is racism per se, the cheapest and basest of all human passions. Tom says amen.

Bigotry has no head and cannot think, no heart and cannot feel. When she moves it is in wrath; when she pauses it is amid ruin. Her prayers are curses, her god is a demon, her communion is death, her vengeance is eternity, her decalogue written in the blood of her victims, and if she stops for a moment in her infernal flight it is upon a kindred rock to whet her vulture fang for a more sanguinary desolation.

Daniel O'Connell

> O'Connell was called the
> Liberator and was the first of the
> great nineteenth-century Irish
> leaders admitted to the British
> House of Commons.

In the early 1990s, the American Jewish Committee, to determine general attitudes toward "others," sponsored a survey of U.S. attitudes toward various ethnic groups, including a fictitious group of *Wisians*. Forty percent of those interviewed rated Wisians unfavorably, only 4.12 on a scale of 9.0, placing them below Greeks, white Southern Africans, and Koreans but above Guatemalans, Iranians, and Gypsies. We naturally believe that others, no matter the basis for their otherness, are inferior and that we are superior, no matter our ethnic, religious, or nationalistic mix. We're a hopelessly bigoted species. The only means of overcoming our bigotry is to remove its causes, which would require the disidentification of any group based on religion, nationality, or ethnic origin. Tom says good luck but seems to lack sincerity.

> Until you have become
> really, in actual fact, as brother to
> everyone, brotherhood will not
> come to pass.
>
> Fyodor Dostoyevsky, *The
> Brothers Karamazov*

> Dostoyevsky was a person who
> would be difficult to claim as a
> brother: short, small gray eyes,
> sickly complexion, nervously
> twitching lips, awkward in social
> settings, compulsive gambler to
> the point of losing the clothes off
> his back, epileptic seizures and
> poverty; perhaps redeemed when
> Stalin called his writing trash.

Bigotry is as inseparable from religious and national affiliation as from race and ethnic groupings. Championing a particular religion, nationality, race, or ethnic group is bigoted in comparison with championing the species. Bigotry unthinkingly or with malice tags outsiders as inferior. Religious bigotry is exemplified by words such as *heathen, blasphemy, devil, infidel, anti-Christ,* and *heretic.* Religious prayers may design death for the disbeliever, eternal hellfire, and blood to avenge *spiritual* wrongs. Nothing is more ephemeral than a spiritual wrong. Nationalistic bigotry is epitomized by words such as *frog, wop, patriotism, Jap,* and *Jew boy,* which often double as racial bigotry with its more vehement labels. Such labels are spawned by wars and hatreds epitomizing the closed circles for which religion, nationalism, and racism are liable. Tom says religion shouldn't be thrown out with the bath. How about organized religion and what exactly is the difference? Few of us feel brotherhood toward our actual brothers, much less toward stereotypical others or those considered enemies because of their nationality, religion, or ethnicity. Until nationality, religion, and race are obliterated from our memories and replaced by the concept of a single species, brotherhood is impossible. Tom says brotherhood is a good idea but hasn't a glimmer how to make it happen except through religion, converting all those misguided ones.

> It's silly to go on pretending
> that under the skin we are all
> brothers. The truth is more likely
> that under the skin we are all
> cannibals, assassins, traitors, liars,
> hypocrites, poltroons.

> Henry Miller

> Miller was a perpetual bohemian
> whose sexual candor had a
> liberating effect on the twentieth
> century.

Under the skin we're patriots, believing our citizens superior to each and every one of those residing outside our borders; we're religious, believing members of other religions inferior and near devils, especially the nonreligious; we're racist, believing members of other ethnic groups are inferior beings. We can't pretend that we're brothers and members of a single species as long as nationalism, religion, and similar racist ideals demand unswerving allegiance. These have no relationship to ethics and are instead the essence of evil. Tom shudders at something.

War and Poverty

> Morality,   thou
>   deadly bane,
> Thy tens o'thousands
>   thou hast slain.

> Robert Burns

> Burns's father worked himself to
> death as a farmhand, dying worn
> out and bankrupt in 1784, making
> Burns a lifelong rebel, perpetually
> satirizing religion and politics as
> inhumane.

Morality slays no one unless in self-defense. But religion, the theoretical beacon of morality, has slaughtered millions of innocent others and plunged billions into poverty. Religion's twofold claim to reverence is its connection with ethics, demanding the triumph of good over evil, and for Westerners, its unverifiable promise of immortality. The Ten Commandments contain four ethical admonitions observed in every part of the world, no matter the dominant religion, two prohibitions against mind crimes, and four commands that have contributed to wars and conflicts since they were written down, including allowing no other gods and slaying those who believe in other gods. Instead of morality, religion seems more intimately connected with war and poverty. Whenever war begins, religion attends with trumpets on both sides. Religion should be clearly distinguished from morality and ethics. Tom says not.

> The   Bible   nowhere
> prohibits   war.   In   the   Old
> Testament we find war and even
> conquest positively commanded,
> and although war was raging in the
> world in the time of Christ and his
> Apostles, still they said not a word
> of   its   unlawfulness   and

immorality.

Henry Wager Halleck

Halleck's 1846 book on military
strategy became the Union
handbook for conduct of the Civil
War; Halleck also helped write the
California Constitution.

The Old Testament dictates somewhere down its list of commandments that thou shalt not kill, and studiously ignores it. No religion, with the exception of a few small sects, literally believes that thou shalt not kill or prohibits participation in war. If all religions prohibited participation in war there might be no more wars, except a war on religion by government. But only then would religion establish a legitimate connection with morality. Tom says we could work toward that.

What characterizes the
Cannibals is that most of them are
born Christians, think of Jesus as
Love, and get an erection from the
thought of whippings, blood,
burning crosses, burning bodies,
and screams in mass graves.
Whereas their counterpart, the
Christians—the ones who are not
Christian but whom we choose to
call Christians—are utterly
opposed to the destruction of
human life and succeed within
themselves in starting all the wars
of our own time.

Norman Mailer

Mailer's first novel elevated him
as a great literary light, but then he
wrote mostly of marginal social
types in a controversial belligerent
and egotistical manner that
antagonized many, including

330

Tom.

Adults should be able to watch out for themselves, but the principle sufferers in war continue to be children. The U.N. Children's Fund counted 149 major wars from 1945 to 1992, a mere forty-seven years. During the last ten years of the period, war killed 2 million children, disabled over 4 million, and left 12 million homeless with millions more orphaned and traumatized. Children are conscripted into military service during war, maimed by land mines and starved; girls are subject to random sexual assault. This is the legacy of war primarily instigated by governments with the enthusiastic support of religion and patriotic hatreds.

> Men never do evil so completely and cheerfully as when they do it from religious conviction.
>
> Blaise Pascal

> Pascal passionately believed in Christianity until he died of a brain hemorrhage at age thirty-nine.

The vast majority of Western civilization calls itself Christian. The rest are Jews, Muslims, the nonreligious, and a smattering of others. Few Christians are cannibals, though most fit the Mailer definition of Christian, being utterly opposed to the destruction of human life but enthusiastic aficionados of any government-decreed war. Most wars, including the Cold War, now revived, have pitted Christians against Christians. Instead of declaring war on Jews, Christians declared open season, urging their destruction until about 1950, when the enormity of the Holocaust finally began to sink into Christian consciousness. The Roman Catholic Church took another forty-four years to grant diplomatic recognition to Israel. Tom says there were political reasons.

> Religion has always sanctified violence and transformed it into a right. It has whisked away humanity, justice and fraternity into a fictitious

heaven, so as to leave room on earth for the reign of iniquity and brutality. It has blessed successful brigands, and, in order to increase their fortune even further, has preached obedience and resignation to their innumerable victims, the people.

Mikhail A. Bakunin

Bakunin practiced anarchism, going AWOL from his Saint Petersburg artillery unit on the Polish frontier and resigning his commission. He barely escaped arrest for desertion.

Religious fervor and belief justify literally anything. When religion says jump and the stakes are as high as eternal life, most everyone jumps as high as the obscene evil of war. If the religious refused to go to war, there'd be no more war. But Christians know that the adherents of other religions have no more scruples about war than Christians, so we cheerfully hug war and its associated evils. Tom says he's not for war, but I remember his stance on the Gulf War and Panama and Nicaragua.

We are always making God our accomplice, that we may legalize our own inequities. Every successful massacre is consecrated by a Te Deum, and the clergy have never been wanting benedictions for any victorious enormity.

Henri-Frédéric Amiel

This nineteenth-century Swiss philosopher was a master of self-analysis in his surviving letters and the personal journal that elevated him to posthumous fame.

332

Our wars are increasingly within a single country, yet religion supports all factions, urging its members to enroll for patriotic slaughter, most recently in Syria. The ultimate religious morality is wartime obedience. Might is right when government and religion say so, overruling individual conscience. The peace sign is the sign of the chicken. Pacifists and humanists, who believe murder is evil under all circumstances except pure self-defense, are painted as evil by the democratic majority of religious patriots. War diminishes us, literally and ethically, endorsing infinite savagery in the name of the father, son, holy ghost, god, Gabriel, Allah, and almighty government. War slaughters the sons and daughters of sheep, who, if they survive, willingly offer their surviving offspring in the next war, always sanctioned and supported by religion. Tom says I'm cynical. Cynicism often reflects reality.

The clergy dispense benedictions for any anticipated war, whether ultimately victorious or suicidal, in self-defense or aggressive. Massacres are venerated by religion. Mass murder is irrelevant, because religion kowtows to government for tax breaks and to line its coffers without fear of being charged with consumer fraud. The god on both sides of any war solemnly sanctifies the murderous instincts of loyalist troops, though the contending parties often worship the same theoretical god, often Christian. Tom says the emperor has no clothes.

> The Master said, One who is by nature daring and is suffering from poverty will not long be lawful. Indeed, any man, save those that are truly Good, if their sufferings are very great, will be likely to rebel.
>
> Confucius
>
> Confucius's parents are believed to have been impoverished nobility who died when Confucius was very young, leaving him to grow up in worse poverty.

Some of the poor, not illogically (though immorally), borrow from richer neighbors whose abundance may stagger the mind. Even were they summarily executed for such acts, when men have no alternative for their survival, then theft occurs. Violent and property crimes will endure as long as poverty is encouraged by religion. We should all have the right to revolt against that which forecloses the opportunity for survival with the blame often traceable to greed, government, and religion. Few of the poor revolt or commit property crimes or crimes of violence, notwithstanding their desperate straits. Most poor act lawfully, perhaps because they know all legal systems have a built-in bias against those who can't afford lawyers. Confucius should have concluded that most of the poor are good because few use their economic status to justify property crimes or crimes of violence. Tom says the bad ones have no excuse for crimes of property or violence. I say amen, except to survive, when it is simple self-defense.

Religious bans on birth control may have fooled much of the planet into poverty. Though extreme poverty has halved in the last twenty years, poverty blankets much of Africa and Southern Asia, plus chunks of Central and South America, with children the most affected. Such poverty is irremediable until organized religions (together with society and government) advocate for birth control and sex education. Because birth control is anathema to the growth of religion, we may be doomed to perpetual and irremediable mass poverty. Tom says poverty is caused by lack of personal initiative and not by religious proscriptions against birth control. Of course, it doesn't help that in 2018, twenty-six billionaires owned the same amount of wealth as half of the world's population, 3.7 billion people.

The Basics of Morality

This chapter examines our ideals of morality, comparing the views of the sages of the species with religious tradition and analyzing their efficacy as compared to the Golden Rule and the Ten Commandments.

> Of all the systems of morality, ancient or modern, which have come under my observation, none appears to me so pure as that of Jesus.

Jefferson was a deist but was against organized religion.

The teachings of those seized upon as the founders of a religion are largely ignored by the resulting religion. Few if any Christians give all they own to the poor, though a rich man can no more enter the kingdom of heaven than pass through the eye of a needle. Most Christians aspire more to abundant riches than abject poverty, and who can blame them? Few Christians forsake their wives and loved ones to serve the Christian god though explicitly commanded to do so by Jesus, a singularly irrational directive. The morality of Jesus includes the Golden Rule, postulated by many philosophers before his time, with several quoted below. The teachings of Jesus, similar to those of other ethical philosophers, contain a mix of good and ridiculous advice, some ethical and some self-destructive. Tom says the teachings of Jesus are ethical but difficult for flawed humans to obey.

> That the saints may enjoy their beatitude and the grace of God more abundantly, they are permitted to see the punishment of the damned in Hell.

Thomas Aquinas

Aquinas is a classic example of

335

childhood indoctrination: He lived
in a Benedictine abbey from age
five through fourteen.

If the fires of hell are mythical, then dead saints will miss nothing, assuming their resurrection, which seems somewhat less than a Jeffersonian possibility. However, if religion is correct that an afterlife exists, then the Aquinas revelation trashes religious ethics. Roman Catholicism has generally abandoned ideas of hell, instead concluding that most everyone goes to heaven. Tom says even I have a chance, though understandably remote.

The sight of hell-torments
will exalt the happiness of the
saints forever.

Jonathan Edwards

Edwards, a colonial American
Calvinist, was home-taught by
religious parents until age thirteen,
when he entered Yale, graduating
at age seventeen. Best known for
his involvement in the Great
Awakening religious revival, he
became the president of Princeton
shortly before his death.

Saints made happy by the hell-torment of their brethren rank with Hitler, Caligula, and Stalin. Sixteenth-century religious belief personified evil as surely as fundamentalists do now, perhaps including religions that bar birth control and sanction war, which is almost all of them. Tom says religion should do neither but doubts the pope is listening.

Do not that to thy neighbor
that thou wouldst not suffer from
him.

Pittacus of Lesbos

Also known as Pittacus of
Mytilene, he was one of the seven

wise men of Greece, helped
overthrow the tyrant Melanchrus,
and single-handedly slew the
Athenian commander, Phrynon.

The Golden Rule and most other Christian dogma originated
long before Christianity. The Pittacus version is arguably superior
to the traditional Golden Rule, which promotes brown-nosing in the
hope of similar treatment by others. Refusing to harm the neighbors,
and even nonneighbors, is superior to optimistic brown-nosing, in
terms of both individual dignity and expenditure of energy. Less
energy is required to refrain from harming others than to beg their
positive treatment. Taking an extreme case, the Golden or Pittacus
Rule would pair masochists with sadists, and require those enjoying
the bite of the horsewhip to inflict it on others. Refusing to harm
others, implied by the Pittacus rule, avoids the absurd and
establishes a crystal-clear guide for ethical behavior. Do as you
please as long as you don't harm others. Many will be pleased to
help others and many won't. Helping others implicates a higher
level of ethics than a foundational ethical rule prohibiting harm to
others. Once an ethical foundation is universally recognized and
established, higher ethics would hopefully follow if we never had
to worry about war or harm from others. Tom says he's still aiming
for the Golden Rule, and if we all did, we might hit my lesser
standard.

When asked how men
might live most virtuously and
most justly, he said, 'If we never
do ourselves what we blame in
others.'

Thales of Miletus

Thales—Semitic founder of Greek
sciences—and his philosophy
were reproached for impracticality
because he was poor; but he
noticed that the weather indicated
an excellent olive crop, so he
cornered the market in olive
presses, made a fortune, and
illustrated the value of common

337

sense.

We couldn't comfortably exist if we never did what we blame in others. We delight in publishing the foibles of others that we can't see in ourselves. Who has never cussed out the driver who made the same stupid move we made yesterday and will make tomorrow? No individual has perfectly objective judgment. By definition, judgment is subjective. We blame others for our own weaknesses while unable to recognize them in ourselves. The Thales of Miletus rule would pry scales from our eyes and require a perfection unlikely on this planet. Tom says spirituality works equally well.

> Tsze-kung asked, saying, 'Is there one word which may serve as a rule of practice for all one's life?' The Master said, 'Is not Reciprocity such a word? What you do not want done to yourself, do not do to others.'
>
> Confucius
>
> Confucius is unknown in China because the word is a European bastardization of his true name, K' ung-tzu.

Reciprocity is the equivalent of doing to others as you would have them do to you, or negatively stated, not doing to others what you don't want them to do to you. The negative formulation is superior by forbidding harm to others, except the suicidal. Confucius also urged repaying kindness with kindness and evil with justice, or an eye for an eye. Many of us prefer to do unto others first, a defensive posture similar to whoever has the gold makes the rules. The golden rule, without provision for self-defense, makes us patsies or sitting ducks. A negative formulation focuses on the actor, excluding analysis of how to respond to actions by others. Adding self-defense to either rule makes a relatively complete ethical system. Treat others as you want to be treated, but tolerate no harm by others. Don't do things you'd not like done to yourself, parrying tit for tat. In other words, harm no one else in their person or property, except in self-defense, which constitutes full reciprocity. Tom says that doesn't sound very spiritual.

God considered not action,
but the spirit of the action. It is the
intention, not the deed, wherein
the merit or praise of the doer
consists.

Peter Abelard

Abelard's doomed love affair with
Heloise overshadowed his writing,
which criticized church teachings
and the monastic life.

The idea that an enigmatic god could clearly communicate
ethical standards seems senseless. Furthermore, intention isn't the
ultimate litmus test whether an action is moral. Negligence and
recklessness are similarly blameworthy, though less culpable.
Intention is important for determining fault and punishment. The
differences between intentional, reckless, and negligent acts mirror
distinctions between first-degree murder, reckless homicide, and
manslaughter. The spirit of the action is irrelevant to the culpability
of klutzes and adolescent morons. Tom says that's a technicality
unrelated to Abelard's point.

See skulking Truth to
her old cavern
fled,
Mountains of
casuistry heap'd
o'er her head!
Philosophy, that
lean'd on Heaven
before,
Shrinks to her second
cause, and is no
more.
Physic or metaphysic
begs defense,
and Metaphysic calls
for aid on Sense!
See Mystery to
Mathematics fly!
In vain! they gaze,

turn giddy, rave,
and die.
Religion,   blushing,
veils her sacred
fires,
and   unawares
Morality expires.

Alexander Pope

Many of Pope's famous quotables,
such as "A little learning is a
dang'rous thing," "To err is
human, to forgive, divine," and
"For fools rush in where angels
fear to tread" are traceable to
sources in Horace, Quintilian, and
Boileau.

Religion destroys morality by crippling truth, philosophy,
and metaphysics, though after Galileo, it can do little with
mathematics or physics. Religion's sacrilege lies in its love-hate
relationship with morality. Religion claims the core of morality,
insisting that without religion morality couldn't exist. Without
religion, morality would prosper. Religion divides us into
permanently contending camps, pitting us against ourselves as if our
eternal lives depended on it. Those outside our religion are against
us. We believe they're either damned or should be. By alienating
the species against ourselves, religion defames knowledge and
corrodes truth. Truth resides in philosophy, metaphysics, physics,
and mathematics, having little relationship to religion, and religion
having small connection with ethics. Tom says that organized
religion is different from religion and he wishes I wouldn't use the
terms interchangeably, that one is spiritual and the other is
bureaucratic. Yes, but they're inextricably intertwined, and there
isn't a single spiritual televangelist, in the sense of anti-
materialistic.

Christianity has waged a
deadly war against the higher type
of man. It has put a ban on all his
fundamental instincts. It has
distilled evil out of these instincts.

340

It makes the strong and efficient
man its typical outcast man. It has
taken the part of the weak and the
low; it has made an ideal out of its
antagonism to the very instincts
which tend to preserve life and
well-being. . . . It has taught men
to regard their highest impulses as
sinful—as temptations.

Friedrich Nietzsche

Schopenhauer   convinced
Nietzsche that life is aimless
suffering and pain.

Instead of taking the part of the weak and low, religion built
fabulous cathedrals and ageless monuments on the backs of the
poor. The higher type of individual has ignored religion throughout
history, except in public, where society demands political
genuflection to religion. Our higher types push the species forward,
making it more efficient, safer, and happier. Toward these ends we
refined the practice of medicine, while religion relied on prayer. We
require strict sanitation, while religion in the Middle Ages prayed
to stem the plague, relegating Jewish doctors to ghettos. Religion
retards us, making us less efficient and more susceptible to
unwanted births, insuring conflicts with those from other religions
and nationalities. Religion develops our fundamental instinct that a
particular religion, ethnic group, and nationality is superior to all
others, coincidentally our own. Our *we* is always superior to their
they. Tom says of course.

He who hates vice, hates
mankind.

Pliny the Younger

Pliny the Younger started out as a
prosecutor, convicting Roman
officials in Africa and Spain of
extortion.

We're a mix of good and evil. The good abounds in most

341

individuals while corruption dominates groups that pit us against ourselves. He who hates vice, hates groups and loves most individuals. Tom says pseudo-slick.

> Nothing will be changed if God does not exist; we will rediscover the same norms of honesty, progress and humanity.
>
> Jean-Paul Sartre

> Sartre's childhood was greatly influenced by the library of his grandfather, Charles Schweitzer (uncle of Albert Schweitzer); his resulting philosophy consisted largely in clarifying the thought of philosophers such as Heidegger and Marx.

The history of the species will likely be unaffected by whether a god exists or religion survives. Without organized religion, honesty, progress, and humanity might spurt forward. We swear that our god exists, that others' gods don't exist, and that those believing in other gods are subhuman compared to us, brandishing bayonets to prove the point. The educated are essentially nonreligious and responsible for our progress. The ethical byline of organized religion is believe, or die and fry. Religion is unrelated to honesty, progress, and humanity, instead rife with dishonesty and superstition, myth and stagnation, internecine war and the perpetuation of poverty in a religious numbers game. Tom says nastily put and quite unspiritual.

> From a psychological point of view, 'Sins' are indispensable in any society organized by priests; they are the actual levers of power, the priest lives on sins, he needs the 'commission of sins.'
>
> Friedrich Nietzsche

Nietzsche studied to be a minister

but in doing so lost his faith.

Though plumbers would be unemployed if plumbing problems vanished, they don't make up arbitrary rules for what clogs pipes. Sin has no particular relationship to ethics, constituting any act decreed as such by religious leaders who interpret otherwise silent and invisible gods. Gobbling pork, bothering cattle, importing rice, masturbating, failing to fondle beads, or forgetting to tithe to support a religious bureaucracy are sins in various religions though completely unrelated to ethics. Without silly sins, religion might languish and morality enjoy a rebirth. Tom says poignant with symbolism.

> Pleasure's a sin, and sometimes Sin's a pleasure.
>
> Lord Byron

Lord Byron fought against the
Ottoman Empire in the Greek war
of independence and is revered as
a national hero in Greece.

Pleasure is often a sin to religions of all hues. The greater the pleasure, the greater the sin, with pleasures related to sex the greatest sins of all, except for paying attention to other gods. The forbidden is particularly tasty, for adults as well as children. Because sin's an artificial religious construct, it may be particularly pleasurable to thumb one's nose at the establishment or the edicts of any bureaucratic, self-appointed, omnipotent, and all-knowing group. Tom admits some experience with such as that.

Another doctrine repugnant
to civil society, is that whatsoever
a man does against his conscience,
is sin; and it dependeth on the
presumption of making himself
judge of good and evil. For a
man's conscience and his
judgment are the same thing, and
as the judgment, so also the
conscience may be erroneous.

343

Thomas Hobbes

The chaos created by Cromwell's
civil war made Hobbes crave
peace and order, trusting
traditional government over the
individual.

Conscience operates erroneously in a few individuals and is
easily suppressed by many, including myself on sundry occasions.
Most of us do things we know are wrong, but it seemed a good idea
at the time, or we got by with it, or no one found out, or no one got
hurt, the last being the ultimate defense. Conscience is more likely
overinclusive of right action than underinclusive, because
conscience, for those who have one, inhibits. An act harming no one
else should never offend the conscience, except to the extent it
harms ourselves. Acts harming another individual in their person or
property should always offend the conscience and never occur
unless in self-defense. Sin is unrelated to ethics, except for those
things that hurt someone else, drawing the clearest distinction
between good and evil. Such an ethical dividing line is brightly lit.
Whether someone else might suffer physical or property harm is
fairly easy to determine and anticipate so that an act tending toward
such harm can be recognized early and avoided. Under these
circumstances, judgment should seldom be erroneous, leaving no
excuse for a guilty conscience. Only we can correctly distinguish
between good and evil. Groups are unequipped to make such
judgments before the fact, except in the most general terms. Without
individual conscience, society would have no means of formulating
a sense of ethics. Tom says religion wrote it down first, and that's
where conscience comes from.

The greatest burden in the
world is superstition, not only of
ceremonies in the church but of
imaginary and scarecrow sins at
home.

John Milton

Milton visited Galileo in his
Italian semi-captivity and as a
result wrote the poem

344

Areopagitica, extolling science;
Milton was a staunch anti-
Catholic Protestant.

After poverty, the greatest burden is superstition, illustrated
by religious outlawing of birth control (nowhere mentioned in the
Bible or the Koran or in any other holy book), the prohibition of
which creates and perpetuates wholesale poverty, and the pitting of
us against ourselves. Not only church ceremonies but the church
itself and all organized religion are founded on superstition, defined
in one dictionary as "excessively credulous belief in and reverence
for supernatural beings."

Sins that harm no one else are superstitious and unrelated to
ethics, though often personally unhealthy. Tom says he wasn't sure
I'd concede the latter.

Sin consists in doing wrong
when we know we can do better,
and it will be punished with a just
retribution, in the due time of the
Lord.

Brigham Young

Brigham Young was president of
the LDS Church, the Mormons,
from 1847 until his death in 1877;
he founded Salt Lake City, served
as the first governor of the Utah
Territory, and had fifty-five wives.
Scary.

Though reaching our highest potential may be a preeminent
goal, it's not a sin to do less when we know we can. Perhaps it's
unethical, in the highest moral sense (far above basic ethics
prohibiting harm to others), to fall short of our intellectual, fiscal,
or social potential, but eternal hell or similar retribution seems an
overly severe punishment for a failure that we all suffer to some
degree. Eternal hellfire overpunishes laziness, occasional laziness,
vacations, and naps. Max Weber called our highest-potential mind-
set the Protestant Ethic, the foundation of American capitalism.
Achievement often requires the sacrifice of family and friends.
Whether it's unethical or sinful to achieve little or nothing when one

has a greater potential is a question far beyond the scope of simple ethics. Whether the adult has a right to waste his or her life must ultimately be left to the individual. Christian dogma properly concludes that we reap what we sow; failing to reach our potential means we can't reap when we don't sow. Sacrificing family and friends to reach our highest personal potential may be sufficient punishment by itself, god or no god. Time is meaningless for gods and immortal individuals. Tom says snideness becomes me not.

> There is no sin except stupidity.
>
> Oscar Wilde

> Wilde was influenced by John Ruskin and Walter Pater, founders of the Aesthetic Movement (of which Wilde became the most famous member), to live life to the fullest.

If the only sin is stupidity, then we've all sinned grievously, though the only unethical act is harming someone else. Harm may be inflicted intentionally, recklessly, or negligently, and only the last is caused by stupidity or inattention. We place a high premium on intelligence, discouraging stupidity, whether natural or negligent. We have few qualms killing or eating animals because they're dumber than we are. The smarter or friendlier the animal the more qualms we have eating it. Stupidity may not be the only sin, but we often act as if it were. Tom says stupidity can't be a sin because it's innate.

> Christian morality (so-called) has all the characters of a reaction; . . . Its ideal is negative rather than positive; passive rather than active; Innocence rather than Nobleness; Abstinence from Evil, rather than energetic Pursuit of the Good. . . . It holds out the hope of heaven and the threat of hell, as the appointed and appropriate motives to a virtuous life, in this falling far

346

below the best of the ancients, and
doing what lies in it to give to
human morality an essentially
selfish character. . . . It is
essentially the doctrine of passive
obedience; it inculcates
submission to all authorities found
established.

John Stuart Mill

Mill was elected the rector of Saint
Andrews University in 1867, but
after a year he retired and moved
to France.

The purpose of the eternal alliance between religion and
government is to exact obedience from citizen congregations. Sheep
tithe and pay taxes, insuring the continued existence of their
shepherds and controllers. Religion bribes government by
demanding that its congregation give unto Caesar that which is
Caesar's, ensuring government protection of religion. The positive,
social, and charitable aspects of religion obscure its totalitarianism,
the limiting of charity to converts or potential converts, strict
forbiddance of birth control miring many in poverty, and supporting
whatever war any government deems yummy. Religion fails
miserably at abstaining from evil, in virtual lock-step with
government. Excluding fundamentalists, most religion has given up
the specter of hell while failing to pursue the good. Instead of
insisting that we refuse to harm others, religion coyly suggests
loving others when the refusal to harm them would be perfectly
sufficient and far easier to achieve. A first step toward religious
goodness would be the establishment of a commandment requiring
the tolerance of all other religions. Tom says good luck, pipe
dreamer.

Moral philosophy is
nothing else but the science of
what is good, and evil, in the
conversation, and society of
mankind. Good, and evil, are
names that signify our appetites,
and aversions; which in different

347

tempers, customs, and doctrines of
men, are different.

Thomas Hobbes

Born prematurely when his
mother was frightened by the
approaching Spanish Armada,
Hobbes grew up to be a timid man
afraid of the dark but a bold and
reckless author.

Good and evil aren't entirely relative terms dependent on
differing tempers, customs, and doctrines, though no less an
authority than Hobbes says so. Good and evil are absolute in the
basic requirement of ethical behavior, that no one else be harmed.
Except for this single inviolate ethical rule, good and evil are largely
dependent on the culture, tradition, and history of ethnic, national,
and religious groups. The only ethical rule, if there is to be at least
one, is that we refrain from harming each other, except in self-
defense. Tom says that's a minimum. Which I would gladly settle
for.

There is . . . only a single
categorical imperative and it is
this: Act only on that maxim
through which you can at the same
time will that it should become a
universal law!

Immanuel Kant

In 1792 the king of Prussia forbade
Kant to publish or teach about
religion, but the king died six
years later, so Kant published his
religious views: a belief in a god
and immortality of the soul.

The only universal law should forbid harm to others except
in self-defense. Other acts generally regarded as laudable instead
become pernicious if universally mandated. If, for example, charity
were universally mandated, it would become the equivalent of a tax

and remove some incentive for personal responsibility. A universal imperative that would create a law enforcing every positive act would create a morass of laws more unintelligible than the millions already on the books. Simply because I enjoy a particular book, movie, or person doesn't mean that everyone should do the same. Only in the negative sense, prohibiting harm to others, does the universal imperative work. Harming no one else physically or in their property, except in self-defense, is a universal maxim that can safely be subscribed to by all. There may be no other safe universal maxim. Unless we can agree on one ethical precept, we can likely agree on none and are left with no ethics at all. Tom says the Golden Rule is okay by him.

> A decent provision for the
> poor is the true test of civilization.
>
> Samuel Johnson

> Johnson practiced what he preached, habitually taking the poor into his home.

The poor who are physically and mentally able should be trained and assisted to provide for themselves and taught along with everyone else that birth control is unrelated to sin. A civilized species provides for its poor, who are no more morally aberrant than the rich and middle classes. The poor should be treated as individuals, instead of a pernicious class. Discrimination against the poor has divided us throughout history. If the poor were presumed to be worthy individuals, treated accordingly, and expected to pay their own way insofar as they are physically and mentally able, we'd become more unified and many of the poor would disappear into the middle class. Tom says utopian.

> I preach not contentedness, but more power; not peace, but war; not virtue, but efficiency. The weak and defective shall perish; and they shall be given assistance: that is the first principle of Dionysian charity.
>
> Frederic Nietzsche

A primary purpose of power is to control other individuals, and when used in this fashion, it should be presumptively counted improper. Peace is superior to war unless self-defense is required. Virtue, in the sense of doing good and avoiding evil or harm to others, together with efficiency, are positive attributes. The weak and defective no longer perish in first world countries. Helping individuals perish, except for those voluntarily and rationally choosing to do so, such as the terminally ill, harms another individual and is unethical. Contentedness, peace, virtue, and efficiency are ethical; Nietzsche seems tipped toward the unethical. Tom says it's been ages since he's agreed with me.

> . . . always fight for progress and reform, never tolerate injustice and corruption, always fight demagogues of all parties, never belong to any party, always oppose privileged classes and public plunderers, never lack sympathy with the poor, always remain devoted to the public welfare, never be satisfied with merely printing news; always be drastically independent; never be afraid to attack wrong, whether by predatory plutocracy or predatory poverty.
>
> Joseph Pulitzer
>
> Pulitzer emigrated from Hungary in 1864 at age seventeen to join the Union Army,. He eventually founded the leading U.S. Democratic newspaper, *The New York World.*

Pulitzer's progress and reform, injustice and corruption, independence and wrong, public welfare and the poor, are subjective concepts, lacking precise definition or common understanding. Our idea of progress and reform may be the opposite of that envisioned by our neighbors. Everyone opposes injustice and corruption in the abstract until defined as including actions by our favorite religion, country, or ethnic group. Pulitzer's statement translates to fighting bad and supporting good, differing widely according to how, when, where, and by whom defined. The most concrete portion seeks drastic independence, warning against conscienceless institutions and groups.   Tom says spiritual groups are okay.

> This is what you should do:
> love the earth and sun and the
> animals, despise riches, give alms
> to everyone that asks, stand up for
> the stupid and crazy, devote your
> income and labor to others, hate
> tyrants, argue not concerning God,
> have patience and indulgence
> toward the people, take off your
> hat to nothing known or unknown
> or to any man or number of
> men . . . re-examine all you have
> been told at school or church or in
> any book, dismiss what insults
> your own soul, and your very flesh
> shall be a great poem.
>
> Walt Whitman

> Whitman's parents were simple
> farm people, his mother Dutch and
> his father English; their farm was
> so small and barren that his father
> became a carpenter to support nine
> children.

Riches should be no more despised than alms automatically given to everyone who asks. Giving alms to all who asked in third countries would pauperize a billionaire. The stupid and crazy deserve neither championing nor derision; they deserve dignity and privacy, the same as any individual. Because they can't easily obtain dignity and privacy on their own, some level of championing may be appropriate. Those who feel good about dedicating their income and labor to others should do so as long as they themselves avoid becoming a public charge. Hate is too good for tyrants; tyrants and those harming others deserve to suffer the harm they mete out to others, or extreme restraint. Gods and superstitions might better be reasoned out of existence, a suggestion at which Tom is aghast. Avoid like the plague the evils caused by and flowing from the idea of gods. Have patience and indulgence toward everyone excepting those intent on harming you. Take your hat off to no one except your heroes. Re-examine everything relating to religious, government, and ethnic groups. Dismiss what insults your conscience, making certain that a refusal to harm others is your center. If all these things can't be accomplished, at a minimum avoid harm to others except in self-defense. Tom says gooey dumb.

> If you were to destroy in mankind the belief in immortality, not only love but every living force maintaining the life of the world would at once be dried up. Moreover, nothing then would be immoral, everything would be permissible, even cannibalism.
>
> Fyodor Dostoyevsky, *The Brothers Karamazov*

> Dostoyevsky was sentenced to death in 1849 for participating in a radical discussion group but the Tsar commuted his sentence as Dostoyevsky was being led before the firing squad, allowing him to enjoy four years hard labor in Siberia where his only reading material was the New Testament, and another four years as a common soldier.

No evidence of immortality exists. Immortality is probably a myth based on fear of death, near-death experiences, and dreams of deceased friends and relatives. A belief in immortality is unrelated to morality. Whether we die or live forever says nothing about whether we're individually good or evil. Religion is perpetually confused with ethics, charity, and love. Disbelief in immortality doesn't make everything permissible, including cannibalism, nor does it make love less possible. The nonreligious embrace cannibalism, child abuse, and murder in the same proportion as the religious, and few seem to believe love worthless, whether religious or not. A belief in immortality, though lacking objective support, is a comfortable way to cushion the mind from death. Any species understanding inevitable death must necessarily design gods granting immortality. Though avoidance of reality may not be a healthy philosophy, the deeply religious on average suffer less anxiety than their nonreligious fellows. Disbelief in immortality might liberate the living force maintaining the life of the world, otherwise known as reality. A disbelief in immortality might convince many to improve life on earth instead of suffering nobly for an unconfirmable reward after death. Religion encourages believers to ignore the temporal life, to embrace poverty and substandard housing, instead concentrating on a heavenly reward. Such behavior encourages immorality by landlords and governments, relegating reality to make-believe and encouraging victims to submit to the snares of the immoral. Only resistance to immorality can slow its course. The living force of life, including love, receives no encouragement from an ignorance of reality. Tom says baloney; immortality is truth.

> It can do no service to blink
> at the fact, known to all who have
> the most ordinary acquaintance
> with literary history, that a large
> portion of the noblest and most
> valuable moral teachings has been
> the work, not only of men who did
> not know, but of men who knew
> and rejected, the Christian faith.

John Stuart Mill

Mill's religion was practicality; by age sixteen, he'd formed the Utilitarians with his friends.

Religion is lightly related to morality, both in the abstract and in the lives of believers. Crime is committed in the same percentage by the religious and the nonreligious. The religious generally lump other religions, or those believing in no religion, as heathens, infidels, heretics, or nonpersons. Individuals advancing society, whether in science, the humanities, or ethics, have a firmer grip on reality and usually exclude belief in the unseen and unseeable, immortality, gods, eternal life, devils, and other spirits indistinguishable from ghosts. Tom says I often give him heartburn.

> That action is best which procures the greatest happiness for the greatest numbers.
>
> Francis Hutcheson

> Hutcheson got crosswise of the Presbyterian Church by suggesting that knowledge of good and evil can precede a knowledge of God. His "greatest happiness for the greatest number" idea preceded Bentham's, and he advised Hume on ethical philosophy.

We can't all (or any of us?) be made happy by the state, society, religion, or any other group. Only the individual can achieve happiness. Trying to construct a state that makes the plurality of its citizens happy may relegate ethnic, religious, and immigrant minorities to unhappiness, poverty, and misery. The purpose of the state is not to provide for the happiness of any one class, though all states operate in this fashion, serving those with the gold and influence while the poor and minorities suffer second-class citizenship. The first justification for government is to promote the safety of all individuals, no matter their ethnic or religious status. Other functions of government come second, if at all. Tom says he also thinks government is bloated.

> Our object in the construction of the State is the greatest happiness of the whole, and not that of any one class.
>
> Plato

> Plato was convinced that democracy couldn't provide the greatest happiness for the greatest

number   because   (without   a
constitution or a bill of individual
rights) it murdered Socrates and
sank Athens into turmoil.

The best government would procure the greatest happiness
and least unhappiness for all, an impossible goal, because of human
nature: Power corrupts, whether religious or governmental. Every
individual deserves privacy and freedom from harm by others, and
this would bring the greatest happiness for all. Tom says he can
already feel the happiness washing over him, rather like a baptism.

Few agree on what happiness is. Happiness is relative and
completely subjective. Happiness may be the ultimate status symbol
unrelated to wealth. Because of its superior status, few individuals
admit they're unhappy, except perhaps revelers in unhappiness,
such as hypochondriacs, masochists, and random mothers-in-law.
Researchers conclude that the best way to define happiness is
negatively: "If you're not unhappy, you're happy." The most truly
unhappy are the abject poor, the imprisoned, and the sick. The
Dominican Republic and India were the only countries with an
unhappy majority in 1995, though it's difficult to believe that
pollsters went door to door in Syria, Afghanistan, Yemen, and
Zimbabwe. By 2018 the Happiness Index found the three health
problems threatening happiness were obesity, the opioid crisis, and
depression. Happiness is unrelated to income or wealth, except for
the horribly poor. Happiness is also unrelated to sex, race, or
religion. Happy people usually have "high-esteem, a sense of
personal control, optimism and extroversion . . . with a statistical
link between happiness and religious faith." Studies conclude that
"Low skills and low challenge produce 'apathy.' Low skills and
high challenge produce 'anxiety.' High skills and low challenge
produce 'boredom.' High skills and high challenge produce
[happiness]." Though 70 percent conclude that religion or
spirituality plays a part in their happiness, the most significant
factors for happiness are spending time with family (43 percent),
travel (23 percent), and spending time with friends (10 percent). The
key to individual happiness may be to let us do as we please,
whether spending time with family, traveling, spending time with
friends, or praying, so long as no one else is harmed. Keeping
authoritarian groups, such as government and religions, out of our
lives without our consent might procure not only the greatest
happiness for the greatest number but also happiness for most and
harm suffered by the fewest possible. Tom says formulistic and

lacking in spirituality.

> So act as to treat humanity,
> whether in thine own person or in
> that of any other, in every case as
> an end withal, never as a means
> only.

> Immanuel Kant

> Kant helped earn his way through
> college by writing sermons and
> playing billiards, hopefully
> treating his opponents as ends and
> not as means only.

The most important rule is to refuse to harm others though they differ by ethnicity, religion, or nationality. Other rules are utopian and difficult to implement or understand, though often delivering an intensely moral ring. Kant's suggestion adds nothing to the Golden Rule. No one wants to be treated as an object, though we may act as if other people are mere objects. We're often too busy and rushed to act otherwise. Privacy is a goal for many, perhaps replacing the desire of an earlier age to be treated as a person rather than as an object. Because religious no-nos against birth control breed poverty, we've come full circle so that many people prefer to be ignored and to avoid the reality of others. Tom says he likes peace and quiet a lot.

> Morality is the observance
> of the rights of others.

> Dagobert D. Runes

> Runes edited *The Dictionary of
> Philosophy,* which included an
> abundance of Chinese philosophy.

The rights of others are a rubbery list, expanding according to the whim of the moment and the momentum of groups demanding special rights. The most important and only necessary rights are not to be harmed by others so long as we don't harm them (unless in self-defense) and a right to privacy, to be left alone. If these two rights were universally observed, few other "rights," if any, would be necessary. Tom's thinking about it.

> Liberty of all, limited by the like liberties of all, is the rule in conformity with which society must be organized.
>
> Herbert Spencer

> Spencer was always an extreme individualist; He coined the phrase, "survival of the fittest."

If we had an inalienable right to control ourselves without interference by groups or other individuals, so long as we harm no one else, then society would be required to recognize the sovereignty of the individual, subject only to the equal sovereignly of all other individuals. We should have the liberty to do as we please, provided no one else gets hurt. Such liberty is unlimited liberty, except insofar as it limits the ability to smack others about. Tom says he finds it tedious to appreciate a broken record, even if correct.

> In every age its [liberty's] progress has been beset by its natural enemies, by ignorance and superstition, by lust of conquest and by love of ease, by the strong man's craving for power, and the poor man's craving for food.
>
> Lord Acton

> Acton was best known for "absolute power corrupting absolutely." His liberalism was rooted in Christianity and hostility to nationalism.

Ignorance and superstition are synonymous with religions that immortalize poverty and the poor man's craving for food. Lust of conquest and the strong man's craving for power are often exhibited by the leaders of religion and government. Love of earned ease is no vice though unearned ease, or laziness, may threaten the progress of liberty. Religion and government are the most formidable opponents of liberty. A minimal level of government, though a seemingly impractical possibility, is necessary to preserve liberty for all. The inherent antagonism of government toward individual liberty has been such that government, together with religion, has done more to erode liberty than to preserve it, with rare exceptions. Tom says American constitutional government is a beacon for the world. Maybe so, but superior "us" connotes inferior "them."

> Hold always the sign of
> blood in horror. Take care not to
> shed or stain thyself with it, for
> the mark is never washed away.
>
> Saladin (advice to his son,
> Dhahir, on appointment as
> governor of Aleppo)

> The first Aryubi Sultan of Egypt, Saladin (1138–1193) was the nemesis of the Crusades, capturing Jerusalem back on October 1, 1187, ending eighty-eight years of Frank occupation, stopping the Third Crusade in its tracks, and uniting the Muslim world.

On a balmy January evening in 1996, an Israeli helicopter swooped down on Hattin, where we were parked in our trusty RV. Hattin, above Tiberius near Lake Kinneret (better known in the West as the Sea of Galilee), is where Saladin finally destroyed the last of the Crusaders. The helicopter pilot had pegged us for subversives and demanded to know whether we were the bad guys. When he realized we were merely foreign-born idiots, he took off with a whoosh. The Saladin quote displays exemplary ethics, as did the helicopter pilot.

> The precepts of the law are
> these: to live honestly, to injure no
> one, and to give every man his

358

due.

Justinian I

> The Byzantine emperor represented the height of sixth-century civilization, building many public works of bridges, aqueducts, forts, monasteries, orphanages, and the yellow mosque (then cathedral) in Constantinople, the Hagia Sophia.

Living honestly and giving every individual his due can't happen without abstaining from harm to others. Justinian's three precepts of law are essentially one: to harm no one else in their person or property except in true self-defense. Tom gnasheth his teeth at the repetition. But I keep it up by pointing out we should harm no one else in their person or property, always holding the sign of blood in horror. Shedding blood is always bad news, even in true self-defense. To remain within the bounds of ethical behavior when acting in self-defense, the violence must be in proportion to that of the originally aggressive act, not in excess of that necessary to repel violence. Tom says that sounds stuffy, like British common law.

> Liberty consists in the power to do anything that does not injure others; accordingly, the exercise of the rights of man has no limits except those that secure to the other members of society the enjoyment of these same rights.

> *Declarations of the Rights of Man and Citizen,* French National Assembly, 1789

The basic idea of liberty, of the freedom to be autonomous, requires that the individual adult be allowed to do anything that doesn't hurt anyone else, except in self-defense. The effects of this conclusion are enormous and unrealized by anyone in any country, ever. Instead, adults have always been prohibited from acts presumed by government and religion to harm the individual, including ourselves. Government and religion assume that the average adult is mentally or ethically incapable of making personal decisions, though they would harm no one else. Acts historically prohibited by government and religion include all victimless crimes, now limited to prostitution, the sale or use of drugs less dangerous to health than tobacco or alcohol, and gambling or gaming without a state license (or as an Indian casino). Government and religion historically and hypocritically impose victimless crime prohibitions on the individual while sponsoring their own gambling, horse and dog racing, lotteries, and bingo. Government is partially supported by taxes from the sale of the two drugs most dangerous to our health, alcohol and tobacco. Prostitution is winked at outside of residential districts because a market economy can't be extinguished, witness the easy availability of drugs in any prison on earth. The inevitability of the market proves the impossibility of diminishing drug use of any kind (except through education), whether addiction to the legal or illegal drugs of television, phone screens, religion, gambling, sex, hang-gliding, or whatever lights our fire. Barbara Holland points out in *Endangered Pleasures* (Little, Brown, 1995) that there are "those who disapprove of idleness, gin rummy, slang, song, unauthorized sex, naps, socialism, and jacuzzies for moral reasons. They enjoy it; moral indignation is a pleasure, often the only pleasure, in many lives. It's also one of the few pleasures people feel obliged to force on other people." No individual or group, governmental or religious, should be able to determine what is appropriate, legal, or sinful for the adult individual so long as no one else is harmed. If government or religion were to prohibit acts most dangerous to others, personal relationships would require full-time monitoring. No entity or force, outside of our own personal responsibility, can prevent harm to ourselves. Religion and government only punish after the fact, seldom if ever thwarting harm. The adult inherently retains the power to injure himself, no matter the number of contrary government or religious decrees, and many of us do so daily. Only through education can government and religion reduce the number who insist on harming themselves, no matter the harm of choice. Punishment is ineffective for many children, and far less effective in controlling adult behavior. Most of us engage in risky behavior, whether through addiction to work, legal or illegal drugs, gambling, religion, sex, or phone screens. Liberty is what religion and government say it is, unless the we escape from society or are similarly discrete. France says government and religion, the primary brakes on liberty, shouldn't be allowed to prevent us from doing anything that doesn't injure others, yet it is lip service only. Harm no one else, except in self-defense, and otherwise do as you please. Ethics and nonharmful liberty are congruent. Tom says spirituality and religion are key players. Not for everyone.

> No woman can call herself free who does not own and control her body. No woman can call herself free until she can choose consciously whether she will or will not be a mother.
>
> Margaret Sanger

> Sanger convinced a Federal Court of Appeals in 1936 to reinterpret the 1873 Comstock Act, which classified contraceptive information as obscene, thus allowing doctors to prescribe and import contraceptives, prescription only.

None are free who don't own and control their own body though it must be said that for those who either avoid sex or use effective birth control, it's relatively easy to avoid pregnancy. Individuals with common sense determine whether they'll have children, notwithstanding general religious prohibitions against birth control. Until women and men are equally free from religious taboos against sex, which inhibit the teaching and societal acceptance of birth control, the species will never be free. Only those who can consciously choose whether to be a mother or a father are truly free. The Sanger quote has no necessary connection with abortion, which harms an organism certain to become a person. With sure and knowledgeable birth control and sex education pushed by government and religion, abortion would become a nonissue. Birth control is the top priority for individual freedom and self-determination until a decision to have children is mutually and rationally made. Religion opposes the freedom of the individual by opposing universal sex education, which is needed as early as possible, and prohibiting birth control. Tom says quite so.

> For us murder is once for all

forbidden; so even the child in the womb . . . it is not lawful for us to destroy. To forbid birth is only quicker murder. . . . The fruit is always present in the seed.

Tertullian

Tertullian introduced ecclesiastical Latin, shaping the vocabulary and central ideas of Christianity, which he thought exceedingly lax.

Harming others, including murder, is forbidden, except in self-defense. The child in the womb, or outside the womb, deserves neither murder nor abortion. The fruit is always present in the seed. The abortion controversy obscures the simple key to its resolution, which is sex education and birth control. Most individuals, though supporting a right to an abortion, believe abortion is morally wrong because terminating a fetus is at least as morally wrong as killing a dog or a horse. Scrupulous use of birth control when no child is wanted would virtually end the abortion issue. Personal irresponsibility shouldn't be used as an excuse for terminating the life of a child in the womb, but most, including myself, would leave the decision to the mother. Many young women, no matter the country, have little power to exercise personal sexual responsibility. Abortion is no business of anyone but the parents, which might mean the father should have a wrongful-death action if a fetus is terminated against his will, the same as he has an eighteen-year child-support obligation if it isn't. Tom says rad.

All ambitions are lawful except those that climb upward on the miseries or credulities of mankind.

Joseph Conrad

Conrad's father was a poet and Polish patriot who served on the late 1850s committee that directed the Polish insurrection against

362

Russia, which got the family
exiled to Northern Russia when
Conrad was a child.

All ambitions (before being realized in action) are moral, as
are all actions except those harming others in their person or
property. We're a herd that has evolved into biological supremacy,
able to extinguish any or all other species at will. Having achieved
that status, we try to eliminate the free and open competition by
which we became predominant. If another species achieved
supremacy, such as antelopes, they might do the same, insuring
survival, basic food, and shelter for antelopes through an antelope
government, multiplying endlessly while other species decline.
Lebensraum would evaporate. When antelopes believe unbounded
propagation is ordered by an antelope god, living conditions
deteriorate. Impoverished antelopes, particularly young antelopes
susceptible to disease or with diarrhea from contaminated water, are
extinguished by the thousands, and millions are too poor to feed
themselves. Religions average less than 1 percent of their budget as
aid for the poor, with 99 percent going to buildings, support of
clergy, administration, and other. Because no religion will open its
financial records, these statistics are based on artful guesswork by
journalists. No one knows for sure. Religion and government prey
on the credulities and miseries of mankind, pitting ethnic, religious,
and national groups against each other on trumped-up charges. Tom
says religion serves the species and preys on no one, though a few
religious leaders may.

There is a violence that
liberates, and a violence that
enslaves; there is a violence that is
moral, and a violence that is
immoral.

Benito Mussolini

Mussolini was a leading Italian
socialist in 1904, but eleven years
later he flip-flopped, founding the
Italian fascist party. By 1922, he
was installed as Italy's youngest
prime minister by the king, who
said, "He is brutal enough to

363

restore order and intelligent
enough to govern."

All violence is immoral and enslaves except the minimum
necessary for self-defense. The only moral violence is
commensurate with the lowest level necessary to repel violence. All
other violence is immoral, whether commanded by presidential
decree, worship of the god of nationalism or the god of religion, by
ethnic hatreds, or any combination thereof. The other primary
justification for war is acquisitive, to expand territory, and gain
Lebensraum, which with ideas of ethnic superiority dominated the
Napoleonic wars, Germany during World Wars I and II, and Japan
in World War II. Both sides in all wars are wholeheartedly
supported by the religious and the patriotic, the worshipers of
governments and gods, with the same god often on either side. The
violence of gods and governments is immoral. Only the defensive
violence of the individual is moral and then only when limited to
the lowest level necessary to repel aggression. Tom says that's
relatively clear and quite moral, but it can't be correct.

It is almost a definition of a
gentleman to say that he is one
who never inflicts pain.

John Henry Newman

Newman was an English cardinal,
as well as a poet who wrote
hymns.

An ethical individual never injures another in his property or
person, unless in self-defense. The infliction of pain is otherwise
inexcusable. Ethical individuals only inflict pain in the sole and
narrow exception of self-defense, which excludes the idea of a first
strike. Gentlemen never strike first. Tom says he doesn't either.

The General's frequent
saying was: live and let live.

Friedrich von Schiller,
Wallenstein's Camp

Schiller was the only son of a

military doctor and was
considered Germany's most
important classical playwright,
writing classics such as *William
Tell*, *The Maid of Orleans* (Joan of
Arc), and *The Robbers*.

Living and letting live requires that no one else be harmed. Harming others almost guarantees eventual harm to ourselves, while the refusal to inflict harm almost guarantees safety and privacy. Generals and popes aren't in the business of living and letting live, but in the business of conversion and conquest, or momentary defense. Armies exist to enforce national policy against foreigners and to extend the reach of the nation beyond its boundaries, only secondarily for defense. Nations fund armies, marines, navies, air forces, coast guards, and space corps out of tradition and for prestige more than necessity. Mexico, for a single example that could be multiplied a hundred times, has no need for an army or navy to repel invasion from the United States or Guatemala, but the Mexican navy and army continue blithely on, draining the economy of pesos that could otherwise be used to raise the standard of living for millions in poverty. Similar nations include all those in existence, save such as Costa Rica, with no military at all, and no one is lined up to invade Costa Rica. To live and let live, all military forces should be liquidated, which would be possible only if they all vanished in the same split second. The first mandate of nations united should be the dissolution of national militaries, so we may all live and let live. Tom says utterly and stupidly quixotic.

The sum of behavior is to
retain a man's own dignity,
without intruding upon the liberty
of others.

Francis Bacon

Bacon's family was wealthy; his
father was Sir Nicholas Bacon, the
Lord Keeper of the Great Seal, but
Francis Bacon always lived
beyond his means and was in
perpetual bondage to money

lenders, dying deeply in debt, which rendered his generous bequests moot.

The key to ethics is to avoid intruding on the liberty of others, refusing to injure others, which is the best means of securing the dignity of the individual. Privacy can be secured only when violence is impossible or remote. When violence threatens daily life, quality dies. The only means of securing dignity is to avoid violence toward others, which is the same as avoiding intrusion on the liberty of others. The foundation of ethics is identical to that required for the dignity of the individual. Tom says it sounds like a neat package, but is it really?

Liberty, then, is the sovereignty of the individual, and never shall man know liberty until each and every individual is acknowledged to be the only legitimate sovereign of his or her person, time, and property, each living and acting at his own cost; and not until we live in a society where each can exercise his right of sovereignty at all times without clashing with or violating that of others.

Josiah Warren

Warren founded the town of Modem Times on Long Island, about forty miles from New York City, in the early 1850s; it lasted until 1862. He also founded philosophical anarchism.

The ideal society or government should as its first principle guarantee the sovereignty of the individual. No society can claim liberty for its citizenry without allowing each adult to do precisely as he or she pleases, so long as no one else is harmed. No government or society has achieved or is likely to achieve this ideal because it's the antithesis of the bossy organized group. Society, government, religion, and ethnic groups can't fully recognize individual sovereignty and survive. Every rule, law, commandment, constitution, code, ordinance, statute, decision, and ruling that fails to limit government and religion infringes the liberty of the individual. The majority of laws viewed singly appear innocuous, because they're either unenforced or affect a small minority, making little difference to most. In the aggregate, however, millions of laws enable any government to enforce any obscure law at will. We must step lightly in the neighborhood of government, religion, and other groups founded on principles of control largely unrelated to individual harm, merit, or ethics. Tom says the individual can legitimately consent to the sovereignty of religion or other groups, though admittedly, government relies on implied consent for its omnipresence.

> If only there were evil people somewhere insidiously committing evil deeds and it were necessary only to separate them from the rest of us and destroy them. But the line dividing good and evil cuts through the heart of every human being. And who is willing to destroy a piece of his own heart?
>
> Alexander I. Solzhenitsyn
>
> Solzhenitsyn was a captain of artillery in WWII but was arrested in 1945 for criticizing Stalin, sentenced to eight years in prison, then labor camp in Siberia, and three years of exile.

The line dividing good and evil cuts through every human heart but is predominantly good in the vast majority, leaving a small percentage, perhaps less than 1 percent, with a heart dominated by evil, though half the population may be willing to get away with whatever can be gotten away with. The distinction between good and evil is determined by a propensity to harm others. The good harm no one else, except to the remote and minimal extent necessary for self-defense. The evil harm whomever hinders their progress toward their chosen goal. They should be separated from the rest of us and rehabilitated, instead of destroyed, if possible. Few have fallen into the evil category: Hitler, Stalin, Amin, and other tyrants, inquisitors, and fundamentalist religions such as ISIS. More problematical are my estimated half of us who, if certain they won't get caught, take advantage of others. A first giant step would be the universal recognition of basic ethical principles, or at least one. Unless we can identify one, we have none. Tom says the last part is logically and undeniably true.

> The great sin by which we all are tempted is the wish to hurt others.
>
> Dr. Karl Menninger
>
> After visiting Mayo Clinic in 1908, Menninger's father started the world-famous Topeka, Kansas, Menninger Clinic; Menninger joined his father's practice in 1920 and had concluded by 1930 that the mentally ill are only a few degrees removed from normal.

The impulse to harm others, or at least slap them around a bit, may strike everyone, but few succumb. Most of us are sufficiently mature to refrain from harm to others except in self-defense or when we're anonymous behind the wheel. Maturity defines morality and ethics. Sin is unrelated to ethics. Sin is an artificial construct of religion and consists of breaking a religious rule. Religious rules are arbitrary, mystical, and historical myths, only coincidentally related to ethics. The greatest breach of ethics that may periodically tempt us all is the wish to shoot another driver. Tom says we're all tempted but few are violent.

> Late on the third day, at the very moment when, at sunset, we were making our way through a herd of hippopotamuses, there flashed through my mind, unforeseen and unsought, the

phrase, 'Reverence for life.' The iron door had yielded: the path in the thicket had become visible. Now I had found my way to the idea in which affirmation of world- and life-affirmation and ethics are contained side by side! Now I knew that the world-view of ethical world- and life-affirmation, together with the ideals of civilization, is founded in thought.

Albert Schweitzer

Schweitzer won the 1925 Nobel Prize for Peace for his effort on behalf of the Brotherhood of Nations. Besides writing widely acclaimed works on J.S. Bach, J. Christ and Saint Paul, Schweitzer built a world-renowned hospital in Gabon, in French Equatorial Africa, and later added a leper colony.

Reverence for human life requires reverence for the individual and a refusal to harm others. Reverence for all life would hold other species sacrosanct. Achievement of the second is less important than the first. If the first were accomplished, our lot would improve exponentially. Murder, rape, robbery, theft, and war would be rendered historical curiosities. Then we could contemplate a secondary reverence for the life of other species. Ethics requires priorities, first protecting the human species and only then deciding whether we should remain carnivorous. The species will likely always (which is an abysmally long time) base its ethics on the intelligence of other species, consenting to the slaughter of worms without compunction while protecting more intelligent species such as whales outside of Japan, porpoises outside of fishing nets, and foxes outside the British Isles. The implications of such an ethical posture are enormous, considering the high likelihood that species more intelligent than ours exist in many parts of the universe. Tom says that's improbable for a species made in the image of God—his capital *G* and not mine—and I refer him back to Hesiod.

Schweitzer also said, "A man is truly ethical only when he obeys the compulsion to help all life which he is able to assist, and shrinks from injuring anything that lives."

Schweitzer was more a Buddhist than Christian-like, at least those Christians who despise immigrants. Philosophy always suggests priorities. Perhaps half of us are inclined to assist anything that lives (Hindus constitute a large chunk of the world population) while most shrink from injuring anything that lives unless already shrink-wrapped. No philosopher has suggested that vegetables are living creatures ethically protected from consumption; only Schweitzer and a few Hindus would protect mosquitoes and flies. What can ethically be eaten is seemingly determined by the former intelligence of that consumed. Vegetables are dumb, whereas cattle and sheep are relatively less so. No one worries about worms, though some demonstrate against the cramped shipment of cattle and sheep, winking at their slaughter. If we could effectively prevent the harm of individuals, except in self-defense, ethics might become sufficiently imbedded that the animal protection portion of a Schweitzer-based ethics would follow. Priorities require that we first stop slaughtering ourselves on pretexts of religion, patriotism and nationalism, racism and ethnic origin, or for any other reason not based on the necessity to defend against harm by another. Wars couldn't begin if harm were limited to self-defense. Tom says Schweitzer took ethics too far and I'm a mere pragmatist. Well, damn.

> Nor does the Anarchistic scheme furnish any code of morals to be imposed upon the individual. 'Mind your own business' is its own moral law. Interference with another's business is a crime and the only crime, and as such may properly be resisted.

> Benjamin R. Tucker

Tucker jettisoned three years of engineering education at MIT and moved to France to study under Proudhon. He was best known for the broadsheet *Liberty,* which he

370

wrote and edited for twenty-seven
years while on the staff of the
Boston Globe.

Some will always count their business as including ours. These are primarily called government and religion. Ethics requires us to mind our own business, harming no one else. Interference with another, including violating their privacy (by prohibiting birth control and foisting indigent children on poor families), is the equivalent of harm. The standard of harm should be objectively judged, which would include the eggshell plaintiff, the easily harmed person. There should be no crime beyond harming another, which means government should have no criminal law function beyond prevention and punishment of privacy invasion, most egregiously debased by the violent crimes of war, murder, rape, and robbery. A capitalistic economic system allows advertising to invade individual privacy, but is chiefly consensual. Minding one's own business could form a broad foundation for ethics and morality, slightly more burdensome than harming no one else. Tom says he'd settle for leaving others alone.

> The foundation of morality
> is to have done, once and for all,
> with lying.
>
> Thomas Henry Huxley

Huxley was the seventh of eight
children from a poor family,
spawning a dynasty of scientists
and philosophers.

Lying is essential to oil social wheels. If we didn't lie and say, "Good morning" every time it wasn't, few might say "Good morning." Lying is often politeness for sparing another's feelings, which is why we tell Jumbo we can't imagine why he wasn't invited to the reception. The only unethical or improper lie is that which harms another. Otherwise, lying may be beneficial or do no harm. Tom says revisionist religion and ethics are often purer than the original sort.

> The cruelest lies are often
> told in silence.

Robert Lewis Stevenson

> Stevenson was dispatched to the
> University of Edinburgh to
> become a lighthouse engineer, the
> family profession.

Cruelty is in the eyes of the receiver. Many prefer fantasy or superstition to truth and reality, and for peace of mind, perhaps rightly so; truth and reality can be depressing. Many prefer silence to depression or confrontation with truth. Few enjoy hurting others' feelings, much less harming others. We're often silent when cruelty might be kindness. The difficulty is distinguishing between cruelty as kindness and cruelty as brutality. What about Jumbo? The kindest lies are more often told in silence than the cruelest lies. Tom says that's hazy.

> [The Church] holds that it
> were better for sun and moon to
> drop from heaven, for the earth to
> fall, and for all the many millions
> who are upon it to die of starvation
> in the extremist agony, so far as
> temporal affliction goes, than that
> one soul . . . should commit one
> single venial sin, should tell one
> willful untruth.

John Henry Newman

Newman relies on pre-Dark Ages ethics, tone deaf to reality. Few if any religious people believe it better for millions to perish of starvation in extreme agony rather than telling a lie to spare someone's feeling, save a life, or escape an unwanted social engagement. Religion always lags behind societal mores, because religious dogma must resist change, with all the main religions having been founded before the Dark Ages. Unless religious change is so slow as to be imperceptible, religious infallibility is glaringly revealed. No religion can risk its infallibility, which might expose a fallible god and disprove the religion. Birth control is forbidden by the largest and predominant religions so they may multiply unto the impoverishment of the earth. Many resulting poor can't escape poverty. It used to be a venial sin for a Christian to lie but not much is heard about the issue these days, illustrating the mutation of religion over time. Religion may eventually relinquish its birth control bars, but by then it will be too late for millions. Religion, race, and nationalism are unable to change core biases that result in insane and irrational competition that negates the individual. It would be better for religion, racism, and nationalism to die in extremist agony than for one individual to be born in poverty or die in war. Tom says that is extreme.

A falsehood uttered for the sake of a righteous end ceaseth to be a falsehood.

The Mahabharata

Hindus knew before Christianity began that some *venial* crimes are less venial than others. Until recently, Christianity required that a mother poised to jump off a cliff be told that her child had just died, no lying allowed. A righteous end is unrelated to whether a falsehood is reprehensible, tolerable, or a positive act because righteousness is subjective. The only proper test is whether the falsehood harms a person other than the utterer. Falsehoods that harm no one else or which confer a benefit with no adverse effects are ethical. Tom says everyone knows that.

Truth, for its own sake, has never been a virtue with the Romish clergy. Father Newman informs us that it need not, and on the whole, ought not to be; that cunning is the weapon which heaven has given to the saints wherewith to withstand the brute male force of the wicked world which marries and is given in marriage.

Charles Kingsley

Newman's "Apology for My Life" was written in response to attacks by Kingsley, who was an accomplished novelist and the first clergyman to accept Darwin's evolutionary theory.

Truth has never been a virtue for any social, political, religious, or ethnic group. Because sex preoccupies the male half of the species much of the time, abstinent male saints may deserve sainthood. Bald truth is eclipsed in importance by the test of ethics: whether an action harms another individual. Because spoken or written truth seldom, if ever, harms others, its suppression is seldom if ever justified. Tom says I beat around the bush.

> In truth lying is an accursed vice. We are men, and held together, only by our word. If we recognize the horror and the gravity of lying, we would persecute it with fire more justly than other crimes.
>
> Michel Eyquem de Montaigne
>
> Montaigne entered the College of Guyenne Bordeaux at age six, studying under the two greatest humanists of his time, George Buchanan and M. A. de Muret.

A lie that harms another individual is immoral. A lie that harms no one is neutral. A lie that benefits someone while harming no one is beneficial and morally correct. Though individuals should have the right to rely on the word of others, the key is whether the lie harms another. Tom says probably true but stilted.

> The intention makes the lye, not the words.
>
> James I
>
> The king of England retained a vivid belief in the devil, was absolutely certain of his own decrees, and enjoyed little money

374

sense.

Harmful lies may be intended to injure. Injurious conduct can be ranked in descending seriousness from intentional to reckless to negligent. This nitpick proves the James I rule, that much of the harm in lying depends on the intention to harm another. Much of the harm in telling the truth also depends on an intention to harm another. Tom says that's truly splitting hairs.

> The essence of lying is deception, not in words; a lie may be told in silence, by equivocation, by the accent on a syllable, by a glance of the eye attaching a peculiar significance to a sentence; but all these kinds of lies are worse and baser by many degrees than a lie plainly worded.
>
> John Ruskin

> In 1854 Ruskin's wife left him, got an annulment (the marriage was never consummated because both were extremely self-centered), and married one of his friends.

A lie may harm, benefit, or leave a person unaffected, making the lie only an attempt to harm. Attempts are treated more lightly by Western jurisprudence, and rightly so, because no one is actually harmed by a mere attempt. When no harm is suffered, harmful intention is relatively innocuous. Silent lies often spring from reticence, instead of intentionally harmful behavior. A lie plainly worded is as bad as any other, whether silent, equivocal, or accentual. Whether a lie is immoral depends entirely on whether it harms another. The means and nuances of lying are unrelated to whether they harm someone else.

> What man in his senses would deny that there are those whom we have the best grounds for considering that we ought to deceive—as boys, madmen, the

sick, the intoxicated, enemies,
men in error, and thieves.

John Milton

Milton's greatest work was the
ten-volume *Paradise Lost*, which
painted a vivid portrait of the
devil, so vivid that Blake and
Shelley concluded two hundred
years later that the devil was the
hero.

A lie is appropriate in self-defense, no matter against whom.
It seems impossible, even for fundamentalist religious absolutists,
to argue that it's inappropriate to lie to those intending harm, in
order to escape harm. Tom says he's no fundamentalist religious
absolutist.

It is double pleasure to
deceive the deceiver.

Jean del la Fontaine

Fontaine inherited the job of
inspector of forests and waterways
from his father but found time to
write volumes of *Fables,* a
masterpiece of characterization
containing 240 poems over an
extraordinary range that covered
the social hierarchy of his time.

Few pleasures are greater than deceiving a deceiver, which
means thumping an unfair competitor. The species is naturally
competitive and combative, regardless of harm. When no harm is
suffered, deceit is not only joyful but ethical. Tom says perhaps.

To deceive a rival, artifice is
permitted. One may employ
everything against one's enemies.

To know how to dissemble
is the knowledge of kings.

Armand Jean du Plessis,
Duc de Richelieu

Richelieu charmed Pope Paul V,
who made him a priest at age
twenty-two; he served as Louis
XllI's chief minister for eighteen
years. Louis XIII nominated
Richelieu as cardinal, and his
leadership spearheaded French
colonization in Canada, the West
Indies, Morocco, and Persia.

The individual should have an inherent and unalienable right
of privacy defensible by concealment, camouflage, or hiding. Lying
that harms another isn't justified, except to defend against equal or
greater harm to another.

The difficulty with basing ethics on friends and enemies is
the fact that our enemies are often determined by religious, ethnic,
and nationalistic bigotries. Most any artifice is permitted in self-
defense so long as the level of defense doesn't impose harm beyond
that needed to repel an aggressor. Tom says yes, but the heat of
contention may excuse an overenthusiastic defense.

If you begin by saying,
'Thou shalt not lie,' there is no
longer any possibility of political
action.

Jean-Paul Sartre

Sartre was awarded the 1964
Nobel Prize for Literature but
refused because he felt it would
compromise his writing.

Whether a statement is a lie, the truth, an accidental lie, or
accidental truth doesn't mean it's similarly perceived. Semantics,
inflection, good faith, and a dozen other factors determine how we
understand a statement. Not all listen carefully or in good faith, the

same as speakers. Political action depends on slippery language and evasion, lawyers and liars, license and privilege. A lie depends as much on the understanding of the hearer as the words and intent of the speaker. Political action is partisan, intended to benefit one faction at the expense of others. Lies may facilitate temporary advantage but when found out, as they usually are, often destroy advantage, though temporary advantage may lead to permanent gain because lies found out too late are often already forgotten. Tom says he thought I was into clarity.

> The more weakness, the more falsehood; strength goes straight . . . weaklings must lie.

> Jean Paul Richter

> Richter, the son of a poor teacher/pastor, studied theology until he was forced to become a private tutor and then a schoolmaster to support himself before becoming famous as a writer.

Lies are often told in weakness. It may be easier to say I have an appointment Sunday next than to accept an unwanted invitation to dine with the parson. Such weakness may be superior to the strong person who instead tells the parson that his company is unwanted, along with his theology and stuffiness. The benevolent lie is necessary for peace and privacy. Lies that harm others are told by spiteful weaklings, particularly the intentionally harmful lie. The strong may be better able to avoid situations where lies are necessary, thus perhaps telling fewer lies. Tom says social and defensive lies are distinguishable from harmful lies, adding *mea culpa*.

> Lying is an elementary means of self-defense.

> Susan Sontag

> Sontag was a regular contributor to *The New York Review of Books*

378

but first came to general public
attention in 1964 with her "Notes
on 'Camp,'" which surveyed
attributes of taste within disparate
segments of society.

Lying is necessary for self-defense from physical harm and
intrusions on privacy. Lying is innocuous unless it harms another
person, other than in self-defense. We have no obligation to
socialize. A lie told to preserve privacy or avoid unwanted social
contact, to avoid fraud or physical harm to self or others, is a proper
lie with no immoral connotations. Tom says yeah, yeah.

> O noble lie! was ever truth
> so good?

> Torquato Tasso

Tasso's restless life of mental
illness, brilliant poetry, romantic
loves, and persecutions made him
a legend who was extensively
written about for three hundred
years after his death.

Lies that prevent harm to others or self, or that preserve
privacy, are admirable, respectable, virtuous, worthy, and noble.
Telling the truth to those who wish to invade our privacy, separate
us from our property, or injure us, is unnecessary; instead, such lies
should be enthusiastically and convincingly told. Such are noble
lies, with truth ne'er so good. Tom says real poetic.

> That a lie which is
> half a truth is ever
> the blackest of
> lies,
> That a lie which is all
> a lie may be met
> and fought with
> outright,
> But a lie which is part
> a truth is a harder
> matter to fight.

Alfred Lord Tennyson

> Tennyson's poetry is remarkable
> for its metric variety, descriptive
> imagery, and verbal melodies,
> though undemonstrated by this
> quote.

Because of semantics, lack of clear thought before speaking, ambiguities, language barriers arising from culture or education, mood, or disposition, circumstance, historical relationship between speaker and listener, and a dozen other factors, the distinction between truth and lie may be exceedingly tenuous. Identifying half-truths is more difficult. Ambiguous language, which includes all language, semantics, fuzzy thought, language barriers, cultural, religious, and ethnic distinctions, and half-truths, are difficult to combat. Every conversation, writing, or communication contains inherent multiple barriers to effective and clear communication. Focusing on whether an untruth is negligent, reckless, intentional, or accidental ignores many other reasons for a failure to communicate clearly, none of which are necessarily related to ethics. Tom abstains.

> The most common lie is that
> with which one lies to oneself;
> lying to others is relatively an
> exception.

Friedrich Nietzsche

We lie to ourselves about our mortality, morality, religion, intentions, motives, worth, values, work, love, achievements, pleasures, and happiness. Because we're with ourselves more than with others, Nietzsche is undeniably correct. We seldom lie to others beyond the perfunctory "Good morning" though it's raining cats and dogs, or responding that "I'm fine" when in the depths of depression. The latter is a dual-purpose lie, to ourselves and to others. Neither we nor others are dumb enough to believe oft-repeated daily lies in our salutations, but we constantly lie to ourselves by preferring make-believe, superstition, or supposed superiorities based on religious affiliation, nationality, or ethnicity. Tom says he still believes one religion is better than others; otherwise he'd have to resign from the priesthood. He also believes the country of his birth is better than other countries, the same as everyone in every county everywhere. Who knew that the vast majority love their government overseers so abundantly?

> The great enemy of truth is very often not the lie—deliberate, contrived, and dishonest—but the myth—persistent, persuasive, and realistic. Too often we hold fast to the clichés of our forebears.
>
> John F. Kennedy

> Kennedy never lost an election, himself becoming a persistent, persuasive, and realistic myth though his presidency lasted only 1,037 days, less than three years.

Myths let us function more easily, providing a cushion against reality. The myths of religion have injured the species by subdividing us into invidious and unfair stereotypes based on religion, similarly accomplished by nationalities and ethnic groups. Racism is a generic category for behavior guided by myth. Any characterization of personally unknown individuals based on their religion, race, or nationality is racist, similar to the clichés of our forebears—that, for example, Anglo-Saxon American Protestant Christians are superior to all others; or, on another continent, that Japanese Buddhist Orientals are best; or, elsewhere, that Northern Ireland Catholic Loyalists are the world's best people . . . or similar rot. These myths have been elevated to actual known fact among the self-exalted, who are us. Self-serving, self-congratulatory, and self-glorifying myths are fed through our mothers' milk and are fatal pap, pernicious, persistent, and persuasive. We, the species, are a single entity. Our primary unethical act is distinguishing among ourselves based on religion, nationality, and race, often resulting in harm to each other. Tom says could be.

Conclusion

Religious controls of the individual retard the species by embroiling us in internecine warfare, overpopulating the earth, and creating a permanent indigent underclass. These controls should, insofar as possible, be eradicated. Unless we can identify a single ethical principle, such as forbidding the harm of others, we have none. The scribes of the species have at least this much to say.

If you liked this book, please leave a review.

Also by David Rich

Sail the World? – An Absurdly True Story, Prequel to RV the World

RV the World, 2nd Edition

Myths of the Tribe - When Religion and Ethics Diverge
The ISIS Affair - Putting the Fun Back in Fundamentalism
Antelopes - A Modern Gulliver's Travels

RV the World: An Excerpt

My earliest vivid memory is of a photo from an old geography book: Vesuvius in full-color eruption spewing fluorescent orange magma, torching rich Romans in Pompeii. This hit me between the eyes. Whoa. I really had to see that in person. What six-year-old wouldn't?

I could never kick this early memory, which evolved into a dream of seeing the world, the whole lot of it. My earliest ambition was finding the world's most fabulous volcanoes, my curiosity spurred by schoolteacher parents with a passion for travel and geography. I inherited a travel addiction, doomed to see the entire world or die trying.

I nagged my long-suffering parents to drive down every road, reasoning that we might stumble across Vesuvius anywhere. Humoring me, they drove down lots of dirt roads, many ending on the edges of deep canyons in Colorado, New Mexico, Utah, and Arizona, the Four Corners area where I grew up. They'd brought it on themselves, infecting me with a travel-and-geography obsession, insisting in return for my see-the-end-of-every-road harassment that I learn context, all the states, their capitals, and the capital of every country on the planet. I was crushed to find Vesuvius nowhere near the Four Corners.

An outlet for itchy feet fortuitously appeared when I was teaching at the local law school. A student said, "Hey, come help me try out my new sailboat." That day one of Arizona's many lakes became a scene of high comedy. By 10 a.m. we finally got the pole up. I later learned it was called a mast. Though we scooted down the lake in half an hour, downwind, it took until sunset to sail back as we cursed gods whose proper names we didn't know—the gods of tacking, coming about, and shifting winds. I was indelibly hooked.

After a few months of torture on my friend's Hobie Cat, including six crazy days sailing down the Mexican coast from Puerto Penasco to Bahia Kino, I finally enrolled—along with my wife, Mary—in a learn-to-sail course at the Annapolis Sailing School in San Diego. Then I tackled the advanced sailing course, which theoretically qualified me to bareboat charter.

Suddenly I wanted to sail around the world. People said, "But you live in Arizona. There's no water, except a few ridiculous lakes." By then everyone knew I'd gone stark raving mad—including Mary, but she gradually contracted the insatiable wanderlust encouraged by my parents.

I captained seventeen charters in Greece, Turkey, Vancouver, Belize, and most of the Bahamas and Caribbean Islands. It was my responsibility to find a proper sailing vessel (best price), set up the charter, organize disorganized friends during bouts of personal disorganization, and then, once we arrived at the destination, find water, fuel, and a likely place to moor or anchor each night. I halfway learned to sail a dozen different sailboats while my accompanying friends coughed up three hundred dollars per person for the pleasure of crewing. Aren't friends fabulous?

The second most glorious day of my life was buying a dreamboat to sail around the world. I named her Grendel. Mary and I spent years flying on weekends from Phoenix to San Diego, putting every toy aboard, from mast steps to radar to a water maker. The big day arrived when, after saving every penny on a ten-year plan that stretched to eleven years, I sold everything and sailed Grendel out of San Diego Harbor.

It became abundantly clear that Dave and Mary sailing around the world was not exactly as it appeared in Romancing the Stone when Michael Douglas and Kathleen Turner sailed into the sunset. No, life on Grendel was more about la problema del dia, the problem of the day, especially for someone who'd flunked grade school shop and was the least mechanically minded in the history of the Montezuma County public school system in Cortez, Colorado. To sail around the world you not only need to know how to sail but also how to fix stuff—all the stuff, including mechanical and electrical— and you need the baksheesh to coax replacement parts through foreign customs.

Hollywood had done me a disservice—or perhaps, like those guys who count landing at an international airport as visiting a country, I was a dope. After a year we were still in Mexico, though far down the Pacific Coast. The Marquesas and Tuamotus islands were next on our itinerary, and as the specter of a thirty- to forty-day ocean crossing loomed closer, I faced up to my terminal ineptness with a multi-meter and a monkey wrench, and Mary admitted to hating unending oceans. A compulsive jogger, she found the deck was too small for laps. We turned north to San Diego, where I experienced my most glorious day, selling Grendel.

By no means was this the end of my dream of seeing the world but instead the true beginning. Living on a sailboat relegated

384

us, two non-beach persons, to the coast, though 90 percent of what there is to see is inland. We found sailing the very best way to spend time fixing stuff in exotic ports, leaving little time for exploration.

We began international RVing in 1994. That year we flew to Germany and bought an RV with the proceeds from Grendel. We lived the next three years in forty countries, spending summers in the United Kingdom, Ireland, Norway, and Scandinavia and winters in Spain, Portugal, Morocco, Italy (where I finally saw Vesuvius not erupting), Greece, Turkey, Israel, Jordan, and Egypt, plus all the countries in between. Seventeen years later, though we have stopped full-time RVing, we're still RVing the world six months a year.

We've visited hundreds of scenic spots available overnight only by tent or RV. Among our favorite experiences have been overnighting within or next to:

- The Horns of Hittite, where the Crusaders met their final demise above Lake Kinneret (aka the Sea of Galilee), where we were visited by a helicopter.
- New Zealand's Mount Cook, framed by our RV's panoramic windows, and Milford Sound, which we had all to ourselves after the tour buses had gone home for the night.
- A remote beach in New South Wales, where we were surrounded by kangaroos.
- The world's most incredible ruins at ancient Petra, and definitely by ourselves in remote Wadi Rum, where Larry of Arabia hung out, both in Jordan.
- Alice Springs in Australia's Northern Territory, where we watched a full eclipse of the moon atop our RV.
- The wind-hewn canyons of the Negev Desert. A French canal and an ancient French monastery in a primeval forest.
- Hobart Bay and Cradle Mountain in Tasmania. Purnululu National Park in the orange-and-black-striped mountains of the Bungle Bungles, and at the confluence of sandstone slot canyons in Karajini National Park, in Western Australia.
- The waterfront in Ushuaia, Argentina, the southernmost city in the world, where we watched ships leave for Antarctica, and in Tierra Del Fuego National Park, outside Ushuaia, at the foot of the last of the Andes, on the Beagle Channel.
- Vesuvius overlooking the bay and the lights of Naples.
- The canals of Bruges, Amsterdam, and Venice. (Unfortunately, the Chinese government prohibits driving an RV to the canals of Suzhou).
- Finland's many   lakes, surrounded by reindeer. The

waterfront in Stockholm, where we camped for a week.

• Lake Titicaca in Bolivia. Another Bolivian favorite is Mount Sajama (21,000 feet), where we camped at 15,000 feet next to hot springs a few kilometers from the border with Chile and a lake perfectly reflected twin Fuji-esque cones.

The week before I quit playing lawyer, several friends said they envied my plan. The brevity of life had been vividly illustrated to them. They, like me, had always treated life as if it went on forever. One guy's brother had been diagnosed with inoperable cancer, a month before his scheduled retirement. Another's father had prostate cancer, chose the operation, and died two weeks after retiring. Mary's boss had dreamed of buying an oceangoing fishing boat but kept putting it off. He needed to add to his retirement kitty. Just before we left he was diagnosed with a brain tumor and died a year later. Do it now, whatever it is you want to do. If we don't do it now, the odds are we never will. Perhaps along the way you'll find the world's most picturesque volcano.

www.ingramcontent.com/pod-product-compliance
Lightning Source LLC
Chambersburg PA
CBHW020148090426
42734CB00008B/734